PRAISE FOR DAN MILLMAN
AND Everyday Enlightenment

"Brings enlightenment down to earth by presenting his own unique expression of practical spirituality to everyday life. I recommend this book to anyone interested in the bigger picture and higher purpose of living."

—John Bradshaw, author of *Homecoming*

"[Dan Millman] pushes the New Age another step closer to practicality . . . full of tips for 'turning your daily life into spiritual practice.'"

—*Dallas Morning News*

"Presents an excellent, useful model for integrating spirituality into one's daily life. If you seek more meaning and direction in your life, you'll want to read this enlightening book."

—John Gray, author of *Men Are from Mars, Women Are from Venus*

"Provides a self-sufficient map and practice of spiritual principles that enhance personal, professional, and spiritual growth. The twelve gateways . . . allow us to serve the world with less fear, more trust and commitment, to cultivate compassion and authenticity in support of fostering the beauty of the human spirit."

—Angeles Arrien, Ph.D., author of *The Four-Fold Way* and *Signs of Life*

more . . .

"Millman has achieved a level of authenticity and courage not often touched upon. It is in the simple, realistic look at living the spiritual life that its radical nature is found."

—*Aquarius*

"Dan Millman demonstrates his dedication to lovingly inspire those of us who open ourselves to his wisdom. . . . This book is indeed a magnum opus."

—Arnold Patent, author of *You Can Have It All* and *Money and Beyond*

"An illuminating and spiritual discussion . . . gives us the knowledge we need for our spiritual journeys and shows us how to translate that knowledge into action."

—*Whole Life Times*

"A brilliant marriage of spiritual vision and practical wisdom. Dan Millman speaks with both tenderness and authority."

—Alan Cohen, author of *The Dragon Doesn't Live Here Anymore*

"Its clear and straightforward structure . . . offers advice for body, mind, and soul."

—*Newark Post*

"Beginning with a personal, transcendent experience, Dan Millman generates a powerful, moving, and practical guide for the individual journey toward spiritual growth . . . a superbly written and compelling map of the winding path to inner balance."

—Dr. Kenneth R. Pelletier, author of *Sound Mind, Sound Body*

"Many thanks for the enlightening headstart! As a college professor who works also in the public schools I find your insights invaluable and want you to know you are also contributing to hundreds of children's lives in California."

—Don Morris, Ph.D., professor, California State
Polytechnic University, Pomona

"EVERYDAY ENLIGHTENMENT had proved to be just what I needed to regain my center and focus. I currently own every book you have ever written and apply the lessons therein on a daily basis at my martial arts school. Thank you for the inspiration to go beyond."

—Robert Hopkins, reader

"Offers a detailed format for the inner journey that encompasses the physical, mental, spiritual, and emotional aspects of life. . . . Millman's personal story helped carry the thread of his message into my everyday life."

—*Unity Magazine*

"I bought your book EVERYDAY ENLIGHTENMENT, and I must congratulate you on your work! I've only read two chapters and I feel like I've discovered gold."

—Anthony Oliver, reader

Books by Dan Millman

THE PEACEFUL WARRIOR SAGA

Way of the Peaceful Warrior:
A Book That Changes Lives

Sacred Journey of the Peaceful Warrior:
Three Selves and the Tower of Life

GUIDEBOOKS

Divine Interventions:
Stories of Mysteries, Miracles and Lives Transformed

Everyday Enlightenment:
The Twelve Gateways to Personal Growth

The Life You Were Born to Live:
A Guide to Finding Your Life Purpose

No Ordinary Moments:
A Peaceful Warrior's Guide to Daily Life

The Laws of Spirit:
A Parable About the Laws of Life

Body Mind Mastery:
Creating Success in Sport and Life

CHILDREN'S BOOKS

Secret of the Peaceful Warrior:
A Story of Courage and Friendship

Quest for the Crystal Castle:
A Journey Through the Forest of Life

For further information:
www.danmillman.com

Everyday
Enlightenment

*The Twelve Gateways
to Personal Growth*

Dan Millman

WARNER BOOKS

A Time Warner Company

Copyright © 1998 by Dan Millman
All rights reserved.

Warner Books, Inc., 1271 Avenue of the Americas, New York, NY 10020
Visit our Web site at www.warnerbooks.com

 A Time Warner Company

Printed in the United States of America

First Trade Printing: June 1999

10   9   8   7   6   5   4   3   2   1

The Library of Congress has cataloged the hardcover edition as follows:

Library of Congress Cataloging-in-Publication Data

Millman, Dan.
     Everyday enlightenment : the twelve gateways to personal growth / Dan Millman.
        p.   cm.
     ISBN 0-446-52279-1
     1. Spiritual life. 2. Conduct of life.   3. Millman, Dan.
     I. Title.
     BL624.M479   1998
     291.4′4—dc21   97-38845
                                                                       CIP

ISBN: 0-446-67497-4 (pbk.)

Book design by Stanley S. Drate / Folio Graphics, Inc.
Cover design by Diane Luger

This book is dedicated to you,
my readers, who lend my words
new meaning and purpose
in your own lives.

*The path of personal growth
leads upward,
through the gauntlet
of human experience
to the peaks of our potential.
On this journey we encounter
twelve gateways.
Their purpose is evolution.
Their arena is everyday life.
Their secret is action.
And their time is now.*
—Dan Millman

Acknowledgments

No one stands alone in this world or accomplishes anything on their own. Even though I've written all the words of this book, I've benefited from the skillful efforts of designers, typesetters, printers, secretaries, software developers, teachers, and countless others—and from the sun, rain, and earthworms who prepared the soil for the trees whose flesh became the pages of this book. Support is everywhere; gratitude has no bounds.

First, I would like to thank my family—Joy, my life partner and editor in chief; my daughters Sierra and China for their support; and my parents, Herman and Vivian, whose generosity of spirit made a difference.

I am indebted to my literary agent, Candice Fuhrman, for her counsel and caring every step of the way; to Claire Zion, my dedicated editor at Warner Books, who, along with Maureen Egen and Larry Kirshbaum, demonstrated a firm commitment to quality; and to JoAnn Davis for her initial faith in the project. Many thanks to local editors Douglas Childers, Tom Grady, and Haden Blackwell, whose sensibilities helped to shape this book, and to my precision copyeditor Sona Vogel. My manuscript readers and friends Jillian Manus, Barry Elkin, as well as my daughter Holly Demé and neighbor Beth Wilson, took time from busy schedules to offer their own insightful suggestions.

The "Constructive Living" teachings and example of author David K. Reynolds—friend, colleague, and mentor—contributed to this work, influenced my teachings, and enriched my life. Dr. Reynolds also gave me permission to use quotations from lectures he gave at his "Constructive Living" certification training. Many thanks to Gregg Krech and Linda Anderson at ToDo Institute in Vermont for their kindness. Appreciation also to my sterling research assistant, Emily Acker, who found the sources of numerous quotations.

The following people kindly gave permission to use material, quotations, or excerpts from their work: Dr. Kenneth Pelletier permitted me to adapt material from his germinal work, *Longevity*. Jim Chamberlain, Pete Dixon, Anne M., Susan Christian, and James Chapman all gave permission to reprint their letters about "the kindness of strangers," most of which originally appeared in the *Sun* literary magazine. Trudy Boyle and Gottfried Mitteregger coined the term "three-question reality check" used in a later chapter. Lynne Twist, a founding executive of the Hunger Project, extended her philanthropic heart to allow me to use brief excerpts on "Service," as well as selected words on "The Soul of Money," based on a New Dimensions Radio interview with Michael Toms. Harry Palmer graciously let me excerpt his words first published in the *Avatar Journal*.

Abiding gratitude also to Oscar Ichazo, founder of the Arica School. In this book I share but a few drops of the oceanic cosmology he has taught—specifically, in the eighth gateway, I present the basics of a deep massage designed to clear fear-produced tension from the body, and in the ninth gateway, I offer a map of the polarized aspects of our character from Professor Ichazo's larger cosmology, in order to clarify universal shadow elements within our psyches.

Deep appreciation to Ivan Smith and Cochrane Thompson, ninth- and tenth-grade English teachers, who convinced me that I could write—and maybe even think. Finally, my thanks to Hal and Linda Kramer, Nancy Carleton, Uma Ergil, Mick Laugs, Jan Philips, and Monique Muhlenkamp for their past and present support in myriad ways; and to Karie Jacobson, Sandra Swedeen, and Danielle Dayen for their quality editorial and administrative assistance.

Contents

PREPARATION:
Stairway to the Soul

Many men go fishing all of their lives
without knowing
that it is not fish they are after.
—Henry David Thoreau

A Flash of Light

One night, years ago, I fell into the depths of despair over a woman I loved and was losing. We had been married for six years and were living in a cottage at Stanford University where we served as dormitory directors. My wife had become enamored of a handsome tennis player. When he entered our cottage to speak with her, as students did on occasion, her eyes sparkled as they no longer sparkled for me. They spoke and laughed into the night, lost in conversation.

I went to bed but slept restlessly, waiting for her to join me. I awoke at two A.M., still alone, unable to sleep any longer. In a dark, disheartened mood, I rose, threw on a shirt and pants, and walked toward the front door. They were still sitting together on the couch.

"I'm going out," I muttered, grabbing my car keys, hoping she would show some concern, even ask him to leave. She said nothing.

Waves of rejection, worthlessness, loss, jealousy, and, most of all, self-pity washed over me as I got in the car. I also felt foolish

1

and weak. Why didn't I tell him it was time to leave? Why didn't I grab her and say, "Enough! This isn't right!" But how can one control the affections of another?

In this desolate mood—the closest I had ever come to feeling suicidal—I drove aimlessly through the night, ending up in a wooded grove. I stopped the car and stared out the window at the muddy earth puddled with rainwater. No reflection stared back at me, only blackness. I didn't know where to go or what to do.

Then it happened.

My awareness suddenly shifted of its own accord. Words fail me here, but at the precise moment I could no longer stand the pain, my consciousness exploded, leaped, broke free, and I was touched by God.

The pain—and this is important—hadn't gone away. The circumstances of my marriage and my life remained the same, yet I had changed in my relation to it all. Suddenly *it didn't matter* what was going on inside my mind or emotions. The hurt feelings remained, but there was no "I" to suffer them. My feelings and thoughts no longer seemed to *mean* anything. They had no significance, power, or influence. I was *free*—free of time, existing not *in* the moment, but *as* the moment. From that state of grace, that transcendent awareness extending beyond the confines of my personal feelings, I thought of my wife and her friend and was overwhelmed by compassion for them both, and for all beings. No, it was beyond compassion; it was a sense of resplendent empathy, of unity. I was not separate from them, or from the trees or the stars.

I began to laugh uproariously, as if life were a cosmic joke and I had just gotten the punch line. If someone had found me in the woods that night, they might have mistaken me for a crazy man. The irony was, for the first time in my life I felt completely sane. I looked around—the night seemed filled with light, reflecting the light within me.

Eventually the light faded and the realization passed, as all things pass. In the months and years that followed, I sought to recapture that sense of unity and divine perfection. I yearned for the light as one might long for a lover. I tried meditation and visualization, seminars, soul-searching, and self-analysis. I had insights and experiences, but nothing matched that simple illumination in the forest grove.

Still, the impression of that experience served as a template of possibility and, I believe, a preview of our collective destiny. It also served as a catalyst in my life, generating within me the desire to share what I had learned. My quest began to shift from what I could get to what I could give. I knew that ancient schools and religious traditions had devised their own methods of personal and spiritual growth, from yoga to meditation to prayer, so I traveled and read and studied, not for my own sake, but to gather gifts I could share with others. In the end, I found the answers I sought not in the temples of the East or schools of the West, but here and now, in everyday life.

The most important understanding that emerged from my experience that night in the forest was that peak experiences fade—and that if I was to make a real difference, I would have to find a universal path, free of exclusive dogmas or cultural trappings. I needed to find a way less dramatic but more lasting than my experience years before. All signs pointed me to everyday life as a spiritual path and practice—and to the twelve gateways.

I use the terms "personal growth" and "spiritual growth" interchangeably because we are spiritual as well as physical beings, and as we mature and grow personally, through the challenges of everyday life, we also evolve toward a deeper awareness of our spiritual nature.

Twelve Gateways to Spiritual Growth

If we never suffered pain or loss—if death did not await us—we might never need to seek a higher understanding, might never wonder about the soul, the hereafter, or the ultimate meaning of life. But life is brief—a flash of lightning, a snap of eternity's fingers. So we question and wonder. While striving for a successful place in the material world, our path eventually leads to the arena of spiritual growth and discovery. We sometimes seek Spirit in churches, temples, or revival tents, but we don't always encounter it there. Some of us look for Spirit in a bottle or a pill, leading either to an early death or unconscious life. Others seek inspiration in sports or sexual relationships. Yet all the time, Spirit has been waiting for us, calling to us, right here, right now in everyday life.

A man once wrote to me, "I *want* to make time for more spiritual practices, but I have a wife, three kids, and a full-time job." He hadn't yet realized that his wife and children and work *are* his spiritual practice—a practice far more challenging and rewarding than sitting in a cave and meditating. I know, because I've done both.

Everyday life is our spiritual school. As you see your reflection more clearly in the mirror of daily life, you will come to know and accept yourself as never before. As you learn from the natural consequences of your actions, you'll find the wisdom necessary to progress on the path of personal and spiritual growth.

As an athlete and coach, I learned to divide goals into distinct, manageable steps. First I applied this method to finding the qualities that constitute a talent for sports. Then I explored the qualities that generate a talent for life, blending elements of psychology, ethics and values, spiritual principles, and practical wisdom. I found a complete map of the territory of personal growth and everyday enlightenment.

The premise of this book is that human evolution—whether we call it personal or spiritual growth—necessarily involves a passage through twelve gateways, like a school from which we graduate after passing twelve core subjects. Twelve seems an auspicious number. After all, there are twelve hours on a clock, twelve inches to a foot, twelve months of the year, twelve days of Christmas, twelve signs of the zodiac, Twelve Step programs, twelve labors of Hercules, twelve jurors to dispense justice, the twelve tribes of Israel, twelve gates to the city of Jerusalem, and the twelve disciples of Jesus—and in some circles, the twelve disciples is a metaphor for the twelve disciplines of life presented in this book.

Inward spiritual practices such as meditation, breathing techniques, and self-analysis generate insights and enhance abilities, but none are so useful as learning to live harmoniously in a committed relationship, being a skillful parent, or juggling the demands of daily life. Spiritual practice begins on the ground, not up in the air. The twelve gateways form our stairway to the soul.

When people ask me abstract questions about time, or space, or reincarnation, I may respond by asking whether they exercise regularly, eat a wholesome diet, get enough sleep, show kindness to others, and remember to take a slow, deep breath on occasion—because it seems important to bring our spiritual quest down to earth. Of course, there's nothing wrong with philosophical speculation. But let's not mistake conceptual thought for the spiritual practice of everyday life. After all, what does it serve to know whether angels wear earrings if we can't hold a regular job or maintain a long-term relationship? What good does it do to pray like a saint or meditate like a yogi if we are unchanged when we open our eyes? What good to attend a place of worship on Saturday or Sunday if we lack compassion on Monday?

This point struck home early one morning twenty-five years ago, as I sat in peaceful meditation until my three-year-old daughter, Holly, tugged at my pants leg, wanting my attention. I hissed angrily, "Don't bother me! I'm *meditating!*" In the next instant I realized that I had missed the entire point of spiritual practice: that picking up and hugging my daughter was a more important spiritual practice in that moment than chanting my mantra.

The Gateways' Higher Purpose: The Liberation of Attention

Most of us experience God or Spirit (terms I use interchangeably) as a sense of *inspiration*. Each time we feel uplifted or inspired, we are touched by Spirit. In fact, Spirit surrounds and interpenetrates us in every moment. Spirit is *always* present, just as the sun is always shining above the clouds. Our lack of inspiration is not the absence of Spirit in our lives, but, rather, a lack of awareness.

From a conventional view, *Everyday Enlightenment* helps you create a more fulfilling life. The awareness generated by this book will reduce or eliminate self-sabotage, strengthen your will, lead to improved energy and health, help to create financial stability, and increase your compassion, perspective, and humor, leading to more loving relationships. But do you truly believe that a satisfying relationship, money in the bank, or good health are *in themselves* the ultimate purpose of life? Or is there something more?

I propose that the "something more" involves a unifying spiritual theme—your evolution up through the twelve gateways. Psychologist Abraham Maslow once proposed that we need to satisfy or resolve lower needs in order to address higher ones, ultimately leading toward what he called "self-actualization." In other words, until we have addressed survival and safety needs, we don't have energy or attention for higher social or spiritual concerns. *As you resolve the issues of each gateway, you release attention previously bound by those issues.* When attention is free, it rises like a balloon to higher levels of experience. The challenges of life remain, but your perception and awareness becomes bright and clear.

Thus, the higher purpose of each gateway is to free your attention so that you become capable of seeing Spirit everywhere, every day, in everyone, and in everything, leading to everyday enlightenment.

> Life is denied by lack of attention,
> whether it be to cleaning windows
> or trying to write a masterpiece.
>
> **—Nadia Boulanger**

Imagine hiking up a mountain toward the summit of your potential. You begin with a knapsack filled with twelve heavy stones. As you pass through and resolve the challenges of each gateway—money concerns, health issues, relationship problems—you release one of the stones, becoming lighter as you ascend. Although the climb can be difficult, the higher you rise, the more wondrous the view, because you see the bigger picture. You begin to perceive and appreciate the bright reality that exists here and now—the same magical world you saw as a wide-eyed infant, gazing into mystery at the soul of life. And as your awareness ascends further up this stairway to the soul, the so-called mystical states begin to occur naturally.

Through the Gateways to Everyday Enlightenment

In the final section of this book, I articulate the practice of everyday enlightenment, the core and culmination of my teaching work. It's natural to want to skip ahead to that section or to those gateways that seem most relevant to your life right now. After all, in everyday life different issues emerge day to day, moment to moment, in random order. But in this book the order of the gateways is not random or arbitrary. I urge you to explore them as presented, because each gateway helps to prepare you for those that follow: *Discover Your Worth* opens you to fully use the other gateways. *Reclaim Your Will* provides tools to transform what you learn into what you *do,* to apply the practices presented in *Energize Your Body,* thus building a foundation to *Manage Your Money* and achieve financial stability, further freeing attention to observe and *Tame Your Mind.* Insight into the nature of mind helps to open inner sight so that you come to *Trust Your Intuition,* thus helping you to *Accept Your Emotions* and create more harmonious relationships, empowering you to *Face Your Fears.* Armed with the secret of courage, you ascend the stairway to the soul to *Illuminate Your Shadow* and reintegrate denied aspects of yourself, thereby liberating energy and attention once trapped in defending your self-image. In *Embrace Your Sexuality* you find deeper pleasure and intimacy by transcending both self-indulgence and self-denial, leading upward to *Awaken Your Heart* and turn love into action as you *Serve Your World,* thereby completing the circle of life.

Each gateway begins with a brief overview or road map of the path ahead. However, instead of piling one point on top of another in building-block fashion, I create overlaid themes and counterthemes that build upon one another—more like composing a symphony than constructing a building. This may at first seem confusing to your left brain, but it has an oddly stimulating effect on your right brain—and in the end, I hope it will play for you in near perfect harmony.

Since these gateways clarify how to live a sane, balanced, healthy, productive life, they are compatible with religious teachings. Still, some ideas here may stir the kettle of controversy, even provoke disagreement. This seems natural and appropriate, since no practice is right for everyone. (If we agree on everything, only one of us is necessary.) Take what is useful and discard the rest. Read with healthy skepticism. Test these ideas against your own experience. My interest is not that you trust me, but that you trust yourself and the process of your life unfolding.

The Twelve-Week Program for Everyday Enlightenment: We learn best by concentrating on one element at a time. Applying this principle to your life, you can create your own twelve-week program by focusing on one gateway each week as you go about the business of everyday life. View each day that week through the lens of that gateway. Reread one chapter. Do the exercises. Apply the principles that stand out for you. Make a few notes each evening in a weekly gateways journal. At the end of twelve weeks— one season of the year—you will have completed all the gateways and created a whole-life make-over. If you repeat the cycle, you will find yourself writing new insights, going deeper, seeing new changes in your journal.

Even if you don't choose to engage in such an intensive program, simply reading this book begins an irreversible learning process. As you read through each gateway, the light of awareness creates an alchemical change within your psyche. Like a beacon in the darkness, this awareness reveals what was always present but unnoticed, infusing your life with clarity, energy, illumination. Everyday life will reveal her secrets because you'll be seeing with new eyes.

These gateways apply to each and all of us. No matter how different our appearances, cultures, or beliefs, we·share in a common quest for meaning—no one is exempt and no one excluded. Taken together, the twelve gateways provide a direct path to your hidden promise and potential, a way to reconnect with your soul's deepest yearnings. As you travel through the pages of this book, expect to find an expanded sense of purpose and direction, toward the summit of human experience, where you can *live* the spiritual truths at the heart of your existence. As you take this journey, you have the opportunity to reflect upon your past, consider your future, while living fully in the present.

Welcome to the path of the peaceful warrior, where everyday life is your journey and adventure. The road is open. Your destiny calls. Spirit waits with infinite patience.

Dan Millman
San Rafael, California
Spring 1997

THE
FIRST GATEWAY

Discover Your Worth

No matter how intelligent, attractive, or talented you may be—
to the degree you doubt your worthiness
you tend to sabotage your efforts
and undermine your relationships.
Life is full of gifts and opportunities;
you will open to receive and enjoy them
to the degree that you begin to
appreciate your innate worth,
and to offer to yourself
the same compassion and respect
that you would give to others.
Discovering your worth
sets your spirit free.

Opening to Life

It is a funny thing about life: if you refuse to accept
anything but the best you very often get it.

—W. Somerset Maugham

Road Map: The First Key to Transformation

Aaron and Charlotte, brother and sister, are born into a two-parent, stable, middle-class household. Their parents are educated, hardworking, caring, have no alcohol problems, abusive habits, or guilty secrets. Aaron grows up successful—earns good grades, wins a junior chess championship, plays sports, and later earns a good income to support a family of his own. Charlotte does moderately well in school but chooses unsavory friends, starts using heroin and other drugs, turns to theft and prostitution to support her habit, which leads to jail time and the hell of withdrawal.

Not all siblings are as different as Charlotte and Aaron, but some of us take higher roads than others. In families all over the world, children grow up differently, make different choices, lead different lives.

Many factors shape our lives, including beliefs, support systems, motivation, relationships, family dynamics, fate, or karma. But the central premise of the first gateway is that our sense of self-worth is the single most important determinant of the health, abundance, and joy we allow into our lives. In the case of Aaron and Charlotte, his behaviors demonstrated his higher sense of self-worth. But the story doesn't end there.

Charlotte, who had always loved children, later found new purpose, meaning, and opportunity for service in her role as a dedicated mother of two. As her children grew, so did her sense of worth. Charlotte got her life together and is doing better all the time.

Not all stories have such a happy ending. Thousands, even millions, of us in all walks of life make self-destructive choices because we have lost touch with our own worthiness to receive life's gifts.

Discover Your Worth is no more or less important than any other gateway. But it comes first because only when you come to appreciate your unconditional human worth will you allow yourself to fully apply and benefit from the gateways that follow. Discovering your worth provides a foundation from which to build, one gateway at a time, a new way of life. Finding your worth is the first step in creating everyday enlightenment.

The purpose of this gateway is to assess your current sense of self-worth, to appreciate the arbitrary factors that created it, to understand how a low sense of worth can generate (largely subconscious) self-destructive behaviors, and, finally, to help you get out of your way and move into a more expansive life.

In the first gateway you will learn how self-worth differs from self-esteem; how your sense of worth impacts the choices you make in life; three ways you can discern your own (largely subconscious) sense of worth; the source and mechanisms of self-sabotage and how to overcome it; and, finally, ways to appreciate your own unconditional worth.

In setting out, bear the following points in mind:

No one else can give you an improved sense of self-worth. Self-worth comes from doing what is worthy. As the Talmudic scholar Abraham Heschel once said, "Self-respect is the fruit of discipline."

This gateway is about discovering your worth, not raising it. Your innate worth has never been lowered, compromised, or touched by fate or circumstance. It exists as a fact of life, like air and trees, and doesn't need to be raised, revitalized, or earned.

The problem is not your actual worth, but your perceived worth. Nearly all of us have lost touch with our intrinsic goodness—allowed it to be covered over by memories of a thousand transgressions, real or imagined, so that we feel only *partly* deserving of life's blessings.

In the gateways that follow, you will find additional keys to resolving and ultimately transcending the critical issue of self-worth. The twelfth gateway provides the final key. We begin now by clarifying the meaning of self-worth, how it differs from self-esteem, and how it impacts the quality of your everyday life.

The Heart of Self-Worth

At its core, your level of self-worth is your answer to a single internal question: "How deserving am I?" Or, to put it more directly as it pertains to your daily life: "How good can I stand it today?" If you observe your life very closely, you will discover that you don't necessarily get what you deserve. Rather, you get no more and no less than what you *believe* you deserve. Only to the degree that you appreciate your innate human worthiness will your subconscious mind open up to life's bounty. Success involves talent, effort, and creativity, but first of all, it requires a willingness to receive. To paraphrase a speech I heard Ram Dass give many years ago, rain may pour down from the heavens, but if you only hold up a thimble, a thimbleful is all you receive.

When a window of opportunity appears, do you pull down the shade? Each of us has a specific degree of pleasure that feels right and appropriate. If that level is exceeded, it makes us anxious.

At a residential seminar I once taught, I encouraged participants to ask for a standing ovation. As each came forward, I noted the variety of ways they responded to enthusiastic applause. Some people opened their arms wide, laughed, even jumped up and down. Others could tolerate only a few seconds of applause before holding up their hands as if to say, "Enough. Please stop. I'm getting uncomfortable."

Self-Worth and Self-Esteem

Because many people assume that self-esteem and self-worth mean the same thing, it seems important to note the distinctions between the two.

Self-worth (associated with self-respect) refers to your overall sense of value, worth, goodness, and deservedness. Your sense of worth can change over time based upon your actions. For example, my sense of self-worth has increased over time as I gradually learned to be a responsible, loving father and husband, and helped others through my writing and teaching.

Self-esteem (associated with self-confidence) refers to liking or feeling good about yourself, your appearance, or your abilities. Your sense of self-esteem may change moment to moment, based on appearance, abilities, or situation. For example, as an experienced gymnast, I felt high self-esteem (confidence) in the gym, but less self-esteem at parties or social gatherings.

Many books offer advice on how to raise your self-esteem and feel better about yourself. *Discover Your Worth,* as you will see, addresses a deeper and more pervasive issue of your own intrinsic sense of value, goodness, morality, and deservedness. By the time you finish your journey through the twelve gateways, you will understand how to transcend feelings of self-esteem and self-worth. Until then, we focus on self-worth and its impact on the paths you choose in life.

The Choices You Make

The central theme of the first gateway is that *you subconsciously choose or attract into your life those people and experiences you believe you deserve.* In everyday life pain is inevitable, but suffering is optional—a by-product of poor choices.

Your sense of worth or deservedness shapes your life by creating *tendencies.*

If you feel worthy and deserving, you tend to make productive choices. ("The world is my oyster.")

If you feel unworthy and undeserving, you tend to make destructive or limiting choices. ("Beggars can't be choosers.")

At each and every crossroads you are free to choose the high road—by being kind to others, working hard, finding supportive partners, and following good role models. Or you may choose the low road—by burning your bridges, using drugs, or choosing destructive relationships. Your sense of self-worth tends to influence whether you choose to learn easy lessons or difficult ones, to strive or to struggle, to cave in to difficulties or rise above them.

Such choices determine your educational and income level, your health habits—even your longevity. Those of us with a strong sense of self-worth are less likely to get caught up in self-destructive habits with tobacco, alcohol or other drugs, or the abuse of food.

Coming to appreciate your worth can, in some cases, dramatically improve your circumstances by changing the choices you make and the actions you take. And as you begin to treat yourself with more respect, other people begin to do the same, since we subconsciously "train" others how to treat us through messages we send through body language, tone of voice, and other subtle cues and behaviors. Discovering your innate worth and living from that place allows you to make more constructive choices—to choose the higher roads of life.

Since you are exploring this gateway, maybe now is the time for you to take stock, to reflect upon your own circumstances and sense of worth, and to determine if your life is working as well as you would like. Are you now where you want to be?

A Self-Worth Wake-up Call

There is a danger of studying self-worth from a distance—exploring the issue the way some people explore Africa from an air-conditioned bus. Keeping a safe distance is more comfortable but far less useful than feeling its impact on *your* life right now.

Since your sense of self-worth (and tendency to self-sabotage) is usually subconscious, *awareness of the problem is part of the solution.* Here are three complementary methods to become aware of your sense of worth.

Life Scan: Rating Your Own Worth

Remember that your sense of self-worth—of deservedness—is related to your perception of your relative goodness. On the scale stretching from a totally bad person to a totally good person, where do you fall? Take a few minutes to scan your life intuitively, taking into account your relationship with your parents, siblings, and others at school, home, and work—the times you have been kind, courteous, generous, and supportive as well as the times you were less so. I am *not* asking you to remember many specific incidents, but, rather, to get an intuitive feel for your life as a whole. Then rate yourself on a scale of 1 to 100 as to your overall sense of worth. On a 1–100 scale, how good a person are you? A score of 100 would mean you deeply believe that you are totally good and therefore deserve a life filled with good things—love, joy, health, success, and fulfillment. A score of 1 would mean that you believe that you deserve the pits of hell. (Most of us fall somewhere in between.)

Stop reading until you have given yourself a rating.

This self-assessment has to do with your *perceived* worth rather than your innate worth. It's important to note that *the most sensitive, self-reflective souls among us—those of us with the highest vision, ideals, and standards—often have the lowest sense of self-worth, because we constantly fail to meet our own idealized standards.* Maybe that's why George Bernard Shaw once remarked that "the ignorant are cocksure and the intelligent are full of doubt."

Whether or not you consciously remember your past behaviors, the fact that you could come up with a number indicates that your subconscious mind has been keeping score. Seminar participants I've asked rate themselves across the spectrum— usually between 45 and 95, with most clustering around 60–80. In any event, if you rated yourself less than 100, you have self-worth issues to address. Welcome to the first gateway.

Self-Reflection on Self-Worth

In order to get a better sense of how your sense of worth impacts areas of your life, consider the following questions, and answer "Yes," "No," or "Sometimes."

- When fortune smiles on you, do you think, "This can't last"?

- Do you find it easier to give than to receive?
- Does your life feel like a series of problems?
- Does money seem scarce and hard to come by?
- Do you find your work unfulfilling?
- Do you find your relationship(s) unsatisfying?
- Do you work long hours but not have much time to enjoy yourself?
- Do you resent or envy people who take frequent holidays?
- Do other people seem to have more fun than you do?
- Do you feel driven to work more, do more, *be* more than others?
- Do you overeat, smoke, drink alcohol every day, or use other drugs?
- Do you feel uncomfortable when you receive praise, applause, lots of attention, gifts, or pleasure?
- Have you turned down or passed up opportunities in education, work, or relationships and later regretted it?
- Do you get sick or injured more than other people?
- If someone asks the cost of your services, do you price yourself lower than others in your field?

If you answered "Yes" or "Sometimes" to more than half of these, then you stand to benefit from your journey through the first gateway.

In the Mirror of Everyday Life

Perhaps the most realistic way to determine what you believe you deserve is to observe your life as it is right now. The state of your relationships, work, finances, education, and lifestyle reflects your perceived worth—how good you can currently stand it. Of course, not every person living in poverty lacks money solely because of low self-worth. There are conditions, such as where you were born or grew up, over which you had little or no control. But as you grew, you chose your *response* to your situation—a response that reflected, and helped shape, your sense of worth.

Money and Self-Worth

Your perceived worth is another kind of belief that impacts how deserving you feel of abundance. Other factors being equal, money scarcity is often related to low self-worth and resultant self-sabotage. For example, lottery winners and others who suddenly receive large sums of money (or fame) sometimes encounter (self-created) troubles if they see their good (but unearned) fortune as undeserved, as illustrated by the following story told to me some years ago by a rabbi:

A little tailor lived in a dingy tenement in a small town in the Midwest, earning a meager existence. But each year he pursued a dream and bought one ticket in the Irish sweepstakes.

For fifteen years his life continued in this manner, until one day he found two men standing in his doorway and smiling. They stepped inside and informed him that he'd just won the sweepstakes—$1,250,000, in those days a fortune.

The tailor could hardly believe his ears. He was a rich man! He would no longer have to spend long hours altering clothing, hemming dresses, making pants cuffs. Now he could really live! He locked his shop, threw away the key, and bought himself a wardrobe fit for a king. The same day he purchased a limousine and hired a driver and reserved suites at the best hotels in New York City. Soon he was seen with a variety of attractive young women.

He partied every night, spending his money as if it would last forever. But it didn't; soon he had lost not only all his money, but his health as well. Exhausted, ill, and alone, he returned to his little shop and started his life over. Everything returned to normal; out of habit he even bought one lottery ticket a year from his meager savings.

Two years later, the two gentlemen reappeared at his door. "This has never happened in the history of the sweepstakes, sir, but you have won again!"

The tailor stood on shaky legs and said, "Oh, no! Do you mean I have to go through all *that* again?"

As the tailor's story exemplifies, how we handle money (or power or fame) often reflects our sense of self-worth.

The Simple Source of Self-Sabotage

If self-worth had no impact on your actions—if it were contained within the feeling dimension alone—its only power would be over your moods. Sometimes you'd feel worthy (a pleasant feeling) and sometimes not (an unpleasant feeling). And that would be that.

However, low self-worth also influences actions, generating tendencies to sabotage your own efforts, so that things just don't seem to turn out well. You may feel unlucky at times or feel as though God is punishing you, when in reality you are only punishing yourself. You do this through behaviors of which you aren't fully aware. Or, like the alcoholic who knows he drinks but doesn't view it as a problem, you may be aware of your behavior without acknowledging its destructive impact.

I have never known anyone who wasn't affected at some time or in some way by self-sabotage or subtle self-destructive behaviors in the arenas of money, relationship, education, or career. The question repeats itself in different forms: How high will you rise? How good can you stand it?

To help eliminate any covert tendencies to sabotage your own efforts, let's examine the simple but profound source of self-sabotage. We need to make this mechanism conscious, so let's look at how it was formed and how it operates.

Your Internal Scorecard

One of the most important steps you can take to improve the quality of your life is to become aware of how your self-assessment has shaped your existence and how you can transcend whatever rating you gave yourself.

To understand the roots of low self-worth and the source of

self-sabotage, we need to examine a universal dynamic that applies to you and to every individual in every culture on earth.

In order to fit into society, your parents (or caregivers) taught you what was considered right and what was deemed wrong.

If you behaved well, you earned your parents' approval and were rewarded with positive attention. If you behaved poorly, you received their disapproval and were punished with negative attention.

Thus, when quite young, you learned the two prime moral directives: *If I am good, I am rewarded. If I am bad, I am punished.*

In an ideal world, these rules would be absolutely fair and consistent. In the real world, however, your parents didn't always notice misbehaviors. Even if they did see every misdeed, they might have been too tired or distracted to respond consistently to your actions.

But there was someone who saw and noted, without fail, every single misstep you ever made. *You* did, and you still do. Not only that, you also saw and recorded every negative, hateful, petty, envious, spiteful, or cruel thought and feeling that passed through your mind. Thus began your issues with self-worth.

Remember the two rules: If I am good, I am rewarded. If I am bad, I am punished. Your parents, however, didn't always do the punishing. So you end up punishing yourself—sometimes for the rest of your life—in the form of self-sabotage or self-destructive behaviors.

The Subtleties of Self-Sabotage

Self-sabotage takes many forms, such as quitting school, taking low-paying jobs, choosing a spouse who abuses you physically or verbally, spending more money than you make, committing slow suicide with tobacco, alcohol, or other drugs, getting involved in crime, working yourself to illness or death, self-starvation, self-inflicting wounds, running away, dropping out, or engaging in other behaviors that undermine your health, success, or relationships.

Fame and fortune have a downside for those who feel undeserving of the adulation. Think of the celebrities who engage in punishing, self-destructive behaviors. It is important to note that those who have garnered fame and success without self-destructing have at least some of the following characteristics in common:

- Someone in their family nurtured them as innately worthy, independent of what they could achieve or do.
- Even when they were treated poorly, they had at least one significant person—a teacher or relative or friend—who listened to, valued, and treated them with respect.
- They felt deserving because they had paid their dues—had sacrificed, studied, and worked diligently over a period of time.
- They developed a sense of perspective and had a sense of humor about themselves; they didn't take themselves so seriously.
- They shared their wealth in concrete ways, donating to charities, working for a cause they believed in.

Consciously you may desire success. You may read books and attend seminars, only to undermine your efforts in ways both subtle and creative. Consider those times friends or loved ones you trusted advised against doing something, but you did it anyway because you just felt you had to.

Of course, sometimes it's best to follow your own counsel. (Where would Columbus have been without it?) But if you see a pattern of blindly stepping into potholes despite others' guidance—like buying a lemon of an automobile when a mechanic friend thought it was a bad deal, getting an expensive item you didn't really need, gambling more money than you could afford to lose, or getting involved in a hurtful relationship—consider this: Haven't you already punished yourself enough?

Taking Charge by Taking Responsibility

While coaching gymnastics at Stanford University, I walked into a workout one day and found Jack, the team captain, lying on the mat, stretching—grasping one of his legs and pulling it toward his chest. As I walked by, I saw him grimace and heard him groan, "Oh, God, I hate this—it hurts so much!" I didn't know whether he was talking to me, to himself, or complaining to God, but I felt as if I'd wandered into a Mel Brooks movie. I wanted to ask Jack, "Who's doing it to you? If it hurts that bad, why don't you just let up a little?" This holds true for your life as well: *If it hurts so much, why don't you just let up a little?*

The moment we recognize the degree to which our difficulties are *self-imposed,* we begin to heal them. We end self-sabotage only by taking responsibility for the choices and actions that created it. Only when we stop blaming our boss or government or parents or spouse or partner or children or circumstances or fate or God can we change our lives and say with conviction, "I chose where I am now, and I can choose something better."

Of course, not every misadventure, injury, or problem is created by your subconscious owing to low self-worth. For all we know, certain difficulties or challenges are gifts from God or arranged by our souls in order to test and temper our spirit. As the old proverb says, "Take it as a blessing or take it as a test; whatever happens, happens for the best." And as it happens, adversities may sometimes contain their own blessings.

The Upside of Adversity

We have all had our share of pain, illness, and adversity. When I was in college, about to fly to Europe to the World Gymnastics Championships, my motorcycle was struck by an automobile and I sustained a broken right femur—my thigh bone was shattered into about forty pieces, according to the doctor. Looking back, years later, despite all the searing pain, disability and depression, and lengthy rehabilitation, I believe it may have been one of the most spiritually useful things that ever happened to me. It shook me "up" and made me consider the bigger picture of life and death. It set into motion some new directions. (I do *not*, however, recommend broken bones, illness, or other injury as a method of personal evolution.)

It's just that we can, if we examine the bigger picture, find blessings in adversity. If we are psychologically healthy, we do not seek pain, injury, or illness, but we can appreciate that everything contains its opposite—an upside and a downside.

Whether or not adversity is a self-sabotage or a spiritual lesson, when a misfortune does occur, something rather surprising can happen. Many survivors of serious maladies—with all the pain and suffering—report experiencing a kind of inner peace they had not felt before. Pain has a way of clearing the subconscious scorecard, as if the adversity and suffering pays off sins real or imagined. It's as if you finally get punished for all those things you said or didn't say, did or didn't do, and the scales are finally balanced. The psyche finds ingenious, sometimes tragic ways to find peace. I raise this topic to make it conscious, so that you can find inner peace through service (as in the twelfth gateway), not through pain.

Most of us have at one time or another experienced a need to do penance, to pay off debts, or to ask forgiveness for past mistakes. As you discover your *innate* worth, you come to see that life is tough enough without adding self-created difficulties; you begin to embrace the joys of life and to bring more joy to others.

The Leverage for Change

Self-worth is not a thing; it is a perception. Just as a gymnast begins a routine with ten points and receives deductions for each mistake, so you began life with a natural, complete sense of worth. (Have you ever met an infant with self-worth issues?) But as you grow, you serve as your own judge, deducting points when you misunderstand the nature of living and learning—when you forget you are a human-in-training and that making mistakes and having slips of integrity and mediocre moments are a part of life, not unforgivable sins.

What follows are some reminders that can help you to score your worth higher in the game of life. By shedding light of awareness and compassion on your own life, you can begin to meet your destiny with arms open wide.

Know That You Are Not Alone

The first step is to realize that you are not alone. We have all made mistakes as part of our life and growth. We have all said, thought, felt, and done things we regret. Our worth is not dependent upon being perfect. Many of us have fallen into self-defeating cycles— behaving badly, leading to a lowered sense of self-worth, leading to more negative behaviors. If we can stop judging our mistakes so harshly, we can also stop ourselves from reactively engaging in the negative behaviors.

Know That You Did the Best You Could

The second realization is that *no matter what your behavior, you have done the best you could every day of your life*. You may not agree with this. So before we tackle that question, consider this principle in relation to your parents or other caregivers: whether they were kind or abusive, they were doing the best they knew how in light of their own limitations, wounds, beliefs, fears, values, and anxieties. Their best may have been wonderful, or terrible, or somewhere in between. In the same way, even though you have certainly fallen short of your ideal many times and made mistakes, you have also done the very best you were capable of at the time.

Apologize and Ask Forgiveness

Most of us have replayed in our minds an incident we wish we could do over. Maybe we could have done better on a job interview, a speech, an exam, or a performance. Or we may wish we could take back hurtful actions—moments of disrespect or dishonesty.

You cannot change past mistakes, but you can avoid repeating them. The past no longer exists except as a set of memories and impressions you keep alive in the present. By focusing on doing what you can do now—by reviewing your mistakes with eyes of compassion and asking forgiveness—you do much to heal your fragmented sense of worth.

If you are sorry for never sending your mother a birthday card, send her a special one *now*. Even if she has passed away, write the card. And ask her forgiveness. If you hurt a brother, sister, parent, or other person, review that memory; then contact them, apologize, and ask for forgiveness. If they will not forgive you, then forgive them for not forgiving you. Then send them flowers or another gift, perhaps with a letter. Going inside and visualizing those you have hurt, and asking their forgiveness, provides a healing that begins to lift your sense of worth as it heals relationships.

Trust Your Process

The next time you feel that something good can't last, remind yourself that evolution moves in an upward spiral and that life can, and usually does, get better over time. You live and learn, stumble and evolve, rise and fall, fail and grow, expand, progress. If you pay attention and strive to improve, you become stronger, clearer, wiser, and more capable. Life is a process of rediscovering your worth and the worth of all beings.

The Power of Grace

Finally, it comes to this: To discover your worth, you have to reach within yourself and find it there. You have to create it through worthy actions. In the twelfth gateway, *Serve Your World*, you will find the ultimate means to rediscover the unconditional worth you felt as a child. The gateways that follow will prepare you for that final step. Each gateway will yield new insights leading beyond self-worth to the practice of everyday enlightenment.

The key is to remember that even though we don't feel very kind, or brave, or even deserving, the roof over our head continues to shelter us from storms, the sun shines upon us, our chairs keep supporting us, and so do our lives. Life itself is an unearned gift—and that is the hidden meaning of grace.

Grace reveals that only this moment is real. That past and future exist only in our minds. Your scorecard is wiped clean in any moment of awareness, humility, or repentance. If you have a debt to pay, then pay it in the currency of kindness to the person it is owed, not by punishing yourself, not ever again. It is not necessary. It never has been.

Next, in the second gateway, *Reclaim Your Will*, you will find another key to overcoming the limits you have placed on your life. Your will provides the power to transcend the tendencies that have limited your choices and your actions, providing your next step on the path to everyday enlightenment.

THE

SECOND GATEWAY

Reclaim Your Will

*Inside you is untapped strength
of will, of spirit, of heart.
The kind of strength that will not flinch
in the face of adversity.
You have only to remember your purpose,
the vision that brought you to Earth—
the vision that will take you to the stars—
to the depths of the oceans and
up the stairway to the soul.
Great strength of will
resides within you,
waiting for expression.*

The Power to Change

When running up a hill,
it is all right to give up as many times as you wish—
as long as your feet keep moving.
—Shoma Morita, M.D.

Road Map: The Gates of Inner Power

Life's greatest challenge—one you face in each of the twelve gateways—is turning what you know into what you do. You know the importance of good diet and regular exercise; you know it's best to treat others with kindness. But until you reclaim your will—assert your power to act upon what you know—even the best plans remain unrealized.

"St. Nike" Was Right

Everything is easier said than done. But no matter how intelligent or talented you are, only your actions shape your destiny. To fulfill the promise of the second gateway, you need know, and act upon, only three magic words: Just do it.

But *how* do we "just do" what we know is best? *How* do we achieve consistent self-control and self-mastery?

This question came to a head a few years ago, just before I walked onto the stage to present a seminar entitled "The Laws of Spirit." A fellow approached me and asked how he could accomplish his goal of losing weight. "A low-fat diet and regular exercise," I answered. With hardly a pause he again asked *how* he could eat better and *how* he could stick with an exercise program. "I *know* I need to get moving," he said, "but I don't have the *willpower*. So how do I strengthen my will?"

31

"You already know how to do it," I said. "Knowing how isn't the problem. Besides, right now you seem to have plenty of will—look at how effectively you've engaged me in conversation while we keep a thousand people waiting."

"Yes, but just one more thing—"

The time had come to apply my own will and begin my talk. So I did.

Something about that fellow bothered me. Then I realized what it was. He reminded me of myself—and of the years I searched for strategies, shortcuts, methods, techniques, formulas, and easy ways to motivate myself to get things done. But life continually returns us to the inescapable reality that the best way to do what you need to do is to just do it. Sometimes it's easy. Sometimes it's tough. But that doesn't change the fact that the only way to get something done is to do it. Reclaim your will and you reclaim your life.

You have free will, but your will isn't always free. Freedom has a price; life has hurdles to overcome. In *Reclaim Your Will* I use the terms "will," "willpower," "self-discipline," and "self-control" interchangeably, because any of them, when applied over time as patience, persistence, and perseverance, lead to self-mastery. This gateway shows how to exert the power of your will to overcome life's obstacles, laying a solid foundation for success both in the material and spiritual realms.

As you pass through the second gateway, you will explore topics such as the power of purpose, the hurdles on the path, the subconscious secrets of motivation, practical guidelines for getting things done, realities about what you can and cannot control, how to transcend tendencies, and, finally, some inspiring reminders about what you are here on earth to do.

Reclaiming Your Power

Difficulties intimidate you only when you doubt the power of your will. Learn from the characters in *The Wizard of Oz*—the quick-witted scarecrow who thought he lacked a brain, the loving tin woodsman who felt he lacked a heart, and the brave lion who feared he lacked courage—all of whom came to realize that they had long possessed the traits they desired. Like them, you have never lacked or lost your will; you have only forgotten its power.

The will is like a muscle; it grows stronger with use. And like your muscles, it needs to move, to exert itself. Your inner strength is waiting to be called upon, to grow stronger still. Now is your chance to remember, rebuild, reawaken, and reclaim your innate powers of will. Welcome to the second gateway.

Assessing Your Willpower

The following questions can help you assess your own relationship to self-discipline and willpower as it operates in your everyday life:

- Rating yourself on a 1–10 scale, how effectively do you turn what you know into what you do?
- How would you compare your self-discipline with that of most other people?
- Do you have a primary dream, wish, or goal right now? How can your will help you achieve it?
- In the past, did you have more or less self-discipline? When and why?
- Can you recall a time you demonstrated strong willpower?
- Can you recall a time you demonstrated weak willpower?
- How might you apply your will to influence your diet?
- How might you apply your will to the area of exercise?
- How would you assess your will in the arena of sexuality?
- Do your budget and finances reflect self-restraint?
- Have people ever called you stubborn or willful? (Did you thank them?)
- When doing something you enjoy, do you need to apply your will? Why or why not?
- What habits would you like to change?
- Have you ever applied your will to act with kindness or courtesy when you didn't feel that way?

● Would you like a stronger will? (How do you know you don't already have one?)

The Power of Purpose

A strong will with nothing to do is like a strong horse with nowhere to go. You need more than willpower to make a journey—you need a direction, a task, a goal, a mission—you need a purpose that has meaning for you.

Your purpose and goals are shaped by a thousand factors, including environment, parents, genetics, talents, values, circumstance, synchronicity, and opportunity. Throw in free will, expectations, a pinch of predestination, and voilà—something appears that you want or need to do this moment, this year, this lifetime. Knowing your purpose and acting in alignment with that purpose unleashes the full force of your will.

Maybe you would like to free yourself from negative habits or create positive ones, to improve your love life or finances, to find more meaningful or rewarding work, to master the twelve gateways. Whatever your purpose, obstacles will appear between you and your goals. Willpower is like an all-terrain vehicle that drives you around the obstacles, past the stumbling blocks, over hurdles, through doubt and uncertainty, sending you onward to your destiny—to the practice of everyday enlightenment.

Paraphrasing Shoma Morita, M.D., from a lecture by Dr. David Reynolds, there are three basic guidelines for living: *Accept your feelings. Know your purpose.* And *do what needs to be done* (in line with your purpose, despite what feelings may or may not be present).

Knowing Your Purpose

Whether or not you know your ultimate purpose, or even your goals for next year, you almost certainly have a clear sense of what you want to do in the next few minutes. When the future is hazy, you can still handle what's in front of you. Destiny has a way of dropping a trail of bread crumbs—one small goal at a time—to mark the path. By paying attention to each day, each moment, you will see what needs to be done right now. Your immediate goals are the bread crumbs leading you toward what you cannot yet see.

Stay flexible. Life sometimes brings surprises, and your path to the summit has many twists and turns, a fact illustrated by the stories of two friends, Lenny and Craig. Lenny went to law school, passed the bar, and began to practice. About a year later, after experiencing a physical problem from distance running, he visited a chiropractor. The moment Lenny walked into the chiropractor's office and looked around, he knew that he had found his true calling, and with it, he found the will to do whatever was necessary to achieve it. Lenny, also a dedicated husband and dad, has become a gifted and successful chiropractor who works with professional athletes.

Craig spent many years of long days and late nights, of sacrifice and dedication, applying his will to become one of the nation's top heart surgeons. At the peak of his medical career, an accident left him without the use of two fingers. His surgical career had ended. So Craig, an aikido master and father of three, applied his will once again, turned lemons into lemonade, and started law school, making the *Law Review* his first year, pursuing another form of service while remaining an active husband and father. This is the power of focus and will.

Summary Points for Clarifying Your Purpose

Knowing your purpose is sometimes all you need to reclaim your will. To clarify your purpose, consider the following action items:

- Pursue your dreams! Creation follows vision; willpower begins with a wish.
- Notice how your goals appear in each moment, at home, work, or school, as things you want to do and as things you need to do.
- Appreciate yourself every time you apply your will each day to accomplish these goals.

- When you lose your will have you actually lost your way? Have you forgotten your purpose?
- Break down a grand purpose into monthly goals, weekly goals, daily goals, and immediate goals—the next step, right in front of you.

In pursuing your purpose, you will find hurdles in your path that may at first look like a lack of willpower. But these hurdles are not indications of a weak will. They need to be handled differently—by calling upon your will and your wits. And by your becoming a hurdler.

Hurdles on the Path

Jean Deeds, author of *There Are Mountains to Climb,* wrote of one harrowing night alone on the Appalachian Trail, listening to a bear snuffling and shuffling outside her tent. Lying very still, she hardly slept, hoping that the beast would not decide to tear into her nylon shelter.

The next morning Jean peeked outside directly into the face of the meandering creature—a cow, calmly munching some wild grass.

A cow is not to be trifled with, but it is certainly not a bear. One responds differently to each. In the same way, when you experience inertia or encounter a difficulty completing a goal, be aware that it may not be weak willpower snuffling outside your tent—it may be self-doubt, the fear of failure, or another impostor chewing its cud.

If you lack a clear purpose, misjudge the size of a task, or feel innate resistance to change, don't berate yourself for having a weak will; rather, apply your attention and will to transcending these pretenders.

Self-Sabotage

As you learned in the first gateway, you may not stretch for your goals because you don't feel deserving of achieving them. Or you may stir up problems around you because you're used to keeping life a little aggravating—because you don't cope well with smooth sailing. As you learned in the first chapter, stay vigilant to be sure you are not sabotaging your efforts to achieve your goal because you aren't yet certain that you deserve to do so.

Unrealistic Standards

Perfectionism may impel you to take on too much. You may decline to follow through with a goal not because you lack the willpower, but because you chose a goal that doesn't match your capacities or reflect your values. You may choose a goal according to what you or other people think you ought to do rather than following the directives of your own heart.

You may also underestimate the effort required to complete a task, begin unprepared, and fail to finish. In such a case, you don't necessarily lack willpower; you lack planning. In contrast, if you overestimate the effort required to complete a task, you may become discouraged or disheartened. (It is unlikely that you will even begin a project or task that you don't believe you can accomplish.)

No task is too formidable when you divide your goals into small, realistic steps and prepare well.

Find Your Focus

Some of us scatter our energy trying to get too many little things done instead of focusing on higher-priority tasks such as writing a book, learning a new skill, or achieving optimal fitness. When you are drilling for water, it is better to drill one hole a hundred feet deep than ten holes ten feet deep each.

When jugglers keep five objects in the air at once, they need focus on only one ball in any given moment. If they scatter their attention among all the balls, the same thing happens that happens to you if you try to juggle too many tasks in your life. You may drop all the balls. So focus on your priorities and handle them one at a time.

If you get mentally scattered, you don't necessarily lack will: you lack focus. So identify your top priorities—write them down, make a checklist—then do them one at a time. By focusing your attention, you focus your will.

Resistance to Change

Nearly all of us have made positive changes only to revert to old habits, with each forward leap followed by a backslide. This is due to a natural, subconscious attachment to familiar patterns.

> To cease smoking is the easiest thing I ever did;
> I ought to know because I've done it a thousand times.
>
> **—Mark Twain**

As a child, you became accustomed to a special blanket, toy, or bedtime ritual. Similarly, your body and (subconscious) mind get accustomed to a familiar weight, activity level, and other patterns of behavior. This applies to good habits (exercising daily), neutral habits (reading at bedtime), or negative habits (smoking). Once a pattern is in place, we all tend to resist change.

Breaking a negative habit or starting a positive one happens in two stages: first, making the desired change; second, maintaining the change. Patterns tend to reassert themselves unless you can maintain the new pattern long enough for it to become familiar. This may take from three months to a year. So apply your will the way you would run a marathon, not a hundred-yard dash. Resistance to change is a fact of life. Understanding this tendency doesn't make change effortless, but at least your attention is no longer tied to the illusion that change should be easy. You can exert your will to overcome your resistance.

Fear of Failure

A fear of failure may look like a weak will, creating inertia with the compelling logic "If I never do my best, I can never fail, because I'll know I *could* have succeeded if I had really tried my hardest." Or the fear may appear as insecurity: "I can do it, but not as well as others, so why bother?" Or as self-doubt: "I'm just not ready yet." Fear is a shape-shifter that appears in many forms, including that of a weak will.

The eighth gateway, *Face Your Fears,* will help resolve this issue and overcome your fears. For now, stop hedging your bets—do your very best. Teddy Roosevelt inspired the Rough Riders with the words "Far better it is to dare mighty things . . . even though checkered by failure, than to take rank with those poor spirits who live in the gray twilight that knows not victory nor defeat."

When something needs doing in your life, you can come up with many good reasons not to do it. But when you look up and around, you may notice that it still needs doing. To overcome the impostors of weak will or any other hurdle in your path, first find your focus, set priorities, know your capacities, and stretch your limits. Then act—because success always boils down to this: Know your adversaries; then apply your will.

Subconscious Secrets of Motivation

In times of urgency, intensity, or excitement—or when you see the habits in your life standing in the way of who you can become—your subconscious mind sends your body a surge of energy, enabling you to break through inner fears and outer obstacles in order to perform beyond your everyday capacities.

In the film *Moon over Parador,* actor Richard Dreyfuss plays an out-of-work actor shanghaied by a small country's secret service chief into impersonating El Presidente, the local dictator, to whom he bears an uncanny resemblance. When the strong-arm SS chief proposes this idea to the actor, he asks, "Well, what if I say no?"

"Then I will kill you," responds the SS chief.

The actor pauses thoughtfully before responding. "You know," he says, "you'd make a *terrific* director."

Most of us would, in fact, find it relatively easy to stop smoking, start exercising, or changing any other habit at gunpoint. Or even for huge sums of cash. We can call forth the best within us during times of crisis because our subconscious mind, working through the autonomic nervous system, releases adrenaline and endorphins into our bloodstream, thereby increasing our heart rate and blood flow, sharpening our focus, raising our metabolism, blood pressure, and vital capacity, and generating instant energy and alertness.

Keys to the Subconscious

If you could find a way to harness the support of your subconscious at will, you would have a head start in generating the energy to reach your goals. How do you accomplish this? By understanding the nature of your subconscious mind and finding out what appeals to it.

The *first key* is that your subconscious mind operates like that of a young child, with values, drives, and interests similar to those of a five- or six-year-old. The better you understand what appeals to children, the better you can access your motivational energy stores.

Children Like More:	*Children Like Less:*
new toys	old toys
fun and excitement	boredom
play	work, chores
treats	things that are good for them
physical pleasure and enjoyment	physical discomfort or drudgery
stable routines	change in a routine
getting things	self-sacrifice

What are we to do with that information? How do you engage, excite, and attract the support of your subconscious mind? You do so by applying the *second key*. To access subconscious stores of motivational energy, you have to provide rewards that address the three vital interests of your subconscious mind: security, pleasure, and power.

Those of us seeking a more spiritual life tend to reject cheap thrills in favor of higher, abstract motives like service to humanity, bettering the world, or achieving enlightenment. Although admirable, such broad and high-minded ideals don't appeal to the simple desires of children—or of our subconscious mind. High-minded motives rarely work to energize us in the trenches of everyday life.

The Realities of Motivation

In my athletic career as a gymnast, I strained and stretched, swung and soared, fell often and sweated with exertion for hours each day. Yet I didn't feel that I needed discipline or willpower, because for me training was fun, exciting, thrilling, and adventurous. Most important, I found a recurring source of motivation.

See if you can deduce which of the following factors motivated me to train with such diligence:

- I intuited that this work might prepare me for my future as a teacher and writer.
- I knew that healthful exercise was good for me and would contribute to my longevity.
- I felt it would build my character and develop excellent work habits—that training in gymnastics was training for life.
- I wanted to attract females.

If you selected the last option, you get an "A" on the quiz, because you now appreciate that to access a wave of motivational energy, you have to connect your goals to rewards such as fun, security, excitement, pleasure, and personal power.

Daydream Magic

When your day-to-day challenges at school or work don't seem at all exciting, you can apply the *third key* to generating motivation:

Use the power of daydreaming to conjure up images of the plea-sures waiting for you when you reach your goal.

Since your subconscious mind doesn't clearly differentiate be-tween what you visualize and what you see with your physical eyes, imagining scenes that appeal to your sense of security, plea-sure, or personal power can stimulate subconscious support. You might want to imagine yourself at work as a highly regarded pro-fessional in your field, or imagine the fruits of your labors—cruising the highway in your dream car (that's paid for), or feel the fresh ocean breezes on the luxury cruise ship or quiet beach, skiing at a European resort. In this way you can restimulate feel-ings of drive and motivation to get through the tough times.

At the same time, you can appreciate that you will also serve people, and make a positive difference in the world, and use your work as a means of spiritual growth. But in the business of moti-vation, acknowledge your basic humanity before you stretch for sainthood.

Daydreaming about pleasurable outcomes has its place in get-ting through the difficult or dry times. But even during periods when you don't feel inspired or motivated, you never lose the power of your will.

Motivation and Will

In this world, persisting toward a goal requires either a *want* or a *will.*

When you *want* something—when you act out of desire—you depend upon feelings of motivation, interest, or excitement to carry you past problems to your goal. You don't need will.

When you *will* something—when you act out of duty, commit-ment, loyalty, or integrity—you depend only upon your power to act. You don't need motivation. You persist because it is the right thing to do, or because of the consequences of not doing it, or simply because it needs doing. You call upon the sleeping giant within you, the power of your will.

Motivation is a welcome wind at your back. But winds are changeable and fickle; motivation comes and goes.

Will is a faithful friend, at your side in both the sunlit days and dark nights of the soul, speaking quietly of what is important and good. You can depend upon your will, because it comes from within you.

So sail the winds of motivation when they blow, but in the calms and dry spells, rely on your will to carry you through.

Motivation in Perspective

In service of a more realistic perspective, I will sometimes seem to contradict something I have stated before. For example, after emphasizing the critical importance of self-worth in the first gateway, I reveal in this and later sections how it is possible to practice everyday enlightenment *whether or not* you happen to feel worthy.

Similarly, in this section, after pointing out how to access the motivational energy flowing forth from your subconscious mind, we return to the central theme that your *will* does not have to rely on whether you feel motivated, that *motivation is helpful but not essential to reaching your goals*. Granted, it seems easier to accomplish a task when you feel motivated (or inspired or confident, for that matter)—and there is nothing wrong with such feelings—but you cannot depend upon them over time.

In a lecture, Dr. David Reynolds related Dr. Shoma Morita's words this way: "If it's raining and you have an umbrella, use it." So *use motivation when you find it, but rely on willpower when you don't.* While writing this book, I sometimes felt inspired, but other times I felt tired, doubtful, or weary; that was when willpower pulled me through.

Effective people are not necessarily smarter or more talented than their less successful counterparts; they are only more disciplined. Many smart people fall by the wayside because they strive only when they feel motivated. Successful people strive no matter what they feel by applying their will to overcome apathy, doubt, or fear. Motivation works in the moment, but you can count on the staying power of your will—persistence, perseverance, and endurance.

Michelangelo had to endure seven years on a scaffold to paint the Sistine Chapel. Vladimir Lenin spent thirty years preparing for his revolution. Inventor Chester Carlson pounded the streets for years before he could find backers for his Xerox photocopying process. Margaret Mitchell's *Gone with the Wind* was rejected by fourteen publishers before it was accepted. No major studio would touch *Star Wars*. Marathoner Joan Benoit had knee surgery seventeen days before the U.S. Olympic trials, but her determination enabled her not only to make the Olympic team, but also to become the first American to win the gold medal in her event. Walt Disney went to over three hundred banks—and was told no by every one—before he found a bank that would take a chance on his theme park idea.

Practical Guidelines for Getting Things Done

Life is training. You can train harder or you can train smarter. Here are some easier, smarter ways to move with will and intention in the direction of your dreams.

Keep It Simple

A little bit of something is better than a lot of nothing. You are more likely to do, and continue doing, what is convenient and simple. Better to meditate, contemplate, or pray for only sixty seconds every day than for an hour once every week.

If you don't exercise every day but would like to start, then get up tomorrow morning and remember to do one jumping jack; then, the next morning do another jumping jack; and the next morning, and the next. That one jumping jack every day is a profound step in the right direction, because it gets your foot in the door—you are forming the habit of dedicating a portion of your day, no matter how small, to exercise. The following month you may decide to trade in your daily jumping jack for a brisk walk around the block or two minutes of free-form movement and deep breathing—or you may even invest four minutes a day to complete the Peaceful Warrior Workout, which you will find in the next gateway. To transform your life, begin simply, with a foot in the door.

Draw Upon What You Have Already Accomplished

The idea of doing what you need to do even when you don't feel motivated to do it may seem unrealistic or out of reach. Yet you have applied the power of your will many times—doing what was necessary in school, at work, or at home whether or not you felt energized, or interested, or motivated. Notice the sacrifices you have made and the persistence you have shown learning a sport or musical instrument, going to work each day, raising children, building a long-term relationship. Recall any accomplishments that required patience and diligence over time—doing what you needed to do whether or not you felt like it—and apply that same willpower to the challenge at hand. Whenever you are tempted to give up, remember that you never have to take more than the next step—and be guided by the English proverb reminding you, "Often the last key on the ring opens the door."

Apply Time-Limited Discipline

Years ago I participated in a forty-day training that required a strict dietary regimen designed to maximize alertness and energy. But Saturday nights from eight to ten P.M. were declared pig nights, when we could eat whatever desserts we wanted. It worked well, because we didn't have to forsake our favorite treats, we just postponed them for a time. Instead of suffering temptation when we walked by an ice-cream shop, candy store, or bakery, we'd look forward to Saturday night.

The same time-limited discipline can apply to cruising the Internet, playing video games, or watching television—any behavior you wish to moderate or limit. You can look forward to enjoying the activity while applying your will and reducing its negative effects by decreasing the time you engage in it.

Apply Quantity-Limited Discipline

For some of us, limiting quantity works better than limiting time. For example, I've always had a sweet tooth. But some years ago it struck me that I was not obliged to finish a sweet or snack. I continued eating whatever appealed to me but allowed myself only one bite per day. I thoroughly enjoyed that bite. Then I gave away or threw away the rest. To paraphrase Epictetus, one should act in life as one would at a banquet—by taking a polite portion of all that is offered.

These guidelines are intended not as rigid formulas that apply in every case, but to help you create your own empowering strategies and apply time- and quantity-limited discipline wherever and however they best serve to reclaim and apply your will.

Just Stop

Some behaviors don't lend themselves to cutting back slowly. If you are a smoker or alcoholic or addicted to other substances, or if you commit violent or criminal acts, you need to stop right now, stop every time you feel the impulse to do it again.

If you want to quit smoking, for example, you have a heroic battle ahead, since nicotine is one of the most addictive substances known. The best method for most people is to just quit—not once, but every time you feel the urge to smoke, until finally the cravings fade and you form the habit of not smoking.

To just stop, you first have to want to stop—really want it in the same way someone drowning wants the next breath. If you decide you want to stop, then you just have to put your life on the line—no safety net, escape clause, or back door. Do it, or die to what you can be. Make yourself an offer you can't refuse. Reclaim your will and regain your self-respect.

Such advice may seem simplistic or unrealistic. But it is far more realistic than looking for tricks, shortcuts, miracles, pills, lotions, self-hypnosis, or magical formulas in order finally to take control of your life.

Work Hard, Play Hard, and Treat Yourself

Another useful willpower strategy is to reward yourself with a treat when you've accomplished a set goal. After completing each chapter of this book, I treated myself to a video rental. When I was halfway done with the book, I treated myself to a massage. When I completed the book—well, that was a reward in itself.

The reverse strategy is to earn each treat through constructive acts of discipline, by completing a task first. If your goal is to lose weight but you also want to eat some cheesecake, go right ahead—enjoy a slice—but only after you've taken a brisk walk around the block. That earns you one thin slice. Want another? Sure, enjoy it! As soon as you return from your next lap.

Make Desired Habits Convenient and Undesired Habits Inconvenient

Make any positive behavior as convenient as possible. To break my habit of snacking in the evenings, I keep dental floss and a toothbrush in the downstairs bathroom near the kitchen. Right after dinner I floss and brush. I'm far less likely to snack, because if I eat something, I have to floss and brush all over again.

Make any negative behavior as *inconvenient* as possible. To smoke less, keep only one pack of cigarettes at home, in a small locked safe under some luggage in the closet in the garage. You might also put the television in that same closet, so you take it out only for special events, and use your old TV time writing that book, painting that picture, or learning a new language. In this way you replace old negative routines with new behaviors, pouring new energy into a new you.

Realities from the Control Tower

The heart and core of will involves self-control leading to self-mastery. Master yourself—your habits and tendencies—and you can accomplish what you will.

Imagine your will as a form of light. If the beam is too broad or diffracted, it does little; but if focused, it can work like a laser, cutting through anything in its path. So rather than applying it to things over which you have less control, you can focus your will intensely on the one thing you *can* control. Consider this version of the Serenity Prayer by Reinhold Niebuhr:

> God, give us grace to accept with serenity
> the things that cannot be changed,
> courage to change the things
> which should be changed,
> and the wisdom to distinguish
> the one from the other.

There is no sense in trying to apply your will to that which you cannot control. In order to use your will effectively, you'll need to determine what you can, and cannot, control by an act of intention. Take out a sheet of paper and make two columns. Consider carefully, then write whatever you can in each column before reading further.

What I Can Control:	*What I Cannot Control:*
Whether or not I speak	The behavior of other people
The movement of my	Whether someone likes or loves
arms . . .	me . . .

In writing your own list, you may have discovered the following:

The list of things you *cannot* control—by willing or intending it—might include the government, the weather, your partner or children, the outcome of a game or business venture, how long you or anyone else will live. (You can't even consistently control your thoughts or emotions.)

The list of things you *can* control should have only one entry: *your behavior*. Your behavior is the only thing in this world you can control by direct application of your will. No matter what you might learn in this or any other similar book, living effectively comes down to applying your will to control your behavior.

Doing so cannot guarantee desired results but will increase the likelihood of living longer, thinking or feeling positively, achieving success, winning a basketball game, creating a happier marriage, and improving your neighborhood, country, or world. You cannot guarantee such outcomes, but you can make the effort. As Shoma Morita, M.D., reminds us, "Effort is good fortune."

In the game of life, you can't be certain of making a basket, but you can take a shot. And in doing so, you celebrate one of life's treasures—a simple act of self-control, the power of your spirit.

Transcending Tendencies:
Your Emancipation Proclamation

Discipline leads to freedom, according to an old spiritual law. This seems a contradiction, since most of us view discipline as doing something we don't want to do and freedom as doing whatever we want. But those of us who have achieved financial freedom, social freedom, the freedom to travel where we wish, the freedom to share the fruits of our labors and learning with others, and the freedom of good health have done so through self-mastery. The greatest human freedom is the power of free will. But we are free only to the extent that we have liberated our will from servitude to our tendencies.

Life Is Full of Tendencies

If you are hungry or upset or lonely, you may *tend* to eat sweets. If you are an alcoholic, you *tend* to have another drink. Tobacco addicts *tend* to have another cigarette. Some tendencies are genetic; others are psychological traits or behavior that you modeled from others. You may tend to underwork or to overwork, tend to eat too much or too little, tend to be shy or outgoing. Tendencies *tend* to shape your life. If you let them, they shape your destiny.

Tendencies describe a certain momentum. Newton's first law of motion states, "A body at rest tends to remain at rest, or a body in motion tends to remain in motion . . . unless acted upon by an outside force."

Or an inside force—the force of your will.

Your tendencies produce patterns that appear fixed, unconscious, and automatic. One of life's greatest challenges and satisfactions involves exerting the force of your will to change your tendencies.

> Give me where to stand,
> [and a long enough lever]
> and I will move the earth.
> **—Archimedes**

To change the course of your life, choose one of two basic methods:

1. You can direct your energy and attention toward trying to fix your mind, find your focus, affirm your power, free your emotions, and visualize positive outcomes so that you can finally develop the confidence to display the courage to discover the determination to make the commitment to feel sufficiently motivated to do what it is you need to do.
2. Or you can just do it.

Daily life provides us with many opportunities to confront and transcend our tendencies, thereby gaining both self-control and detachment. Here are some you might try—not habitually, of course, but on occasion:

- The next time someone offers you dessert and you want it, decline; and if you don't want it, accept.
- Be especially kind to someone you dislike.

- Drive or move even slower when you are late.
- If you like to hit the snooze button on your alarm, get out of bed immediately after the alarm rings.
- In any challenging situation, ask yourself, "What would my strongest, bravest, most courageous, most loving part do right now?" Then do it. Do it right. Do it right now.

Do It or Don't—But Hold the Excuses

Don't be a master of "If only"—if only I had more time, more money, a better opportunity, different parents, a more understanding spouse, no children.

Life is tough. Be tougher.

Reclaiming your will isn't easy, but life is not about easy; it's about finding inner strength you didn't know you had. And remembering that you didn't come here for "easy."

It would be nice if we could master life from our armchairs—achieving our goals through positive thinking or creative visualization alone. But the power to change depends not on what you hope or wish or think or feel or even believe; it depends on what you *do*. Doing can be tough, and life can be difficult. It's supposed to be, at least some of the time, because life develops in us only what it demands of us. Daily life is a form of spiritual weight lifting, and you are here to strengthen your spirit.

If your purpose in life is to make life easier, don't get married, don't have children, avoid responsibilities, work minimally for basic subsistence needs, and learn to live cheaply. Don't commit and never volunteer. Don't own things, because they break. Hitchhike through life. Rely on the goodwill, charity, or tolerance of others. If you run out of family or friends to help, there's always the government.

I've known a few people who live like that, sitting out the dance, taking an incarnational vacation. Sometimes these vagabonds are interesting characters, but for the most part they are not exemplars of human potential.

Only the most courageous souls come to this planetary school.

And only awakening souls pick up a book like this. If you have read this far, you have all the will you need.

Reclaiming your will can make or break your life. Just stop looking for easy ways. Instead lay it on the line—picture yourself standing on the edge of a cliff with your habit right behind you, ready to push. Visualize your tendency holding a gun to your head, for in a way it is. Imagine having to choose between continuing your habit or saving the life of a child (and that child is you). Then make your stand. You may feel like giving in to a habit or tendency; you may miss it, want it, or believe you need to do it because you feel so much pain. Accept that your feelings are natural. But know your purpose, your will, and your power. And know that all your angels and ancestors, all those who came before you, are watching and cheering you on. Then do what you have set out to do. If you backslide, love yourself anyway and hold your course. Your cheering section is still with you. Build a new way of life, one day, one hour, one minute, at a time.

Take inspiration from people like Helene Hines, who was diagnosed with multiple sclerosis. She had sought medical treatment when she first experienced weakness in her legs; it turned to numbness, and finally, at age thirty, she had complete paralysis. After undergoing electrotherapy to tone the muscles of her legs, she began an intense period of rehabilitation, first walking, then running. Helene still has MS. But she is now a 4:20 marathoner, inspiring thousands who run with her in the New York City Marathon every year. Helene's husband reports, "No matter how lousy Helene feels, she goes out every day and does what needs to be done."

Winning the Battle of Will

Wherever there's a will, there's a won't. You know that accomplishment takes effort, even sacrifice.

Even if you know something is good for you, even if you know you really ought to do it, even when you ardently want it to happen, even if you agree with the value of accepting your feelings, knowing your purpose, and doing what needs to be done—

won't-power sometimes wins out over willpower. So be gentle with yourself. It can take time to awaken your will. The time you take is entirely up to you. Negative thoughts and feelings may continue, but your power will grow until one day, one moment, you discover that even when you *can't* do something, you have done it anyway.

Following Higher Will

Throughout history, and into the new millennium, those who have engaged mighty endeavors—missions to discover new continents or explore new worlds—have drawn upon not only their own inner strength, but also a higher will that takes them beyond their own personal power. When you strive to go beyond yourself, even in everyday life, or to struggle against immense odds or difficulty, you can also call upon a higher will. Countless people in a life-and-death battle with alcohol or other drugs have found strength in the prayerful words "Not my will but Thy will be done."

Whether or not you believe in an external God or relate more to a universal Spirit or life force, by surrendering your will to the will of your higher self, or Spirit, or God, you can find infinite strength. That strength can support you as you begin to serve its source, surrendering your individual desires to the higher purpose of serving family, society, and humanity. Instead of asking, "What do I prefer? Is it in my best interest?" you begin to ask, "What is for the highest good of all concerned?" This question spiritualizes your relationships and creates newfound meaning and connection with your family, your business associates, and the larger world in which you live.

As you leave this gateway, remember that you too are on a mission—exploring inner space and discovering new worlds as you pass through the twelve gateways. Every life has its heroic struggles. By reclaiming your will, you find the power to persevere in the face of odds or obstacles. The power of your will is a master key to everyday enlightenment, and to all the gateways to come.

THE

THIRD GATEWAY

Energize Your Body

*Your body is the only thing
you are guaranteed to keep for a lifetime.
It forms the foundation of your earthly existence.
Energizing your body
enriches your life
by enhancing every human capacity.
If you lack vitality,
nothing else really matters;
if you have your health,
anything is possible.*

A Foundation for Life

Your body is the ground and metaphor of your life,
the expression of your existence.
It is your Bible, your encyclopedia, your life story.
Everything that happens to you
is stored and reflected in your body.
In the marriage of flesh and spirit
divorce is impossible.

—Gabrielle Roth

Road Map: Beyond Good Advice

If you haven't yet achieved optimal energy, vitality, and health, it is not because you haven't read or heard good advice on the topic. Most of us are on information overload. The world is filled with guidelines and principles. But how many of us turn what we know into what we do?

Good advice isn't enough. You can read a never-ending stream of principles and programs in books and magazines, but you will benefit only from what you do each and every day. That is why it's so important to keep it simple and practical. That is why, in the third gateway, you will find not only practical methods for energizing your body, but also practical ways to apply these methods in everyday life.

Here's an example: Take one slow, deep breath—as slowly and deeply as you can, without strain, expanding first your belly and then your chest—and feel yourself relax as you exhale slowly. In the same manner, take two more deep breaths before proceeding. And from now on, for the rest of your life, take at least one deep, deliberate breath every hour. Take a nice deep breath right now and you've begun; you've hardly stepped into the gateway and you have already learned an energizing practice for life worth infinitely more than the price of this book—if you do it.

This book, like this life, represents a wonderful opportunity or a waste of time, depending upon what you do with it. We benefit from an exercise machine, or book, or seminar, or lifetime only to the extent we use it.

In this gateway we come back to the body basics—a tour through the holy trinity of health, exploring seven dietary principles for increased immunity, longevity, and energy, and how to maintain a higher energy level. You will also learn the vital secrets of conscious exercise, breath, and relaxation, culminating in the Peaceful Warrior Workout—the most efficient routine of flowing movement, deep breathing, and tension release you may ever learn.

Back to the Body

Many of us have a love-hate relationship with our bodies. We indulge them, deprive them, stuff them or starve them, overwork and underwork them, spoil them, punish them, enjoy them, suffer them, and, at times, feel betrayed by them. How many of us wish to fly free of our physical mortality, to travel out of our bodies before we've fully gotten into them—to reincarnate before we've fully incarnated?

> If you don't take care of your body,
> where will you live?
> **—Unknown**

Energize Your Body begins by making peace with and coming to love and admire the body you've been given. In fact, your body is the *only* thing you are guaranteed to keep for an entire lifetime. You can't say that about your spouse, children, home, car, money, or beliefs—only your body. It is your only real possession, so it pays to treat it well. If you do so, many other things fall into place. No matter where our flights of fancy take us, we return to a fundamental truth: The human journey begins and ends with the body.

Energy Assessment: The following questions are not in any way comprehensive but are intended only to stimulate initial reflection on your body, health, priorities, and energy in everyday life.

- Are you completely satisfied with your own body?
- If not, what would you rather change, your appearance or energy level?
- On a scale of 1–10, how would you rate your average energy level?
- Does your body function as well as you would like?
- How much time, out of each twenty-four hours, do you spend on the health and fitness of your body?
- How much time do you spend maintaining or improving your physical strength, your stamina, and your flexibility?
- Consider your priorities: How much time, energy, and attention do you spend on health, fitness, and energy compared to your primary relationship, your children, your education, your worth, recreation, entertainment, and sleep?
- Do you listen to your body?
- Do you treat your body with care and kindness?
- What three things do you like most about your body?
- What three things do you like least about your body?
- What can you change, and what can you learn to accept and appreciate?

There are no right or wrong answers, but considering these questions opens you to make the best use of this gateway.

Higher Outcomes and Hidden Benefits

This gateway combines body and spirit to offer both practical and transcendental outcomes. The functional practices and principles presented here will help you build a foundation of physical vitality and health. And by cultivating an energizing lifestyle, bringing your body to a state of dynamic balance, you also achieve three higher outcomes:

1. **Liberating Your Attention:** When your body rests in dynamic balance with energy coursing through you freely, you feel a deeper connection to life and you begin to ascend to higher states of attention and awareness.
2. **Amplifying Your Capacities:** Increased energy enhances your strength, mental alertness and brightness, charisma and personal presence, sensitivity and intuition, and even the ability to heal yourself and assist in the healing of others.
3. **Preparing Yourself for the Gateways to Come:** This gateway provides a foundation for all those that follow, because energy is the common denominator that provides the stamina, fortitude, and focus necessary to face the challenges ahead.

Managing Your Energy

Energy is the most abundant substance in the universe; in fact, it is the universe. You are made of energy; you take it in at the gross levels from the food you eat and, on more refined levels, from the air you breathe and from the people and living things around you.

Why, then, do you feel so little energy at times? There are several explanations for this, both physical and psychological, including (1) a weak link in the trinity of health—poor diet, insufficient rest, lack of exercise—resulting in toxicity, enervation, imbalance, and compromised immune response; and (2) low motivation—a lack of compelling purpose, resulting in a depressed autonomic nervous system (the "blahs").

The key to managing your physical energy is actually threefold:

- how much (and how efficiently) you *assimilate* energy through the food you eat and the air you breathe
- how much (and how efficiently) you maintain and *channel*

energy through your body through exercise, stretching, relaxation, and massage

● how much (and how efficiently) you use or *spend* energy in
the world.

As you will explore in the next gateway, *Manage Your Money,* an
often ignored financial principle states that no matter how much
money you take in, you remain poor if you spend more than you
make. This same principle applies to the arena of vital energy.

You may recall the story of the man who stood on a mountain-
top and cried up to God, "Fill me full of light!" A voice thundered
down from the heavens, "I'm always filling you—but you keep
leaking!"

Even now, abundant energy flows through the world, swirling
around you, flowing through you. Your primary task in managing
energy is to clear internal energy leaks so you can maintain a
higher energy level.

Energy leaks can stem from mental sources (including anxiety, worry, regret, and preoccupation), emotional sources (including fear, sorrow, and anger), or physical sources (including
illness, injuries, postural imbalances, overloaded digestive systems). All of these produce tension and discomfort, which reduce
physical vitality.

To understand how and why you have developed energy leaks,
imagine a flowing river whose water represents the energy flowing through your body. A free-flowing river has great energy and
power, but if trees or boulders obstruct the flow, it creates turbulence. In your body you experience these obstructions—this turbulence—as tension and discomfort, which in turn drain your
energy.

There are two primary ways to reduce the discomfort: (1) you
can clear the obstructions; or (2) you can lower the level of energy
(water), resulting in less flow, less turbulence, and less discomfort.

Few of us have learned how to clear the mental, emotional,
and physical obstructions in our bodies, so we often resort to the
second solution: finding ways to lower our energy level, thereby

reducing tension and discomfort. The obstructions (problems) remain, but by lowering the flow of energy, we reduce the symptoms and don't feel them as intensely.

The most common forms of tension release include exercise, sexual climax, creative endeavors, physical and mental overexertion, thrill seeking (including gambling, suspense films, and video games), overeating, and the use of alcohol or other drugs. The problem with any of these methods is that once we release the tension and feel better, the energy begins to build again and the discomfort increases, so we need to release it again. This repetitive cycle is commonly known as addictive behavior.

The twelve gateways teach a more lasting solution to this problem by showing you how to clear away your obstructions. Doing so enables you to

- experience more joy, bliss, and spirit in everyday life.
- reduce or eliminate addictive drives and compulsive behaviors.
- increase your physical strength, mental alertness, intuitive sensitivity.
- strengthen your immune system, living a healthier, more energized life.

Open Secrets of Vibrant Health

Vibrant health is essential to removing the obstructions that create our tension and devitalize our bodies. The cornerstones of energy include moderate, regular exercise; a simple, healthful diet; enough fresh air, fresh water, and rest; and engaging in some form of creative activity. You also want to avoid the following three factors, which can compromise your immune system, resulting in illness:

1. **Toxicity:** Toxicity here refers to how we feel after eating or drinking more than we can effectively process, burdening our liver, kidneys, intestines, and eliminative organs. We all know the dull, heavy, tired, or queasy feeling that follows a bout of overindulgence. To avoid toxicity, enjoy quality, not

quantity. Eat less, exercise more, and hydrate your system with fresh water, herbal tea, and fruits and vegetables, which aid waste elimination.

2. **Enervation:** To enervate means "to weaken or destroy strength or vitality." Enervation refers to chronic, stressful fatigue, such as the exhaustion that arises from overworking at a job you don't enjoy. To avoid enervation, combine moderate, stress-releasing exercise with sufficient rest. And make sure you take at least three vacations each year; they are worth their weight in gold.

3. **Imbalance:** Your body maintains delicate temperature, sugar, hormonal, acid-base, and respiratory balances that can easily be upset. To avoid physical imbalance, remember to take some slow, deep breaths regularly, avoid extreme temperatures unless you are prepared for them, and make the following three keystones your holy trinity of energy and health.

The Holy Trinity of Health

Whenever people ask me for advice about problems ranging from the mundane to the metaphysical, I ask them three questions:

- Are you eating well?
- Are you exercising regularly?
- Are you getting enough rest?

These three questions constitute the holy trinity of health. All three, taken together, balance your body and generate vitality that enables you to meet the challenges of everyday life and the twelve gateways.

> I am convinced that a light supper,
> a good night's sleep, and a fine morning,
> have sometimes made a hero
> of the same man who,
> by an indigestion, a restless night, and rainy morning,
> would have proved a coward.
>
> **—Lord Chesterfield**

It is not enough to know about or merely appreciate the trinity of health. For you to benefit from them, these three elements—diet, exercise, rest—must become absolute priorities. Unless you make your health more important than your work, your money, or watching television, you will always find something more pressing to do instead. Each day you choose whether to make a nutritious meal at home or get some fast food, whether to get up early to exercise or sleep in because you stayed up late watching television. And let's face it, it's easier to watch television, sleep in, skip exercise, and grab some fast food. But ask yourself, "When I look into a full-length mirror, what do I see?" You see your living habits reflected back at you. So don't wait until you have time—*make* time.

Eating for Optimal Energy

Most of us know—and research supports this belief—that what we ingest affects our physical energy, our mind and moods, and our longevity, so we need to pay attention to what, when, and how we eat. But be wary of making diet too great a preoccupation. As my old mentor, Socrates, once said to me, "If you get too obsessed with discipline and purity—hell, the *stress* is gonna kill you."

Don't get lost in the details of food—how many calories this or that food has or whether the protein and carbohydrates are balanced. Instead I recommend focusing on the key principles that follow in this section. But first, let's overview how your diet can impact both the length and quality of your life.

Diet and Longevity

Some scientists suggest that longevity depends almost entirely upon genetics. Other scientists disagree. Studies of the diets, physical activities, and lifestyles of other cultures whose people live long lives suggest that our genetic inheritance may create a *tendency* to live a longer or shorter life, but that we have the ability to maximize our genetic potential through our habits. My conclusions are based in part on the research of Dr. Kenneth Pelletier, who studied the Vilcabamba people in the Ecuadorian Andes, the Hunza of northern Pakistan, the Abkhazanians in the former Soviet Union, the Mabaans of Sudan, and the Tarahumara Indians in northern Mexico, where he found enough people living in the 115–130 range to be worthy of serious study. Most important, Dr. Pelletier found that the same factors that contribute toward *quantity* and energy of life also contribute to its *quality*. Long life for its own sake means little, but when that life is filled with joy and vitality, each day becomes another opportunity to practice everyday enlightenment.

One of the most effective means of increasing the quality and quantity of life is through your diet.

> Never eat more than you can lift.
>
> —Miss Piggy

Seven Enlightened Dietary Practices

The following guidelines don't require sudden changes in your lifestyle, because abrupt changes have a way of changing back to old habits. Instead these practices involve a graceful adaptation to a new and enlivening lifestyle as you pay attention to what you eat and how you feel afterward, find what foods work best for you, and avoid swings from self-denial to self-indulgence. You create this lifestyle by applying the following principles:

1. **Eat less food.** Moderate, systematic undereating—smaller portions and less caloric intake—may be the most important dietary practice of all. Long-lived peoples consume 1,800–2,000 calories per day, in contrast with the average Westerner's 3,200–3,500 calories per day. (This practice of systematic undereating does *not* apply to growing children, people with very lean body types, pregnant or lactating

women, those with high metabolic or caloric expenditures, such as athletes or laborers, or those with eating disorders.)

2. **Eat less protein.** Many of us worry if we're getting enough, but long-lived peoples consume about *half* the amount of protein as the average Westerner. Nearly all are vegetarians or near vegetarians whose protein comes mostly from grains, legumes, and dairy products. They almost never eat red meat and only small amounts of fish or poultry. Long-lived peoples have far lower cholesterol levels, less coronary disease, and virtually no osteoporosis.

3. **Enjoy a variety of foods.** In the United States we genetically select uniform grains for high yields—the same kind of wheat, for example. A field of wheat in the Caucasus region of Russia, home of the long-lived Hunza people, contains different colors and sizes of plants, genetically diverse wheat with a variety of amino acids that combine into complete protein. This principle applies to far more than wheat, of course; anyone who eats a varied diet of different, seasonal fruits, vegetables, grains, and legumes is guaranteed sufficient protein, vitamins, and minerals.

4. **Experiment, and trust your instincts.** Young children, relying on instinct alone, will, when exposed to a variety of food groups over time, choose a well-balanced diet with the nutrients they need. Few of us trust our instincts, relying instead on what we have been taught by parents, sold through advertising, or theories from a variety of diet books. Our instincts have been distorted by such outside influences as a limited selection of food in the home, television advertising, and peer pressure to eat or behave according to tribal fashion. You can sharpen your instincts through exercise and fasting, as well as by adding or subtracting kinds (and amounts) of foods from your diet, then paying attention to how you feel after eating. This is one of the surest ways of combining instinct and awareness and finding an optimal diet for you. Trust your body over any theories or systems.

5. **Practice periodic fasting.** Fasting, or going without food

for one or more days (while drinking plenty of water and fruit juices), is a time-honored practice in nearly every spiritual tradition. Fasting provides a rest for the digestive system, generates a physical cleansing-detoxifying effect, improves immune function, affords extra time for reflection and contemplation, and relieves subconscious fears by providing the secure knowledge that if you ever have to go without food for days, you can do so. Fasting is *not* recommended for growing children, pregnant and lactating women, those with eating disorders, or lean body types with high metabolisms. Nor is it a weight-loss method. Before starting a fast, be sure to read one of the many books about this practice. If you have doubts or health problems, consult a health professional familiar with fasting.

6. **Enjoy more raw fruits and vegetables.** Increasing the proportion of fresh, uncooked vegetables and fruits in your diet provides unprocessed nutrients in their most direct form, with a full array of enzymes that help you assimilate the food you eat. These high-water-content foods also provide fiber necessary for good elimination. Eating mostly or exclusively raw foods naturally promotes weight loss, while ensuring high-quality nutrition and vitality. Eating only raw fruits and vegetables for a period of time has much the same cleansing effect as a fast.

7. **Pay attention to how you eat and drink.** How you eat is nearly as important as what you eat. A few simple habits can enhance your digestion and help you get the most from your food. Form the habit of chewing well and breathing deeply while eating, savoring the taste and aroma as you chew. Eat each bite as if it were the only one you will get all day. Put down your fork or spoon between each bite as you chew. (I'm still working on this one.)

Ultimately you are the final authority over how you feed your body, and you have to find what works best for you. Favor experimentation over rigid rules; diet involves lifelong learning and practice. The same applies to the arena of exercise, to which we now turn.

Energizing Exercise

How we define fitness determines the kinds of exercises we perform in order to achieve it. When strength was king, we lifted weights for fitness; when we decided that cardiovascular health was most important, we began running, race-walking, and practicing aerobic dance. As the definition shifts to neuromuscular balance, meditation, stretching, and relaxation exercises will form the core of our fitness training.

The Four S's of Physical Fitness

I've found four physical areas that contribute not only to total fitness, but also to what we commonly refer to as "physical talent." You can achieve complete and balanced fitness as well as increase your physical talent by conditioning all four of the following:

1. **Strength:** muscular power and control; the ability to move effectively even against resistance in the field of gravity
2. **Suppleness:** flexibility, elasticity, or optimal range of motion
3. **Stamina:** endurance; the ability to persist over time
4. **Sensitivity:** including balance, rhythm, timing, reflex speed, coordination.

As you develop the four S's of talent, you balance and open your body to the light of Spirit—literally enlightening your body—which is why athletics can, with a conscious attitude, become a form of spiritual practice.

Conscious Exercise

You exercise every time you move in the field of gravity—walking, sitting down and standing up, lifting and carrying groceries, climbing stairs, cleaning the house, gardening. As long as you are using your limbs, working your muscles (including your heart), and breathing deeply, you are exercising. By taking the stairs instead of the escalator, by parking your car a little farther from the store, you develop an energizing lifestyle. What counts is not only what you do for an hour at the gym, but how much you have moved by the end of each day, the end of each week.

Sports also provide some exercise, but competitive games are designed to release tension—to provide enjoyment, recreation, and skill development—not necessarily to provide balanced fitness training. In fact, most sports provide only limited and random fitness benefits.

Conscious exercise, in contrast, is designed *specifically* to improve the overall balance and development of the body. Conscious exercise

- develops a balance of all four S's of physical talent.
- combines movement, mind, and breath.
- makes ease and relaxation a priority.
- energizes rather than fatigues.
- involves an awareness of breathing patterns.
- creates symmetry (balances both sides of the body).
- includes specific elements of deliberate tension followed by relaxation (in order to release chronic tension).

Different forms of conscious exercise include hatha yoga, certain martial arts, Arica Psychocalisthenics, schools of noncompetitive gymnastics, trampoline, aerobics, dance, and the Peaceful Warrior Workout presented at the end of this chapter. Done regularly, and in moderation, conscious exercise can balance, rejuvenate, and energize your life.

Inspiration: Breathing for Energy and Longevity

You can live for weeks without food, days without water, but only minutes without breathing. For most of us, breathing is a relatively automatic, unconscious act. You don't usually notice your breathing unless you have a problem with it. One of the goals of spiritual practice is to make conscious what was previously unconscious. You don't suddenly have to pay attention to every breath you take, but you benefit by expanding your breathing capacity and control. A growing body of research links vital capacity (how deeply you can breathe) with longevity.

Breathing Basics

Your lungs are passive organs, like sacks. By expanding your thoracic (chest) cavity, you create a vacuum and suck air into the lungs. You do this primarily with the intercostal (between-the-rib) muscles. But the primary mechanism of full and relaxed breathing is the diaphragm (pictured below), a bell-shaped muscle separating the thoracic and abdominal cavities. When the diaphragm flattens as shown, it pulls air into the lungs; as it relaxes or moves forcefully back up, it pushes air from the lungs.

When infants breath in their natural, relaxed way, you will see their bellies move in and out, since they principally use the diaphragm (belly breathing). Most of us also breathe in this relaxed way when asleep. Diaphragmatic breathing is associated with a state of ease, serenity, and repose. Shallow or fitful chest breathing (using only the intercostal muscles to expand the upper chest) is associated with anxiety and tension.

Try this simple exercise.

1. Sitting up, place one palm on the center of your upper chest and the other palm against your lower abdomen, below your navel.
2. First, breathe with only your upper chest moving. (Your lower hand on the abdomen should not move at all.) Take

rapid and shallow breaths. With what emotional state would you associate this feeling?

3. Next, breathe with only your lower abdomen moving. (Your upper hand on your chest should not move at all.) If you tend to be very busy and tense in your life, breathing just with your belly may feel awkward or strange. If you have trouble feeling this, try lying on your back with one or two hardback books on your abdomen, and breathe so that the books rise (on inhalation) and fall (on exhalation). Once you get accustomed to it, you'll notice that (diaphragmatic) belly breathing almost immediately relaxes the body and creates a more serene state. In fact, since you usually experience emotions as a tension or contraction in your chest or abdomen, you will literally find it difficult to feel angry, afraid, or sad breathing this calming way.

4. Turning this relaxing, rejuvenating belly-breathing practice into a form of meditation, imagine yourself filling with light and energy as you inhale; and as you exhale, let your entire body relax, and imagine that you are breathing out toxins, negativity, or troubles.

It is natural to belly-breathe when sitting in repose, reading, relaxing, meditating, studying, talking with a friend. But you will also want to use your entire breathing apparatus, including your diaphragm, chest, and back muscles, when you are actively engaged in life—moving, climbing stairs, carrying groceries, or exercising. At times like these, you want to feel as if you are filling your lungs from the bottom up, like pouring water into a glass. So, in taking a deep breath, you begin by filling your belly (using your diaphragm), then your lower chest, and, finally, your upper chest. As you exhale, let the air flow out naturally. With this sense of full breathing under your belt, so to speak, you are ready to apply it in the most natural way in the world.

Walking and Breathing—Nature's Best Exercise

Walking is one of nature's best exercises and has myriad benefits. It is low impact, you can do it every day for your entire life, and you already have all the skills and equipment needed.

In severe weather you can walk indoors on a treadmill. Whenever possible, however, walk outdoors in the elements. Moving through the natural world, greeting neighbors, seeing the changing textures of light and shadow, can be a joyful, even spiritual, experience.

Breathing to a Count

The following practice, which combines walking and conscious breathing, is one you can easily integrate into your everyday life:

1. As you walk, inhale and exhale to a specific number of steps. Begin by inhaling for a count of two steps, then exhaling for a count of two steps (inhale-one-two, exhale-one-two), and continue this until you get used to the rhythm of breathing to that count. Now you are ready for the entire exercise, beginning with the two-count you've learned.

2. Inhale for two steps; exhale for two steps; then inhale for *three* steps; then exhale for three steps; then inhale for *four* steps and exhale for four steps; continuing with *progressively slower and deeper breathing,* increasing the number of steps to each long inhalation and exhalation until you reach your maximum count (perhaps up to ten or more steps to an inhale and exhale), stretching to the top of your comfort zone, but not straining.

3. After working up to as many steps as you can, work back down. For a long walk, when the progression is complete, maintain a comfortable rhythm, such as four steps to each inhalation and exhalation for the duration of the walk, creating a kind of meditation.

4. If you plan to walk only a short distance—say, from the parking space to the supermarket—try parking at the outermost corner of the lot and do the breathing-to-a-count exercise by twos: inhale for two steps and exhale for two, then four steps, then six, and so on.

5. Experiment to see what works for you. If you are inside,

you can do this exercise walking in place, on a jogging trampoline, with a stair climber, or on a stationary bicycle.

By expanding your vital capacity and energizing your body, you will improve your chances of living a longer and healthier life. You'll literally breathe easier for having done it.

Relaxation: Excellence with Ease

A woman recently asked if I could offer in one sentence some practical advice that would improve the quality of her life. I responded, "Breathe deeply, and relax as much as you can in everything you do."

If breathing is a key to longevity, relaxation is a key to energy.

Relaxation is one of the most important life skills you can learn, because the ability to relax enhances your strength, elasticity, grace, coordination, reflex, speed, sensitivity, sensuality, awareness, balance, peripheral blood circulation, breathing, and overall sense of well-being.

As infants, we were models of relaxation-in-action. As adults, our minds impose tension on our bodies. Regrets, anxieties, worries, and preoccupations—replaying unpleasant scenarios in our minds—create neuromuscular tensions. Nearly all of us carry some degree of chronic tension, which rises and falls in the course of everyday life, resulting in headaches, neckaches, sore lower back, chronic fatigue—classic energy leaks. By consciously learning to relax, we can return to a natural state of ease without tension.

Dynamic Relaxation

We normally associate relaxation with the stillness of sleep, trance, or meditation. But life is *movement,* so relaxation-in-motion is the highest form. The ancient swordmasters of China and Japan, living and moving in the moment of truth, had to relax or die. You and I, in our own moments of truth, can learn to relax into life. This is the highest practice, and also the most difficult.

Awareness and Relaxation

While you can't always control whether you feel peaceful, you *can* learn to let go of muscular tension at will. But your muscles can relax only if they remember what relaxation feels like. Many of our bodies have forgotten what it means to sit, stand, and move with the ease of a cat. Some of us attain a degree of relaxation only when asleep or self-medicated with tranquilizers, alcohol, or other drugs. Once your body experiences deep relaxation, your right brain can more easily duplicate that state at will, even in the midst of potentially stressful daily activities.

If possible, take ten minutes right now to do the following exercise, which is designed to induce deep relaxation:

1. Begin by lying comfortably on your back. If you wish, place pillows under your knees, arms, and head—whatever helps you find the most comfort.
2. Become aware of your body pressing down into the bed or floor, and notice the bed or floor pushing equally back against your body.
3. Allow yourself to feel a pleasant sense of weight, as if your skin, your bones, and your whole body is heavy.
4. Without concern over whether the process is working, or whether you are relaxing yet, let your awareness begin at your feet, feeling *your skin, bones, and whole body become heavy,* repeating this idea to yourself as your awareness, and the sense of heaviness, expands from your feet, up through your calves, knees, thighs, abdomen and lower back, chest and upper back, up through your torso to your shoulders, upper arms, forearms, out to your hands and fingers.
5. Then, releasing any residual tension, let the heaviness continue through your neck, jaw, ears, chin, mouth, nose, eyes, forehead, and scalp.
6. While in this pleasant state of relaxed heaviness, free of the usual tension, you have the best opportunity to feel and visualize yourself practicing a sport or musical skill. Once you are freed of interfering tensions, the skill you imagine

is imprinted more clearly on your right brain or body consciousness. I would often do this when I was a gymnast,
with excellent results.

7. Before you come back to everyday awareness, scan your
body and remember that you can return to this state of
profound ease just by thinking a key word or phrase such
as "Relax" or "Let go."

8. When ready, take three deep breaths, each breath deeper
than the last, and with a third deep breath, feeling re-
freshed and alert, stretch like a cat and sit or stand, remembering how relaxed you can feel in stillness or in motion.

Slowing down for Ease and Energy

Slowing down in life, deliberately moving in very slow motion,
amplifies awareness and expands time, enabling you to be conscious of every part of a movement—to notice and release any
tension of which you would otherwise have remained unaware.

The following exercise helps illustrate this principle:

1. Perform any familiar skill, such as hitting an imaginary
tennis shot, throwing a ball, playing part of a musical score,
or swinging a golf club, at three speeds: first at regular
speed, then at half speed, then in slow motion—moving so
slowly that someone observing you from a distance would
hardly see you moving.

2. As you move, notice your breathing, your balance, how
your weight shifts from one foot to the other, the relationships among your different body parts. Especially notice
any extra tension you are holding, and in each moment see
if you can let it go and relax even more.

Once you become aware of tension, you automatically take
steps to release it. This results in more efficient movement, so that
when you move at a normal (but unhurried) tempo, you do so
with greater ease, lightness, and energy. Try it. You may be pleas-
antly surprised.

Alignment in the Field of Gravity

Watch how young children sit, stand, and move. Notice how well their pliable bodies have adapted to gravity, sitting and standing straight, with each section of the body balanced in correct alignment above the other. As the years pass, because of injuries and stresses, our bodies become misaligned to one degree or another. This is a chief source of physical energy leaks.

When you rise out of bed in the morning, your body becomes a stack of building blocks, moving through space. Moving correctly saves vast amounts of energy; moving and standing incorrectly produces tension, wasted energy, and pain. Good posture—sitting, standing, and moving tall and aligned in gravity—has a very real energy payoff.

To illustrate how misaligned posture creates tension and pain, picture eight children's blocks stacked on top of one another. If you push down on that column when it is out of alignment (see next page)—with some blocks forward, others back, some twisted or turned—the blocks will fly in every direction. If your posture mirrors those misaligned blocks, the energy and muscular tension it takes to hold yourself together in the course of a day drains energy. (Imagine just holding your arm muscles slightly tense all day—it drains energy just as a dripping faucet leaks water.) To experience how this works, do the following:

1. Bend slightly forward or sideward at the waist and hold that position for thirty seconds. Notice that it doesn't take too long to feel the muscle strain. Where there is strain, there will be pain and energy drain.

2. Sitting down, stick your chin out or tilt your head forward, the way many of us do habitually as we talk, watch television, or read. If you hold that position, you'll begin to notice a tension at the back of the neck, creating a headache and neck pain. The same thing happens if you hunch forward over studies, reading or working at a desk. (When you bend forward while sitting, do so from the hips, keeping your back straight.) Hunching over makes it more difficult to

take a deep breath. Poor posture, if chronic, leads to inhibited breathing, which contributes to other health maladies.

If the building blocks are in proper vertical alignment, you could place a heavy weight on that column of blocks, and because the structure is sound, it would remain strong. Similarly, when your body is properly aligned with gravity, with your head balanced naturally atop your spine (as if a wire from the sky were attached to the top back of your head, pulling up), this proper alignment frees up tremendous energy. At first it seems to require conscious attention and effort to hold your head tall and your chin slightly in, but once you get used to this posture, it becomes natural and effortless.

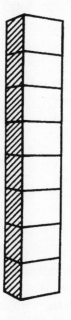
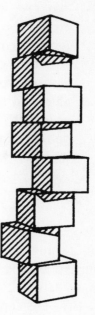

In realigning your posture, you will find that your body immediately feels lighter, freer, younger, and more elastic. You will breathe easier as your chest opens and belly relaxes. There are several methods to regain your youthful posture.

- The first method is *awareness*. Check your posture in a mirror. Awareness and a (literal) period of self-reflection can serve as a reminder to sit, stand, and walk tall. Self-consciousness can turn to consciousness.

- The second method is *bodywork*. Ultimately, any exercise you do to balance the body is a form of bodywork, but *deep-tissue work* such as Rolfing or Hellerwork is a specific form of bodywork that helps to realign your body in the field of gravity. Unlike massage, which can be wonderfully relaxing but addresses only the symptoms of misalignment, deep-tissue work provides longer-lasting relief by lengthening, realigning, and unifying the structure and relationship of your different body parts.

- The third method is to work with a practitioner specializing in *movement awareness* such as Alexander Technique, Feldenkrais Method, or Aston Patterning; another form of awareness training such as yoga, martial arts, or other forms of conscious exercise.

- You can perform the following method of bodywork yourself. As described, it takes very little time, is pleasurable, and brings immediate results. I've done it daily for years with wonderful results. Each morning and evening, do it to relax and realign the body by reversing the force of gravity.

Beating Gravity at Its Own Game

This simple and enjoyable practice instantly transforms gravity from a compressing, degenerative force into an elongating, regenerative one. This practice realigns and balances the body by providing natural traction. It also helps to prevent or reduce the severity of osteoporosis in older people. It strengthens your forearms and grip, reduces wear, tear, and pressure on the spine, and opens up and decompresses every joint in your body.

What is this miraculous exercise? It is simply *hanging*—a natural, enjoyable, even instinctual activity. All you need is a doorway hanging bar, available at most sporting goods stores—the kind of bar with brackets that screw into the sides of the doorjamb, for security.

- Each morning upon rising and each evening before retiring, grasp the bar (bending your knees if necessary) and hang.
- If your grip is not strong enough to hold the bar while supporting your weight, stand on the floor or a chair to support part of your weight (but as little as possible) until your grip becomes stronger (which usually takes a week or two).
- Start out hanging for five or ten seconds; then increase up to thirty seconds or more, breathing slowly and deeply and feeling your arms, shoulders, and entire spine stretch out. (Hanging for thirty seconds provides the equivalent of a fifteen-minute massage.)

The Peaceful Warrior Workout™

More than a decade ago I designed an efficient routine of flowing movement, deep breathing, and tension release that incorporated elements from calisthenics, dance, gymnastics, martial arts, and yoga. Most important, I made sure that once you become familiar with it, you can complete the routine in less than four minutes a day, in a relatively small space. It's nearly excuse-proof. I have done it every morning for the last decade to jump-start my day. Other people tell me it's a perfect warm-up for any sport or game or just to loosen up after a busy workday—a relaxing yet energizing transition between work and home. If this workout is the only part of this book that you put into practice, you will still experience tangible benefits that increase over time.

This routine of conscious exercise goes beyond most fitness regimes in its style and purpose. Consistent with the higher purpose of the twelve gateways, the Peaceful Warrior Workout provides an efficient and balanced fitness routine, developing elements of strength, suppleness, stamina, and sensitivity.

It also operates at more subtle energetic levels. To understand this, consider the following: Although your body is the most visible aspect of who you are, you are surrounded and interpenetrated by an energy field (also called an aura) that connects the physical self to the Light that is always emanating from Spirit.

The planet Earth, like the human body (and all living things), has an energy field, called the biosphere. If the Earth's energy field is polluted by radiation or toxic gases, it affects the physical body of the planet. In the same way, negative thought forms— regrets, worries, resentments—will pollute the human energy field, creating weak or sensitive areas that then are susceptible to injury or illness.

A strong energy field means a strong body. The flowing movements and deep breathing of the Peaceful Warrior Workout liberate energy and attention to enhance your functioning on physical, mental, and emotional levels. As you complete this workout, your energy field becomes larger, brighter, and cleaner, like the atmosphere after a good rain. You will feel more expansive, alert, and relaxed.

While no four-minute exercise routine can equal an hour at the gym, this workout is unique in integrating all elements of fitness in an efficient package and helps to create a more energized body.

Remember that you gain only from what you can sustain. You are more likely to maintain this workout over time because it is relatively easy to learn, doesn't take much time or space, and feels good. Four minutes a day, every day, can go a long way. Keep it short, sweet, and simple. Experience the power of relaxed movement and deep breathing. Make it the foundation of an energizing lifestyle.

General Guidelines for Learning and Practicing the Series

- Respect your body's learning process; go gently at first.
- If you have any physical problems, consult with an appropriate health professional. Problems that result from muscle weakness, inactivity, or lack of flexibility will improve over time as you progress. If you feel discomfort or if a

particular element feels too difficult at first, find a way to make it easier for yourself—work around the problem area.

- Do all (or some version of all) the exercises, and in the order presented. You'll benefit most from the elements that give you the most trouble, so don't skip them.
- Each time you flow through the workout, ask yourself, "How can I do each movement a little better?" That way you are always improving.
- Do the workout outdoors or in a carpeted space about six by six feet, clear of furniture.
- To complete the series in four minutes or less, do the number of repetitions indicated. Ultimately, the number of repetitions is entirely up to you and may vary, depending on your needs or energy that day.
- Enjoy the routine to music or in silence, as a moving meditation.
- Perform the movements vigorously or in slow motion, very consciously, as in hatha yoga or the Chinese martial art of tai chi chuan.
- Do the Peaceful Warrior Workout each morning or at another regular time so it becomes a natural part of your daily routine. The key to making this routine part of your everyday life is to commit to doing it every day for thirty-six days. At that point your subconscious will recognize it as a habit. If you skip even one of the first thirty-six days, the next day is day one as far as the subconscious is concerned.

Specific Guidelines

- Exercise is only as beneficial as the posture in which it is performed. Relaxation, breathing, and posture are key. If possible, use a mirror for the first few days to check your technique.
- For moves done to both sides, you can begin to the left or to the right, but stay consistent.
- Pay special attention to deep breathing as you flow through the elements. Breathe as deeply as possible without strain,

coordinating your breathing with each element; feel as if the breath is moving the body. Inhale through the nose; exhale through the nose or mouth.

● Pay attention to the foot widths as shown. For each standing exercise, the feet are parallel and one, two, or three foot widths apart, as shown.

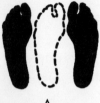

A	B	C
(one foot width)	(two foot widths)	(three foot widths)
NARROW	SHOULDER WIDTH	WIDE

The Peaceful
Warrior Workout

1
Stretch-Back Swing-Down

Directions:

- Palms are together in front of you as you inhale and raise arms overhead.
- Still inhaling, squeeze your buttocks as your arms bend and drop behind your head and you stretch gently backward.
- Begin exhaling as you straighten your arms and body, then continue exhaling as you swing your arms forward and down in a wide arc, bending your knees and letting your head drop and relax forward.
- As you finish your exhale, your arms swing back behind you and you momentarily straighten the knees for a stretch.
- Then bend your knees and begin inhaling as your arms swing forward, palms together, rising upward into the second repetition.

Reminders:

- One foot width
- Three repetitions
- Inhale up and back, exhale down
- Buttocks firm when stretching back
- Bend knees on down- and upswing
- Straighten legs momentarily at end of downswing

Benefits:

- Inspiring warm-up
- Gentle stretch of the spine
- Invigorates entire body
- Frees obstructed energy for exercises to follow
- Begins to clear tensions around heart and solar plexus

NARROW

Start

a

b

c

d

e

f

g

h

i

Finish

85

2

Squat-Down Side-Stretch

Directions:

- With your back straight, exhale as you squat halfway down and rest the back of your forearms on your thighs.
- As you begin inhaling, rise directly to the left side-stretch position, facing front (not twisted or turned), arms stretched sideways, and elbows behind your ears.
- Exhaling, squat back down as in the beginning, then rise to your right, as shown, and repeat.

Reminders:

- Three foot widths
- Three repetitions
- Inhale during side-stretch, exhale down to squat
- Keep weight evenly balanced
- Hip stretches opposite direction of arms
- Face front squarely with upper elbow behind ear
- Forearms rest on thighs during squat
- Rise directly to side-stretch rather than standing straight up, then leaning

Benefits:

- Opens rib cage and expands lungs
- Sideward stretch of the spine
- Generates vitality
- Clears energy around the head and shoulder areas

WIDE

a

b

c

d

a & c
(Side View)

3

Neck Release

Directions:

- Standing in a natural posture, inhale as your head moves forward and down in a relaxed manner—do not force the movement—then exhale as you relax in the forward position.
- Inhale as your head tilts directly left (nose and chin facing forward, not twisted), and exhale as you relax in that position.
- Continuing to move when you inhale and relax when you exhale, place your head gently backward by lifting chin, with teeth closed but not clenched; do not force movement.
- Inhale directly to the right, and relax in the position.
- Then inhale as your head returns to a forward hanging position and exhale as it relaxes.

Reminders:

- Two foot widths
- One repetition each position: front, left, back, right, front
- Inhale moving to position, exhale/relax in position
- Let weight of head do the stretch rather than forcing head
- As head bends sideward, keep opposite shoulder down
- Gently lift chin rather than forcing head back, with teeth closed

Benefits:

- Relaxes tensions of jaw, neck, and shoulders
- Opens the lungs
- Clears tensions related to the weight of responsibility

SHOULDER WIDTH

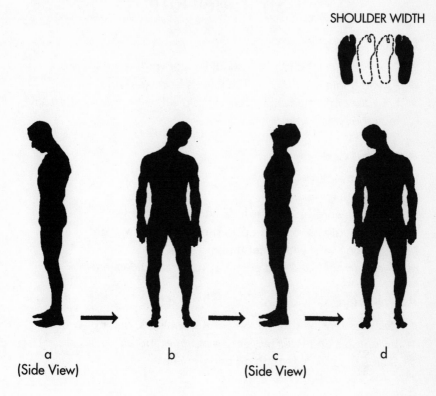

a
(Side View)

b

c
(Side View)

d

89

4

Shoulder Roll

Directions:

- As you begin inhaling, pull shoulders forward, then upward.
- As you begin exhaling, pull shoulders backward and down.
- Let your arms themselves remain relaxed, with one hand grasping the other wrist behind you.

Reminders:

- Two foot widths
- Three repetitions
- Inhale forward-upward, exhale backward-downward
- Circle shoulders forward-upward-backward-downward
- Grasp one wrist with other hand
- Keep arms relaxed and passive, and let shoulders move

Benefits:

- Releases tension around the chest, shoulders, and upper back
- Invigorates and frees movement of upper thorax
- Clears emotional tension around the heart

SHOULDER WIDTH

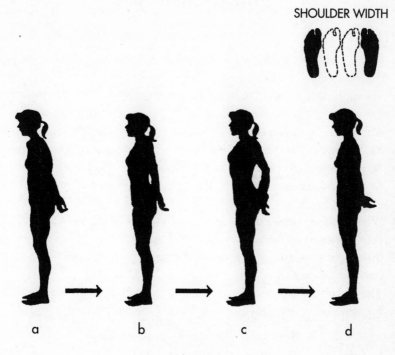

a   b   c   d

(Side View)

5

Spine Swing

Directions:

- Hold your arms straight and sideward at shoulder height, forming a straight line.
- Throughout the exercise, your hips remain square to the front: in other words, the turning is done at the waist; your hips do not move.
- Also, your arms remain in a straight-line, 180-degree relationship as if a broom handle were tied across your chest and to both arms.
- As you inhale, pull your left arm behind you and turn your head left so that you can see your left hand (this also exercises your neck as it turns).
- When you've turned as far as you can to the left, exhale rapidly as your upper torso turns back to face front and so you have time to then inhale as you pull your right arm behind you and turn your head to the right.
- The breathing is the most challenging part, as each inhalation pulls an arm behind you, followed by a rapid exhalation to the front.

Reminders:

- Three foot widths
- Six to ten turns each side
- Inhale going back (to right or left), exhale rapidly coming back to center
- Keep knees relaxed and slightly flexed
- Keep hips square, facing front to stretch waist
- Head turns to look back as arm pulls back
- Hands and arms form straight line as if broom handle were tied to both arms

Benefits:

- Benefits internal pelvic organs
- Prevents atrophy of lower spine (associated with aging)
- Clears energy field from knees to top of head
- Increases vitality

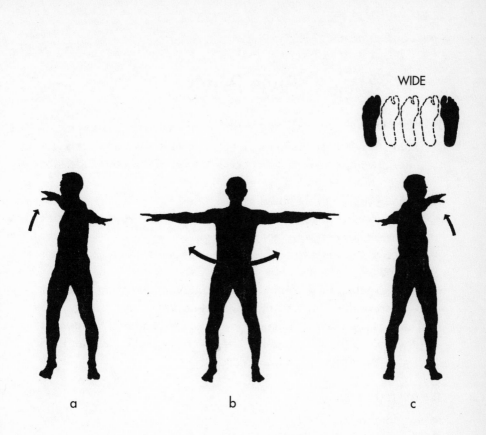

WIDE

a   b   c

6

Elvis Pelvis

Directions:

- During this exercise, imagine that your pelvis is like a bowl, and feel it tilt forward, sideward, or backward, then to the other side in a circular, hulalike motion.
- Begin by relaxing your knees.
- As you inhale, let your pelvis tilt forward (so that your lower back arches slightly and your rear protrudes).
- Then, as you begin to exhale, move your pelvis around to the left (it will tilt to the right).
- Then, exhaling fully, continue the circular motion as you tuck your pelvis forward and under (the bowl tilts back).
- Then, as you begin to inhale, move your pelvis around to the right (it will tilt to the left), forming one complete circle. You can then continue circling, or reverse direction.

Reminders:

- Two foot widths
- Three circles each direction
- Inhale as pelvis circles back, exhale as pelvis circles front
- Knees relaxed with head tall and still
- Pelvis (not belly) moves in circular movement

Benefits:

- Frees movement of the pelvis
- Releases tension in lower back and hip fascia
- Aids digestion by moving intestines
- Clears energy field from knees to navel
- Frees blocked sexual-creative energy

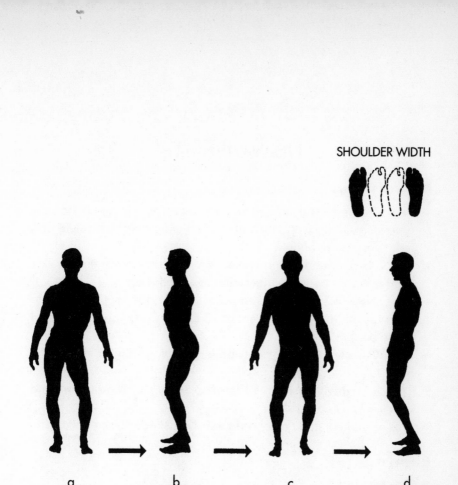

SHOULDER WIDTH

a
Hip Left

b
Hip Back
(Side View)

c
Hip Right

d
Hip Front
(Side View)

95

7

Heaven-Earth

Directions:

- Begin by inhaling as you bend your knees slightly and bend your arms as if lifting a weight with both hands; hold the inhale and tense your entire body.
- As you begin to exhale and relax, extend your left arm directly skyward and your opposite (right) arm toward the earth.
- Note that whatever arm is upward, you lift the opposite knee to waist height with your leg bent at 90 degrees and your toe pointed to the earth.
- Return to original bent-knee tension position as you inhale and hold.
- Then raise the opposite (right) arm up with your left arm down and your left knee up, as shown.
- This movement can be done vigorously or slowly, for balance.

Reminders:

- One foot width
- Three repetitions each side
- Inhale and tense entire body as knees bend slightly and arms curl
- Exhale and relax-extend as one arm stretches up and the other arm down
- Knee lifts to waist height same side as down arm
- Watch a spot in front of you to help balance
- For extra challenge, rise up on the ball of your foot as you stretch upward

Benefits:

- Invigorates entire musculature
- Enhances coordination and balance
- Floods energy field with strength and vitality
- Releases numerous points along energy meridians

NARROW

a

b

c

d

a / c
(Side View)

b / d
(Side View)

8
Cross-Country Ski Hop

Directions:

- This smooth, low-impact, but lively scissorslike movement is intended to stimulate the cardiovascular system as you gently jump from a left-leg lunge to a right-leg lunge.
- Begin in a lunge position, forward knee bent about 90 degrees, with either the left or the right leg forward.
- Both feet face forward with the back heel off the ground.
- When first learning, don't be concerned with your arms; just practice jumping and scissoring smoothly from a left-leg lunge to a right-leg lunge.
- Once the legs move easily, add your arm movements, as in walking, with the opposite arm and leg swinging forward (in other words, left leg and right arm).
- Breathe in coordination with the hops, starting with two hops to an inhalation and two hops to an exhalation, later increasing to three or four hops to an inhalation/exhalation cycle.

Reminders:

- One foot width
- Ten to twenty repetitions
- Back and torso vertical
- Inhale for four hops, then exhale for four hops
- Gentle, low-impact sliding motion, right lunge to left lunge
- Weight equal on both feet or slightly more on front leg
- Your weight is evenly distributed on both legs in each lunge position
- Relax and let the movements happen smoothly
- It may take a few days to master opposite arm-and-leg forward

Benefits:

- Stimulates cardiovascular system
- Increases power of legs
- Enhances coordination
- Expands energy field
- Contributes to improved rhythm, timing, vitality

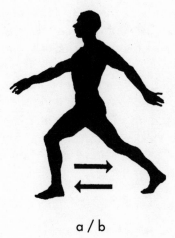

a / b

9
Buns Down, Buns Up

Directions:

- Begin as in a push-up position, arms straight and shoulders directly above your wrists, with the arms parallel and back straight.
- Your arms remain straight throughout the movements.
- Then, as you inhale, let your hips (and buns) sink down toward the floor, letting your back arch as you look forward and slightly upward with your eyes.
- Then, as you exhale, lift your hips (and buns) up toward the ceiling as you press your heels toward the floor and bring your head forward between your arms so that you can see your belly.
- From this piked or jackknife position, begin inhaling as you let your hips (and buns) drop back down toward the floor, beginning the movement once again.

Reminders:

- Three repetitions of complete movement
- Inhale as hips (buns) lower toward floor and back arches
- Exhale as hips (buns) pike upward
- Arms remain straight at all times
- As you arch your back (buns down), lift your head gently, eyes looking up
- You may at first need to take an extra breath between the movements; no need to strain

Benefits:

- Improves flexibility of spine and legs
- Releases tension in lower back and abdomen
- Strengthens shoulders, wrists
- Opens creative area of solar plexus

a

b

10

Rock and Roll

Directions:

- This rhythmic backward-then-forward rolling motion stretches the upper and lower spine.
- From sitting position with knees bent and arms extended, pull arms back and roll backward, exhaling and bringing bent knees upward until arms push above and behind you against floor and your bent knees are near your forehead as shown.
- Then roll forward as you inhale.
- Exhale once again as you reach and stretch forward, letting your head drop forward and down, placing the soles of your feet together and your knees stretched sideward. You are now ready to begin inhaling as you roll backward to repeat the entire movement.

Reminders:

- Three repetitions of complete forward-and-backward rolling movement
- Inhale during roll back and roll forward
- Exhale when all the way back and when all the way forward (stretching)
- Back remains rounded for smooth rolling action (may thump when first learning)
- Don't force; roll smoothly; range of movement improves over time
- On roll back, straight arms extend up and back, behind ears to protect neck, with legs together, knees bent toward forehead
- On roll forward, knees spread sideward, soles of feet together, head relaxing forward and down, arms reaching forward

Benefits:

- Invigorates lymphatic and vascular circulation
- Increases flexibility of upper and lower spine and hips
- Releases stored tension
- Stimulates release of energy

Finish

Start

e

a

d

b

c

103

11
V-Ups

Directions:

- Begin flat on your back.
- As you inhale, lift your head and shoulders up and forward, followed by straight* legs, to a point of momentary balance on your tailbone at the top of the inhale and movement, so that you balance like a "V."
- Exhaling down, place your heels on the floor, then uncurl the upper spine until your head finally rests on the floor. Head up first, down last.

Reminders:

- Three repetitions
- Inhale on upward movement
- Exhale on downward movement
- *You may want to first learn V-ups with knees bent slightly before performing with your legs straight
- Make sure that your head comes *up first* and goes *down last;* this serves to press the lower back to the floor, protecting it while you are doing the leg-lifting movement; lift your head high enough to see your belly before you lift your legs; and on the way down, watch your heels touch the floor before you lower your spine, then head back to the floor
- When you come down, uncurl one vertebra at a time, from the lower spine and working up

Benefits:

- Strengthens lower and upper abdominal muscles
- Improves balance and coordination
- Supports lower back and frees tension
- Moves viscera and enhances digestive processes

a

b

105

12

Cradle Rock

Directions:

- Begin learning this exercise by lying flat on your back with your knees bent and your feet on the floor; then grasp the back of your thighs with your hands and rock gently back and forth; minimal movement is best.
- To increase the difficulty, release your thighs with your hands and, breathing normally, rock very gently, minimally, back and forth.
- Note that your head remains held high and forward in order to press the lower back into the floor.
- Before you finish the movement, tap your abdomen vigorously with your fingertips to feel the muscle tone.

Reminders:

- Ten small rocking motions, holding position
- One complete breath for each rocking motion (quick inhale, quick exhale)
- Keep head up, eyes on abdomen, lower back pressed to floor
- Beginners can grasp back of knees with hands; later, do without holding on; less knee bend equals more rigorous exercise
- Just before completing the cradle rock, tap your abdomen with fingertips

Benefits:

- Strengthens core of body, making it more resistant to stresses
- Makes you more ready to face the rigors of life
- Improves overall endurance
- Stabilizes life force and entire energy field

13

Swan Dive

Directions:

- Begin by lying flat on your belly.
- Inhaling up, let your arms, head, chest, and lower legs rise up off the floor.
- Hold that position for three deep breaths.
- Keep your knees straight.
- On the final exhale, relax back down to a resting position, ready to repeat.
- This exercise feels difficult for most people, because our backs are relatively weak. If it feels difficult for you, you stand to benefit from it the most.

Reminders:

- Three repetitions
- Hold arch position—chest and knees off the floor, legs straight—for three deep breaths
- On last repetition, scissor-kick legs as in a swimming pool

Benefits:

- Strengthens entire back, an area often ignored and left stagnant
- Releases chronic tension from lower back, upper back, and shoulders
- Contributes to improved posture and more youthful presence

14

Free Movement

Directions:

- There are few guidelines except moving and stretching freely and spontaneously.
- Stay as relaxed and aware as possible throughout.
- Breathe fully and deeply (avoid holding the breath).
- Explore all height ranges: sometimes close to the floor (as in rolling and stretching) and sometimes stretching tall.
- Move continuously for approximately thirty seconds.

Reminders:

- Maintain deep, even breathing
- Stay relaxed, aware, and at ease
- Keep movement spontaneous, without thinking or preplanning
- Vary some of your movements day to day

Benefits:

- Complements all other movements of the series
- Stimulates all energy meridians
- Activates energies of creativity, strength, grace, emotional expression
- Enhances self-trust and spontaneity
- If you did no other exercises from the workout, do this one

15

Letting Go

Directions:

- Lying flat on your back, let go of everything but your breath.
- Experience a brief but profound sense of release and relaxation.
- Remain in a relaxed posture for three to ten deep breaths or until your heart rate returns to normal.
- Experiment with crossing legs at ankles or hands on chest or belly.

Reminders:

- Do not skip this final exercise
- Allow yourself to stop the world for three to ten breaths, letting go of concerns, goals, everything—no doing, just being

Benefits:

- Reestablishes normal metabolism as a transition back to daily activities
- Provides rest, relaxation, and release
- Opens the body and mind to blessing, balancing, healing; receptive to the energies of life

Quick Reference

1. **Stretch-Back Swing-Down:** Inhale up, exhale down; bend knees on downswing and upswing.

2. **Squat-Down Side-Stretch:** Exhale on squat, up to side, weight balanced, face front.

3. **Neck Release:** Inhale as head moves, exhale on rest; don't force—keep neck relaxed.

4. **Shoulder Roll:** Inhale as shoulders go forward and up; exhale as shoulders go backward and down; relax arms.

5. **Spine Swing:** Inhale on twist each way; exhale rapidly to front; head turns; hips square.

6. **Elvis Pelvis:** Breathe rhythmically, naturally, deeply; move pelvis not belly; relax knees.

7. **Heaven-Earth:** Inhale and tense with knee bend; exhale and relax as you lift opposite knee/arm.

8. **Cross-Country Ski Hop:** Inhale and exhale each two to three lunges; opposite arm/leg forward; gentle slide.

9. **Buns Down, Buns Up:** Inhale on arch; exhale and press heels/head down on hip lift.

10. **Rock and Roll:** Exhale front and back; inhale on movement; knees bent, arms overhead in back.

11. **V-Ups:** Inhale up; exhale down; head up first and down last; learn with knees bent first.

12. **Cradle Rock:** Head up; lower back pressed down; knees slightly bent; tiny rocking motion.

13. **Swan Dive:** Inhale up; hold position for three breaths; legs straight and together; arms up.

14. **Free Movement:** Express your creativity, breathe deeply, experience free movement.

15. **Letting Go:** Ten to thirty seconds; release all tension, let the body go.

Hit the Showers!

After your workout you can enjoy a final energizing practice—a hot shower or bath followed by a brief cold shower. This is a stimulating form of hydrotherapy that has a tonic effect on your circulatory system and entire body. It also helps acclimate you to cold weather and provides a psychological lift, tempering your spirit in the same way the samurai warriors would pour a bucket of icy river water over their heads in midwinter. It's best to begin with a hot (not lukewarm) shower; then, when finished, turn the water to cold for a few moments. You can acclimate to this practice gradually, turning the water from hot to cool (but not cold) and with each shower turning the water cooler for a few seconds. Begin with only two or three seconds, then work up to five or ten seconds. Follow this invigorating practice with a brisk towel rub and feel tingling, awake, and alert.

The point of this and every exercise in *Energize Your Body* is to show how ordinary, everyday practices can energize your body and temper your spirit. The holy trinity of health—balanced diet, exercise, and rest—serve to enlighten your body by strengthening, opening, clearing, integrating, aligning, and liberating energy and attention, preparing you for the gateways that follow.

THE

FOURTH GATEWAY

Manage
Your Money

Money is neither god nor devil,
but a form of energy.
Like love or fear,
it can serve you or bind you,
depending upon how you manage it.
By clarifying your goals
and using your gifts,
you can make good money,
doing what you enjoy,
while serving
the highest calling of your soul.
Using money wisely, and well,
you increase the material
and spiritual wealth
with your world.

Sufficiency and Spiritual Practice

There's a certain Buddhistic calm
that comes from having . . . money in the bank.

—Tom Robbins

Road Map: The Flow of Money

With the arrows of worth, will, and energy in your quiver, you are better prepared to meet the challenge of managing your money. Self-worth tends to improve net worth. Self-discipline provides the power to apply the principles herein. Free-flowing energy in your body increases the flow of money in your life. Of course, reading the first three gateways is not the same as mastering these arenas in daily life, but it does provide a beginning, a foundation, and a map.

Before you proceed further, let's explore the meaning of money. In the context of personal growth, money is more than a means of exchange or ready cash. Your relationship to money reflects your relationship to energy and service and spirit, your ability to function in society, your openness to pleasure and abundance, your reality check. Money mirrors the quality of your interactions with other people, your ability to receive and to give. Money represents survival, security, safety, shelter, food, family, livelihood.

More complex, it turns out, than balancing your checkbook.

If spiritual life begins on the ground, money forms a foundation on which to build. Shivapuri Baba, an Indian saint and yogi who walked around the world on a pilgrimage when he was over

100 years old, was once asked about the best way to begin a spiritual life. He advised, "First build a foundation—manage your money." (Through hard work and simple living, he had acquired a small bag of gems in his younger years; he drew upon these gems as needed.)

Money in Everyday Life

Pam, a friend who read an early version of this manuscript, thought *Manage Your Money* should come later in the book. "Surely," she said, "money can't be more important than taming your mind or facing your fears or some of the other gateways—" Abruptly she looked at her watch. "Oh, my gosh, look what time it is! The bank's closing in ten minutes!" Wondering about why money was so important, Pam had to run to the bank.

Yet her question was a good one, so I answer it here: No gateway is more important than any other, although some may seem more relevant to different people at different times. But just as you need to crawl before you walk, and learn the alphabet before you read or write, each gateway prepares you for those that follow.

On the way to the bank, Pam later told me that she realized how much of her time, thoughts, and attention revolved around money—paying the bills, balancing checkbooks, discussing costs of the room addition for their growing family. After the bank, she went food shopping, then stopped by the furniture store to check prices on a new bed for one of her children—all activities dealing with money. Like Pam, most of us have money concerns of one kind or another: striving to make more or make do with less, learning to live simply, comfortably, spiritually.

Poor people may be forced to think about money a lot of the time, related to food, shelter, subsistence, and survival. Rich people may also think about money a lot of the time, related to status, travel, freedom, influence, and options. But managing your money does not depend upon becoming wealthy or declaring vows of poverty. Rather, it is about creating *stability* and *sufficiency*—a balanced flow of monetary energy through your life.

This kind of management liberates you from survival issues, so that money concerns no longer occupy your mind or monopolize your attention. When money flows in, you spend it in a matter-of-fact way where it needs to go, where it will do the most good. You pay bills gladly, knowing that your money helps to support other people who in turn provide services for you. If something breaks, you write a check and get it fixed without further concern. Free from cycles of scarcity, your attention can ascend to higher levels of awareness and experience.

> Money, it turned out, was exactly like sex,
> you thought of nothing else
> if you didn't have it
> and thought of other things
> if you did.
>
> **—James Baldwin**

Managing your money begins by examining limiting beliefs and negative programming, then exploring such topics as your hidden relationship to money, how your perspectives and beliefs can suddenly shift, money as energy, money and spirituality in the East and West, keys to career success, and five simple principles for sufficiency.

Programming and Prejudice: Freeing Your Mind

Spiritual illumination necessarily involves the expansion of awareness—letting its light penetrate your body, mind, and emotions. Our unexamined (subconscious) beliefs are like minefields of conflicting ideas, desires, and aversions—especially in the realm of money and spirit.

While you may consciously desire to increase your wealth, unexamined beliefs can stand in your way. Thus you benefit from the following material only to the degree that you have overcome such mixed emotions and self-defeating attitudes. As in the other gateways, the purpose of this one is to make such beliefs conscious, releasing their power over you.

An Attitude Assessment

This inventory clarifies your current attitudes and circumstances in the arena of money, providing a chance for self-reflection:

- Do money issues periodically monopolize your attention?
- How much time and energy do you spend struggling to balance income and expenditures?
- Do you believe money makes you happy?
- Do you believe money makes you unhappy?
- How much money would you like to earn each year? Why not more?
- Does money seem very hard to come by or burn a hole in your pocket?
- Does your financial life swing between feast and famine?
- How do you feel about wealthy people?
- How do you feel about wealthy spiritual teachers?
- Do you believe that seeking or having wealth hinders your spiritual life?
- What do you spend more time thinking about—money or love?
- Do you tend to spend more than you make? Are you in debt?
- If you are in debt, is it the result of insufficient income or overspending?
- Are the best things in life free?

As in other self-assessments, there are no right or wrong answers here, only a chance to shed light on your beliefs about money, especially as they relate to spirituality.

Another direct and practical way to assess your priorities and values is to read your financial journals—your checkbook registers and monthly credit card reports—for the past year. These are clear and objective records of the priorities, needs, values, and spending habits that paint a telling portrait of your life.

Your beliefs about money are the key determinant—more than education or talent or even opportunity—of your level of financial stability. There are plenty of stories of well-educated and talented people who suffer in poverty, consciously seeking financial support while unconsciously avoiding it—and an equal number of others with less education who seem to attract money like magnets.

The irony of negative beliefs about money is that we did not choose them, but were programmed by religious and cultural assumptions, and by mass media imagery in films and literature, about the relationships of money and spirituality.

Spiritual Stereotypes

You can probably conjure up images of pure and holy people quite easily—monks with begging bowls, Indian ascetics, priests and nuns from every tradition who have renounced money in order to live a more spiritual life free of worldly distractions. Images of Jesus expelling money changers from the temple and quotations about money being the root of all evil and rich men having a tough time entering heaven are quite familiar. Such images and ideas help create stereotypes that equate poverty and spirituality in the minds of many.

> I don't like money, actually,
> but it quiets my nerves.
>
> **—Joe Louis**

Managing your money begins by acknowledging any mixed feelings, guilt, or negativity you may have about money and about those who possess it in abundance. If you associate voluntary poverty with humility, goodness, and spirituality, then with what do you associate wealth? It is worth pondering, because what you believe about money will determine in large part your effectiveness in acquiring it.

Money, Movies, and Mass Beliefs

For centuries, literature, theater, and more recently film have depicted the rich as villains and the poor as everyday heroes, as if wealth were a sin and poverty a virtue. Take, for example, "A Christmas Carol," which contrasts the misery of the frugal, hardworking, but humorless Ebenezer Scrooge with the poor, loving, but happy Cratchit family. Or take George Bailey, the eternally poor and struggling family man in *It's a Wonderful Life*, who embodies the spirit of sacrifice, duty, and love, while the rich Mr. Potter, who owns the bank and most of the town, is the epitome of evil and greed. Film and literature do, of course, portray kind, industrious, generous, and moral wealthy people, but such imagery is more the exception than the rule.

Popular entertainment themes associating poverty with spirituality create unexamined assumptions that take on the power of hypnotic suggestions. Simple awareness of such beliefs can help to clear them. When you *know* you have a negative belief about money, you are free to examine it and discard it if you choose. No such choice exists for unconscious beliefs or unexamined attitudes.

A Financial Wake-up Call

Over the years I've had to deal with my own money issues—to overcome profound money aversion, fear, and negative beliefs. Several years ago, while channel surfing, I paused to watch Barbra Streisand on *Lifestyles of the Rich and Famous*. Ms. Streisand was graciously giving the viewing audience a tour of her home. She stopped in one room to show a very thick, intricately designed, custom-made wool carpet that would cover the entire bottom floor of my house—and probably cost as much. She lifted the corner of the carpet to reveal a marble floor beneath with exactly the same design as the carpet, so that when the rug was sent out to be cleaned, she could still enjoy the beautiful design. I found this display of wealth ostentatious and offensive; I righteously calculated how many people could have eaten for a year for the cost of the marble floor alone.

I was, at that moment, unaware of my own negative associations, prejudice, and naive judgments. I might have then turned away and gone about my business, but in an instant of self-reflection I realized that I didn't know Barbra Streisand at all. In fact, all I knew about her for certain was that she had earned her money through years of hard work, talent, and creativity. Later I learned that she had raised and donated more money to charities in one year than most people give in a lifetime.

I also realized that if I felt so negatively about her just because she had a lot of money, then *I* certainly wasn't going to attract much of it. As a matter of fact, during this period of my life I was working two jobs to support my family, earning about $7 an hour. I had to work eleven-hour days just to get by and was going deeper into debt with no light on the horizon.

That night, when I saw my beliefs clearly and realized that I had created my own obstacles, a door opened up inside me. And with the goal of creating stability and sufficiency for my family (and the dream of one day starting a philanthropic foundation), I began to direct myself with the full force of my being to make good money, creating fulfilling work, providing a valuable service.

Unless you are independently wealthy or dependent on others, you will need to earn money to live in this world. And your needs will be determined by the choices you make—where you choose to live and whether you are single or supporting a family, for example. Some of us choose a life that requires a higher income, and others of us choose voluntary simplicity.

Mohandas Gandhi, a wise and courageous man who inspired millions of people in India and around the world—and who is often associated with voluntary poverty and simplicity—is often reported to have advised people to live simply, so that others may simply live. This sentiment is far better known than a comment attributed to a wealthy industrialist who supported Gandhi's cause: "It cost me a fortune to keep Gandhi simple."

Managing your money doesn't require magic or miracles, but it does require an honest examination of the values, beliefs, and inner hurdles that may stand between you and sufficiency or abundance.

Reflections on Money

This gateway now leads through a long tunnel, like a hidden mine where random, multifaceted gems, reflections on money, sparkle from the crevices. (But watch your step!)

On Money and Worth

Before you ask for a raise, before a potential client asks, "How much do you charge for your service?" you should ask yourself, "How much is my time, my service, my talent, worth?" And you should come up with a clear and realistic answer that reflects the realities of the marketplace as well as a clear sense of your value, talent, and energy.

As your actions begin to flow from an expanded sense of innate worth, you accept, attract, and receive more from the world—not just money, but friendship, love, and attention. As you become aware that you have been actively declining such blessings, you put out a welcome mat where before you had a "Not Home" sign. You become willing to accept and to work for every kind of abundance and respect; more important, you are willing to enjoy it. And since our subconscious minds communicate with one another through body language and other subtle cues not yet fully understood, other people begin to support you in new ways as they begin to get "Yes, call me, my star is rising" messages instead of "No, I don't see myself doing that" signals from you. As you manage your money, you manage your life.

> It is better to have a permanent income
> than to be fascinating.
> **—Oscar Wilde**

Money forces you to confront your sense of self-worth. It takes courage—because of the fear of rejection—to place a fair but generous price on your time and accept only those clients who value your service. Of course it has to be a realistic fee that the market will bear. Yet in any service field, some will charge more and some will charge less.

Don't Charge Less—Give More

In my own seminars and trainings, I have always worked toward the goal of giving participants more than their money's worth. When you dedicate yourself to raising the top (quality) rather than lowering the bottom (cost), everybody wins. If you charge very little (and give back in kind), everybody loses. Bump up the energy level! Ask a fee that says, "I value what I offer." (If *you* don't, why should anyone else?)

Larry, who had a small tax accounting firm, kept his fees low "in order to be competitive," he told me. Indeed, he did attract those customers looking for low-end fees. He confided that he had received many complaints about his fees nevertheless. One day, after studying the fees of other accountants in the area, Larry raised his fee toward the mid- to upper range. At the same time, he upgraded his services, moved to a nice office nearby, redecorated, and hired another assistant.

He lost nearly half of his clients—nearly all of the complainers, he noticed. Within a year their spaces were filled with clients who appreciated people who value their work. Since then his client base has doubled with a different kind of clientele. And he rarely receives a complaint about his fees.

Don't charge less. Give more.

Be wary of the idea "I don't want to charge so much that people of limited means can't afford me." Charge enough so that you can afford, if you choose, to subsidize those of limited means. During the fifteen-year period I taught the Courage Training, I charged enough so that I would attract stable, energetic people from all walks of life. The price turned away the vaguely curious or uncommitted. (One young man saved a dollar a day for three years to attend.)

Money as Energy

I can use my physical energy to tune up my car, or I can take some currency or a piece of plastic out of my wallet and use that energy to get the job done. Money can get the lawn mowed, the house cleaned; it can create Christmas presents, pay school tuition, or provide food for children in Africa and around the world. It can also create a stable foundation from which to climb out and extend yourself in the spirit of creativity and service in the world.

However, as with any form of energy, money needs to move, to be channeled wisely and well. Like any form of energy, money is morally neutral. It can serve the highest and the lowest. Money doesn't care who has it; it has no prejudices. As energy, money only amplifies whoever and whatever you are.

Guilt and the Dollar Dynamic

Some wealthy people feel guilty when they think of others who live below the poverty line. Since money is energy, do you also feel guilty if you have more energy than your neighbor? Does having more energy make you a bad person? It's commendable to feel compassion for less fortunate people in the world. But are you not to eat until all the world is fed? Will you help others by remaining poor? Suffering is a fact of life. Even if we are able to end chronic hunger in the world, there will always be people who, for any number of reasons, have less than others.

By first creating sufficiency for yourself, you can better assist others and be a force of light in the world. When you pay a bill you are supporting hardworking employees of that business; when you pay a gardener or babysitter, or generously tip a server at a restaurant, you are offering support, trust, and appreciation.

The Eastern Solution: Escape from the Material World

While the Western solution to managing money is to pursue it, the Eastern solution is to avoid it. Disillusioned with the outward drives of the Western world, some of us turn to Eastern spiritual philosophies and practices, confusing the idea of letting go of attachments with giving away all earthly goods.

Detachment is much more challenging than simply divesting yourself of all external possessions, because it means giving up your internal possessions, preferences, and points of view. The practice of detachment means seeing things as they truly are, in proper perspective. Giving everything up doesn't mean giving everything away. Rather, it involves living a simple, functional, ordinary life without clinging, craving, or holding on.

Making Money, Making Choices

Most people grow up, find work, spend money on themselves for a while, maybe even save or invest a little money, eventually settle down with a partner, create a household, and pay rent or a mortgage.

Based on our choices and priorities, our needs expand or contract over time. Shall we get married? Have children? Buy new clothing or used clothing? Live in the suburbs and commute to work? Send the children to public or private schools? State or private colleges?

If you earn a bare subsistence income, your choices are relatively few. The more you earn, the more choices you have. Those choices, even more than your income level, will determine your financial present and future. If you make choices that result in spending less than you earn and saving even a little money, regularly and consistently, you are well on your way to mastering one basic skill of money management: Spend less than you earn; earn more than you spend.

Meanwhile, notice the choices you make.

> Man's greatest riches
> is to live on a little with contented mind
> for a little is never lacking.
> **—Lucretius**

The more money you make, the more you will seem to need. You'll find that you can quickly grow accustomed to a different level of service and experience, moving up from three- to four- to five-star hotels. A rowboat becomes a motorboat, a cruiser, a yacht. Desires are infinite. Escalation can be endless.

What Money Cannot Buy

Money cannot buy security, because security is a psychological state. To some, it means having enough food to eat, clothing on your back, a shelter over your head, or someone who loves you. To others, security requires millions of dollars in tax-free accounts around the world.

Money can't buy happiness, either. In one telephone survey, 275 people in the San Francisco Bay area were asked if they believed that they would be significantly happier if they had a million dollars. Seventy-six percent of the respondents replied, "Yes. Absolutely." Then the research company contacted ten millionaires and asked them, "Did making your first million dollars make you a happier person?" The response was unanimous: "No."

The best things in life—the sun in the morning and the moon at night—are free. And money doesn't guarantee happiness. But financial abundance does offer a number of practical benefits. Sleep, for one thing: very few affluent people stay up late worrying about having too much money. Money also buys privacy, space, and silence.

Wealthy people do have problems, but they have less to do with survival. There may be some forlorn rich people and some delighted poor people, but on the whole, managing your money certainly gives you a leg up.

Earning a Living: The Right Career

Most of us need to produce income. Why not do so in a manner that uses your talents and interests while providing a tangible service to others? It can be nearly any kind of work, from the high-paid pressure professions to part-time hourly wage earners, or the all-important work of caring for and raising children.

Soul Work

Banish the illusion that certain professions are inherently better than others. A job or profession is only better or worse for *you*, depending upon your tastes and values. There are people in every field who are happy with their work and others who are unhappy with it. The key is finding work that matches your values and challenges your capacities. Finding the inherent meaning in any work is one of life's great blessings. More accurately, you don't *find* meaning in work; you bestow meaning upon your work. We have become befuddled by status professions and star power, while the Eastern traditions are filled with stories about master butchers, Zen bakers. I once met a very interesting old gas station attendant. And there was another man, I recall, a carpenter by trade. . . .

Finding or creating the most suitable livelihood—or making the most of your current occupation—can become one of life's most creative challenges. Relatively few of us figure out what we want to do when we are young. Most of us happen upon it, the same way the winds of fate carry us to our spouse or home. Still, the better you know yourself, your interests, and your values, the easier time you have finding your soul work.

Psychologists who do career counseling offer vocational interest tests that help you evaluate what vocation might be for you. You can also consult Richard Bolles's career hunter's classic, *What Color Is Your Parachute?*

In the meantime, take a few minutes to consider and write down a list of ten of your primary values (such as health, solitude, group interaction, financial or spiritual rewards, or the right geographic location). Sort them from the most to the least important, and let these values guide you in any job searches or changes.

It can be said that the goal of life should not be to get rich, but to enrich the world. The secret of satisfying work is to provide quality in whatever you do. Appreciate your work as a means of spiritual development; use it to serve, connect, lend a helping hand, and make your labor an offering for the good of the community.

> He is well paid
> that is well satisfied.
>
> **—William Shakespeare**

Trampoline and Career Change

Our income flow has its ups and downs just like bouncing on a trampoline. There may come a time when opportunity calls but entails a pay cut. Unless you are prepared to tighten your belt and simplify your life, you may miss the boat.

Stay flexible. Don't get locked into your standard of living, current purchasing power, lifestyle, location, and options. Sometimes the only way you can rebound to a higher plateau is if you are willing to drop down for a while. Life may require you to back up in order to get a running start.

If You Can't Find the Perfect Career, Create Your Own

I enjoy telling the true story of Ron Kaufman, a friend who loved nothing more than to play Frisbee and see those plastic disks glide through the air. But he was thirty-five years old, and his parents suggested he grow up and find a real job. In addition to tossing Frisbees, Ron had a larger vision of promoting world peace. One day it occurred to him to combine his passions. He contacted the representatives of the Wham-O Company and asked if they would sponsor him to fly to the then–Soviet Union and provide him with five hundred Frisbees imprinted with the words "World Peace" in English and in Russian. They agreed, and Ron became a Frisbee goodwill ambassador, teaching people throughout Russia to play the game and talk about peace. Ultimately Ron formed a company that led goodwill Frisbee tours to Russia, where he also met his wife. Doing what he loves, serving other people, Ron thrived, along with his business. The moral is simple: If you can't find a career that satisfies you, invent your own.

Those who view money as an incidental benefit of work they enjoy for its own sake seem to be the most satisfied with their lives. Ask yourself this: "If I had enough money to live on for the rest of my life, what would I do with my time?" *When you have the answer, find work in that area if you can.* If you became wealthy and would nevertheless spend some of your time doing just what you now do for a living, you are fortunate indeed.

Every kind of work that provides a service has innate meaning. It doesn't have to make you famous, or dispense charity, or be connected directly to healing or spiritual teaching. If you provide a helping hand, whether behind the counter of a grocery store, building automobiles, cleaning someone's home, doing market research, mowing lawns, working in sales, or practicing law, your work, and the relationships you develop with the people you meet through it, can shed light and provide a vehicle of transformation.

My friend Lou was a stockbroker and insurance salesman— but the way he saw it, that was just an excuse to get in the door and meet people, and maybe provide a service. Maybe they did business and maybe not, but Lou considered himself successful only if he shared some laughter and some light. Maybe that's why Lou was such a successful person. He was also a very good stockbroker.

Simple Principles for Sufficiency

In *Walden* Henry David Thoreau described how by living frugally, growing his own food, building a hut with scrap lumber he'd found on some land near Walden Pond, he would have to work for only six weeks a year to earn enough to live a quiet, contemplative life. There is much to admire about his experiment (which lasted a season or two), but such a life is not for everyone. You may not want to follow Thoreau to Walden Pond, but here are some simple principles that you *can* follow:

Live Below Your Means

Many of us believe our main money problem is how to make more of it, but how we spend it is in fact more important. Because as our income increases, so do desires and expenses. It's all a matter of scale. Many wealthy people end up in debt.

Money is so easy to spend that an alarming number of us have put away little or nothing toward our later years. Applying fiscal discipline is a central part of managing your money. Most affluent people become and stay that way owing not to extraordinary incomes, but to an unassuming lifestyle and the self-discipline to spend less than they earn, while investing the rest.

According to Thomas Stanley, author of *The Millionaire Next Door,* the road to financial independence is paved with frugality— letting consumption take a backseat while you doggedly cultivate financial stability. Twice as many millionaires have a credit card from Sears than from Neiman Marcus; most drive Fords. On the other hand, many with moderate incomes often fail to create wealth because they spend money on things of relatively little lasting value, like flashy cars and clothing or expensive vacations.

Pay Yourself First

Make it an ironclad rule to pay yourself by putting away ten cents of every dollar you ever earn until you are seventy years old, and teach your children to do the same. Before you pay the bills, before you pay the IRS, before you give to charity, put that money away as if it never existed and learn to live on the rest, no matter what. Put aside that 10 percent in a safe nest-egg account or very conservative investment and let compound interest work for you all day and all night over the years. Never mind the fancy investment strategies, schemes, and experts. If you do have money to experiment with, that's icing on the cake. In a true emergency, give yourself a few days to decide if you really need to draw out any of the principal to spend. Never draw out more than half of the principal. At the age of sixty-five or seventy, it is yours to do with as you wish.

Earmark Your Money

Whether your income is derived from a salary with taxes withheld, or whether you are self-employed, one of the most practical steps you can take in managing your money is to create a budget, clearly earmarking your money for distinct purposes. Once you've created the budget, stick with it. While this is not a radical idea, obviously few of us put it into practice, given the level of credit card debt in this country. Unless you already have tax withholding at your work, divide your income—every $1,000 you make—as follows:

- Immediately put away 10 percent of every dollar you earn into your savings.
- If you are self-employed, put aside whatever percentage of your gross income (20–40 percent) that goes to state and federal taxes, and social security.
- If you donate a share of your income (say 5 percent) to charities, earmark that fund next.
- Put 5 percent into an account for Christmas, Hanukkah, or other holidays.
- Put another 5 percent into a vacation account.

In the preceding model, that means immediately setting aside from 45 percent to 65 percent of your income (depending on your tax bracket) toward retirement, taxes, charitable donations, holidays, and vacations. The remainder (35 percent to 55 percent) of your income goes to monthly living expenses: the mortgage or rent, food, utilities, medical care, and so on. The precise percentages may vary from household to household, but the principle is the same—earmark and budget your money. Exerting this financial discipline will eliminate a great deal of pretax as well as postretirement stress. Such fiscal discipline is far easier than the live-for-today, if-you-have-it-spend-it approach, but you gain self-reliance and self-respect by taking responsibility for managing your money in this way.

The Two Essentials of Business Success

In order to succeed in nearly any business enterprise, whether you work for a large corporation or are self-employed, you must operate on these two principles:

1. **Be good at what you do.** That means ongoing study, practice, innovation, and refinement. Treat your work as a form of skill training. Never believe that you are as good as you can get. Each day, each year, strive to master your work. No matter what you do, if you become one of the best in your field, you will do well (if you also pay attention to the second principle).

2. **Be good at promoting what you do.** There is no telling how many exceptional, gifted people exist in every field who are not successful because they were unwilling to promote themselves. I know extraordinary musicians whose songs will never be heard by more than a few people, while the top forty charts include many forgettable but well-promoted clichés. It's a sad irony that those most dedicated to their art or craft, who most love what they do, understandably want to spend their time getting better at what they do but fail to grasp the need to promote themselves.

Ask yourself: "Am I good at what I do? Do I provide a valuable service?" If the answer is "No," then stay out of sight and work at improving what you do. But if your answer is "Yes," then blow your horn! You can't help anyone if they don't know you exist.

Whether or not you have any innate interest in promotion and marketing—whether or not you enjoy it—it has to become at least half of your job, your energy, and your attention at the beginning stages of a new venture. Promoting your business helps you to help others and provide a valuable service in the world as *only you can do it*.

The Soul of Money

It is easy to get lost in the practical details of managing money and forget the higher purpose of this gateway: to provide a foundation for spiritual practice and to free your attention from the task of survival. Lynne Twist, cofounder of the Hunger Project, put it this way to Michael Toms on New Dimensions Radio:

> Money is an inanimate object [but] we can assign to it a spiritual meaning and voice and power if we choose to, and give it some soul. Money doesn't have any soul, but *we* do, and we're the people through whom money flows and with which money speaks. . . . And when our spirit is unleashed, what's unleashed is the prosperity of the soul, of the heart . . . and in that truth, the whole world belongs to you.

When I became committed to teaching whatever I learned, more information poured in. In the same way, as you contact the joy of sharing your abundant spirit, more spiritual wealth pours down from the heavens, bathing you in its light. Managing your money provides another arena of practicing everyday enlightenment.

From that point of awareness, we turn now to the source of all beliefs—the mind. It serves as a prison for some, but for you it can also hold the key to freedom.

THE
FIFTH GATEWAY

Tame Your Mind

❧

You perceive the world
through an obscure window
of beliefs, interpretations, and associations.
The world is therefore
a reflection of your mind.
As your mind clears,
you perceive reality
simply as it is.
What does your experience of life
reveal about your filters of perception?

Inner Peace and Simple Reality

We are what we think.
All that we are arises with our thoughts.
With our thoughts,
we make the world.
—Buddha

Road Map: In the Realms of Thought

In his *Republic* Plato describes a group of people living deep within a dark cavern far from the light of day, seeing only their shadows, cast by firelight upon the walls. These dark shapes are their only reality, because they have never ventured outside the cave—indeed, they are unaware that there *is* an outside.

Plato's allegory of the cave goes on to describe how someone escapes from the cave into the sunlight of the real world. Having seen the light, he returns to the cave and tries without much success to tell the others imprisoned there about the real world outside. His words make no sense to anyone but a few adventurous souls who dare to venture with him, upward, into the unknown, toward a brighter, shining reality.

We are each living within the caves of our dimmed and distorted perceptions, seeing not the world, but our own minds. *Tame Your Mind* shows how to grasp reality as it is, beyond the shadow-play of thought.

Reality is not what you think.

A Fresh Approach

Now that you have seen the tip of the mind's iceberg, you are ready to look beneath the surface and gain access into the heart

141

of the mind—see its all-pervading influence in every facet of your life experience. If thoughts are a muddy river flowing past, this gateway provides stepping-stones that allow you to cross to the other side, to a place of simple reality, humor, and peace.

This gateway reveals how to tame your mind—not by subjugating it, controlling it, or trying to quiet it, which you will see is fruitless, but by making peace with it.

We begin by exploring the hidden *anatomy of the mind,* including original, intuitive material I believe will one day be supported by scientific research. We then move on to several key areas, including filters of your mind and how they influence your perception, communication, and relationships; the nature of thought and the illusion of a quiet mind; a radical approach to finding inner peace; a fresh look at meditation; why no one can control thoughts; directing attention as a realistic approach to taming the mind; and, finally, a return to simplicity by living in the moment.

A Simple Self-Assessment

As in the other gateways, self-reflection and assessment prepare you for the territory of the mind. A self-assessment makes the material relevant and personal. If you are going to tame a lion, you had better know something about lions. The same applies to your mind. So consider the following:

- Would you describe your mind as busy or calm?
- Do you believe you have a clear grasp on reality?
- What do you do when you have troubling thoughts, such as worries, concerns, guilt, or anxieties?
- Do you believe your life would be better if you had better control over your mind?
- Have you tried to quiet your mind? What happened then?
- Do you try to think positively? Have you successfully done so with any consistency?
- Should people be held responsible for petty, jealous, negative, or sadistic thoughts or ideas?

● Would you like to live a more simple life? What might this have to do with your mind?

Anatomy of the Mind

First a word on *thoughts,* since I use this term often. Thoughts are those subjective pictures, sounds, and words—and the beliefs, associations, interpretations, opinions, and meanings—that pass through our mind or hold our attention. The mind is an ocean of awareness through which thoughts pass, sometimes like flotsam and jetsam, sometimes like sailboats or speedboats.

We can deliberately think thoughts, as when we rehearse a speech, remember a shopping list, or solve a puzzle or math problem. Clearly, such deliberate thinking is a profound and useful capacity of the human mind—a boon, not a problem.

The thoughts we need to transcend, the mind we need to tame, are those random, problematic gremlins that interfere with clear thinking, with the silence of clear perception, and especially with our relationship to ourselves, to others, and to everyday life. This is the discursive mind, the wild monkey-mind that must be tamed.

Even as you read this, ongoing research into the human brain is expanding the frontiers of scientific knowledge. Yet few of us have insight into the anatomy of our own *mind*—its structure and function. So to begin that process of insight, I present here a speculative model about the right and left hemispheres of the brain (which I'll refer to as the right brain and left brain). Although both sides of the brain interact to form a whole, each side has general functions and responsibilities different from the other.

Your *left brain* functions in a more linear, logical, rational, structured, mathematical (conceptually based) fashion; it deduces, reasons, processes, weighs data, sorts values, compares, and analyzes to come to decisions.

Your *right brain* functions in a more primitive, childlike, suggestible, symbolic, visual (sensory-based), spatial, holistic manner; it instantly processes information through instinct and intuition rather than logical thought.

These facts are well-known. What is not commonly known, but what I also believe to be true, is that

- your *left brain* functions as the center of your ego or *conscious* mind—your personal identity and intellect. It learns—takes in and processes information, data, beliefs, and values that you can access at will.
- your *right brain* functions (in ways we don't yet understand) as the center of your *subconscious* mind—unexamined beliefs, data, values, and associations that you cannot or do not readily access at will.

Later in this book you will learn more about the right and left brains' roles in intuition and in our sexual character. In this gateway we will focus on the role and influence of the conscious and subconscious minds in the quality and clarity of our life.

For now, understand that your brain and your whole body function best when both hemispheres work together, forming a whole greater than the sum of the parts, expanding both your powers of reason and your full creative capacities.

Shedding Light on the Subconscious

One important aspect of expanded awareness, healing, balance, and wholeness is making what is subconscious, conscious. That includes beliefs, thoughts, and memories.

The *un*conscious mind is that of which you are normally unaware and *cannot* usually access—the place of deep sleep, silence, stillness, and mystery. The unconscious mind is so mysterious, in fact, we don't know whether it even exists.

The *sub*conscious mind is that of which you are normally unaware but *can* access—dreams, intuitions, beliefs, images, and other material. (The subconscious mind is the unexamined or uninspected mind.)

In this gateway (as in meditation), we direct the light of

awareness into new and unexplored territory, illuminating the darkness, turning shadows into three-dimensional reality.

You have already learned that your subconscious mind also functions as your instinctive body wisdom and controls autonomic (involuntary) processes such as immune response and vital energy reserves (through endocrine and hormonal secretions). You also know some of the childlike qualities of the subconscious mind as it is related to motivation and will. (Those who refer to their "inner child" are actually pointing to their subconscious mind.) You need familiarity with your subconscious mind because the subconscious is the stream of random, discursive thoughts—the same field we access in dreams and in meditation.

Thoughts arise of their own accord, in a subliminal flow. Sometimes they get your conscious attention (you notice that you are thinking thoughts), but mostly they pass unnoticed, like a subconscious stream. These thoughts manifest as subliminal whispers, becoming moods, emotions, desires, and impulses. When unnoticed, they operate like hypnotic suggestions to influence your behavior. When you observe them consciously *as* thoughts (as you do in meditation), a healing takes place, because thoughts—fears, beliefs, and associations—are clarified in the light of awareness, lose their power to distort your reality, control your moods, or limit your life.

Filters of the Mind

An ancient spiritual proverb says, "The mind is the slayer of the real." What does that mean, and how might it be important to your life? Look around you right now. What do you see? Listen to the sounds around you. What do you hear?

You experience the world through five primary senses: visual (sight), auditory (hearing), tactile (touch), olfactory (smell), and gustatory (taste). But you do not take in these impressions directly, objectively, as they are. They pass through multilayered filters, colored and often distorted by your interpretations, expectations, assumptions, beliefs, associations, fears, desires, and opinions. You also perceive through cultural, religious, professional, educational, racial, and gender filters, created by your unique life experience.

Thus, for example, you don't just see or hear or taste. You see a barren or sad or interesting sight; you hear glorious or disappointing music; you taste delicious or bland food that reminds you of Grandmother's cooking. Reality becomes *your* reality; what *is* becomes replaced by what you *think* it is. A key principle to remember in taming your mind is that reality is not what you think.

If you happen to be hungry while walking in the city, eating establishments stand out. If you need money, you see banks. And as Ram Dass once said, quoting one of his teachings, "If a pickpocket stands in a crowd of saints, all he sees are their pockets." (This makes me wonder what a proctologist sees.)

Having different filters, none of us see or hear exactly the same world. We view the same objects but perceive different meanings. As an unknown poet once wrote on a prison wall, "Two men looked out of prison bars; one saw mud and the other saw stars."

Pictures about Reality

We do not see reality as it is; we see reality as *we* are—through the filter of our own personal experience. Two people ride a roller coaster; one screams with delight, the other with terror. One person imagines the next curve to be even more exciting; the other anticipates the car flying off the tracks. Our experience of life depends upon whether we have formed the habit of mentally sorting for—or expecting—pleasures or dangers.

Expectation determines perception. If you walk through a reputedly dangerous neighborhood, every large male stranger may look like a potential mugger. I recall a public service announcement that brought this point home. The television screen displays a photo of a serious-looking man of African heritage. Imagine this somber face as you read the following words: "Andrew Coombs: Vandalism and petty theft—14 years old. Aggravated assault—16.

Grand theft auto—17. Armed robbery—20. Sought for murder at 24. Pursued and apprehended by Federal Marshal Bob Jones—*pictured here."* Suddenly our assumptions are shattered.

To the degree your perception is distorted by a filter of associations or beliefs, you experience misunderstandings and miscommunications. Simple reality, as it unfolds in the present moment, is clouded by meanings, troubles, hurts, interpretations, and confusion.

Different Worlds

If you could see life through the eyes of someone else, the world might appear so different that you would think you were hallucinating. A chair would still be a chair, and an automobile would still be an automobile, but your thoughts, feelings, and associations about them might differ so much that you would have a radically different experience of them.

Even when we speak the same language, our personal filters account for much of the difficulties in communication. The same words have different meanings for different people. Try this simple experiment: Picture a horse in your mind's eye. Is it a mare or a stallion? Is it all white, or does it have markings? Where? How large is it? Approximately what age? Any other characteristics? Now put down the book and ask someone nearby to visualize a horse and to describe it to you. Chances are it will be a very different horse from the one you picture. Not only that, the two of you will have different feelings and associations about horses.

Given that we live in different worlds, it seems amazing to me that we understand one another at all.

Filters and Communication

Conflicting filters can cause communication problems in our relationships. Case in point: Reba's teenage son, Alex, gets home from school, goes directly to the refrigerator to pay homage to the God of Food, and then crashes on the sofa, television remote control in hand, for a few minutes of space time. Enter Reba. She sees Alex and remembers that he has a big exam coming up. Reba knows that Alex is a good student, with conscientious study habits. She is busy with her own project but wants to show interest in her son's life and studies, so before she returns to her office, she says, "Hi, Alex. How are your studies coming for the history exam on Friday?"

"Get off my back, will you, Mom?" Alex says defensively. "I'll get to my studies soon!"

Reba's intent was to show Alex that she is interested in and cares about what he is doing. When she says, "How are your studies coming?" Alex interprets these words through his own filter, hearing, "Hey, couch potato, why are you sitting here watching *Idiot Youth Mating Rituals* when you have *work* to do?"

When you understand your mind, or at least begin to recognize the filters you see and hear through, you will no longer suffer the illusion that you are hearing or seeing the real world. Rather, you are creating your own meanings, interpretations, and associations.

Setting aside subjective filters takes a little practice. The following two exercises are designed to provide an experience in objective listening, observing, and speaking—without subjective interpretations.

Listening Objectively

"Did you hear what I said?" All of us have heard that phrase, because few of us listen attentively to what people tell us. So we end up responding to what we heard (through our own filters) rather than to what was said.

> The first duty of love
> is to listen.
>
> **—Paul Tillich**

You can practice objective listening by asking someone to tell you about themselves and their life and by paying close attention to precisely what is being said. As you hear the words, *repeat* them silently to yourself. By focusing in this way on what they actually say, you better understand their meaning rather than *your* meaning.

Seeing and Speaking Objectively

This exercise is both challenging and revelatory. For maximum benefits, do it with a partner and then do it alone.

First, sit facing your partner, observe his or her face closely, and then describe what you see without interpretation or value judgments. Name exactly what you see—shapes, colors, textures, tones, lines, not how it looks to you. Avoid subjective value judgments like "pretty, attractive, ugly, weird, or interesting." Ask your partner how objective you were. Then ask your partner to describe you in the same way.

Next, stand alone before a mirror and observe your own face closely, then describe it objectively. Speak aloud. Notice carefully whether you are describing exactly what you see rather than interpreting what you see. This exercise clarifies the meaning of objective observation and also gives a rare chance to see yourself clearly.

By reducing the influence of your interpretations and associations on your perceptions, bringing you in more intimate contact with reality—and with other people—objective listening serves to tame your mind and bring you closer, in moments of attention, to everyday enlightenment.

The Two Kinds of Beliefs

There's an anecdote about an American Indian brave who asks his young son the color of a nearby pony. "It is white with brown spots—on this side." This is a tale of knowledge based upon direct experience. He described only the side he could see.

Many of us believe that we operate, act, and make decisions based upon knowledge and direct experience. In reality we operate on innumerable beliefs and assumptions rather than on direct experience.

Unconscious beliefs are those we mistake for truth or reality. We don't say, "I believe this is so." We say, "This *is* truth." Unconscious beliefs lie at the root of fundamentalism; true believers zealously defend their beliefs and ideas as ultimate truth, confusing their opinions with the word of God. Such fundamentalism exists not only in the arena of religion, but in any field, any place, any time we are convinced that our way, our method, our ideas, are universally true.

A magnificent leap of awareness occurs when our beliefs become *conscious,* the instant we recognize them as *our* truth rather than as *the* truth. This is the first step in recognizing the illusory nature of thought. Thoughts, like the stuff of dreams, arise mysteriously from the psyche as naturally as waves on the sea. Thoughts are not a problem; it's only when we *believe* them, mistake them for reality, that we get into trouble.

Suffering Is Optional

In any moment, your attention resides in one of two worlds: the objective world of what is happening or the subjective world of your thoughts and interpretations *about* what is happening. Only one is real.

Physical pain, for example, is an objective function of your nervous system. Mental and emotional pain are your subjective creation, based upon your own meanings and interpretations. Life has no consistent meanings except as you project your own meanings onto life. Good and bad depend upon your point of view. A Chinese farmer's son breaks his leg; this is bad. The army comes but cannot take him for war; this is good. The broken leg was first bad, then good.

Pain and Suffering

Pain is a relatively objective, physical phenomenon; suffering is our psychological resistance to what happens. Events may create physical pain, but they do not in themselves create suffering. Resistance creates suffering. Stress happens when your mind resists what is. If your spouse or lover leaves you, the amount of stress or suffering each of you experiences depends upon the meanings each of you places on the event. If you believe it to be good, that you are now free, you suffer less; if you believe it is bad, that you are now alone, you suffer more. The only problem in your life is your mind's resistance to life as it unfolds.

> The mind . . . in itself,
> Can make a heav'n of hell,
> a hell of heav'n.
>
> **—John Milton**

By accepting an event as it occurs—not passively, but by making the best of it—and by accepting your thoughts and feelings and acting constructively, you can reduce suffering and create greater ease and flow in your life. Such acceptance is the practice of everyday enlightenment. You tame your mind not by changing your world, but by changing your response.

Liberating Attention at the Source

As you pass through the twelve gateways, a central and recurring theme is the liberation of attention. We've seen how your attention can become trapped or monopolized by issues in each gateway. The most subtle and insidious attention trap, however, is the mind itself.

Imagine a television set turned on all day in the background of your mind. The volume moves up and down as your attention channel surfs through inner dramas. Sometimes you pay attention to what is going on in the world around you, to daily tasks and activities. Much of the time, however, you are drawn back to your internal television world.

When something happens in your world that demands your full attention, it pulls you away from the inner television world.

At such times you feel you are living fully, intensely. Yet in any moment, you have the power to tame your mind by liberating your attention from the internal programs and dialogues simply by looking up and becoming more aware of the beauty of the real world.

Many of us drive down the highway of life for minutes or hours or years, lost in thought, daydreaming, worrying, wondering, in a kind of half-awake reverie, until we notice we have missed our exit, and most of the scenery on the way. The party continues, but we never quite show up. But when we recognize the subjective mind as a purveyor of illusions, we come to our senses. And instead of napping our way through life or flying on autopilot, we wake up and come alive.

The Illusion of a Quiet Mind

Most of us view the world through the mind without seeing the mind itself. Arising thoughts and impressions become *our* thoughts and impressions—become our truths. We believe our beliefs and interpretations the way a young child believes a movie is real. But at some point we wake up enough to suspect that the filters of our mind might actually be the source of our difficulties.

At this point we become interested in fixing, improving, or quieting our mind. As our insight grows, we notice how the mind plays like a radio tuned mostly to the noise of worries, concerns, regrets, and anxieties. We become seekers of positive thoughts or inner silence. And for the first time, we form an interest in meditation.

Meditation: A Fresh Look

Many respected teachers who make the mind their specialty offer meditation techniques for quieting the mind.

The only problem is, none of them work. In fact, the mind seems only to get busier. Despite temporary efforts, techniques, or strategies, thoughts continue to arise. You can, however, redirect your attention so you don't notice arising thoughts, in the same way you might concentrate on a good book so that you don't hear people talking around you.

Meditation does, however, have a number of benefits, which include

- deep rest and relaxation, and neurological fitness.
- moments of stillness that balance a life of activity.
- the practice of detachment (taming your mind).
- insight into the nature of subjective thought.

Meditation is *not*

- a special, higher spiritual practice.
- an elevated state of being set apart from everyday life.
- an exclusively Eastern, esoteric, mystical, or religious exercise.

Meditation is a simple and ordinary, yet endlessly challenging practice that requires vigilance and commitment to stay fully aware of what is happening in the moment. Sitting meditation is no more and no less inherently spiritual than paying attention to how you walk, eat, breathe, exercise, make love, or tie your shoes. In fact, the essence of meditation, of enlightenment, is paying attention. What makes the period of time you set aside for meditation a little special is that in everyday life we rarely pay full attention to anything, whereas in meditation practice we commit ourselves exclusively to doing just that. When you pay full attention to anything (or to nothing), it becomes a spiritual practice.

Like physical exercise, meditation is only a means to an end. You may find it helpful to meditate as an essential part of your fitness routine. Even sitting for only one minute at the end of a workout or after you shower can make a difference. As with exercise, a little of something is better than a lot of nothing. Research indicates that regular meditation can lower and stabilize blood pressure, reduce tension and anxiety, enhance creativity, lower the risk of both hypertension and heart attack, and aid in lowering addictive drives.

How Meditation Works

The principles of meditation vary from tradition to tradition but generally include the following:

- Sit in a balanced, stable, comfortable posture with your spine straight and your shoulders relaxed. (Recommended postures range from a variety of cross-legged postures, to sitting on the knees, to sitting on a chair, or even to lying down.)
- Keep your eyes closed or half-open; experiment to find what works best for you.
- Keep your tongue on the roof of your mouth.
- Relax and breathe with your belly.
- Choose an object of attention. It may be a mantra or chant, the act of counting or watching your breath, visual images (internal or external), internal or external sounds, or, in the practice called mindfulness or insight meditation, noticing whatever sensations, emotions, images, or thoughts arise spontaneously in your field of awareness.
- There are different and equally valid views on how long to sit. Some say as long as you are interested in sitting. Others say define a definite time, perhaps setting a timer with a bell. You may wish to set a minimum time such as ten or twenty minutes, or start simply, with three to five minutes, and work up from there. Experiment as you would for any other practice.

Meditation for Relaxation

If the main reason you meditate is to discover a sense of inner peace, you may want to focus attention gently on a mantra, or the breath, or listening for internal sounds. Your thoughts will continue to arise but will then fade into the background as you gently return your attention to the mantra, breath, image, or sound. The body relaxes into a sense of silent timelessness.

Meditation for Insight

Insight meditation involves noticing (that is, becoming mindful of) everything that arises in your awareness. The practice of meditation is the practice of enlightenment as you become awareness itself, observing thoughts, images, inner and outer sounds, voices, emotions, physical sensations as they arise without judgment or expectation, simply noticing whatever arises and letting it pass on.

The complete practice of meditation involves a threefold process of (1) attention, (2) insight, and (3) surrender. Surrender means letting go rather than clinging to what arises in your awareness—images, sounds, feelings, physical sensations, insights, fantasies, fears, joys, sorrows.

This is easier said than done. Perhaps you've seen the highly disciplined Buckingham Palace Guards in England, who stand gazing directly ahead with a sober expression on their faces despite the children who try to distract them. In meditation your awareness is like the Palace Guards, and your thoughts are like these children.

The beauty of insight meditation is that you can do it any time, in everyday life, with your eyes open, using whatever task is at hand as your meditative object. This is the key to understanding all Zen arts, including serving tea, arranging flowers, calligraphy, archery, swordplay, and other martial arts. All are forms of meditation. In fact, anything you do in daily life with real attention is a means to tame your mind and a practice of everyday enlightenment.

A One-Minute Meditation

This simple exercise offers a powerful way to reset your attention and regain your balance—taming your mind in the moment—a kind of instant meditation in everyday life. Do the following:

At any point in your day, especially when things get frantic or stressed, *stop* whatever you are doing, take a deep breath, and practice *one minute* of deeply felt meditation or prayer. (Prayer may be an ardent request for guidance or simply a heartfelt remembrance of Spirit.) The key is to connect your heart, attention, and feeling (a practice more fully developed in the eleventh gateway). This is a moment of remembering, of perspective, of pure feeling, that washes through the mind the way a fresh breeze sweeps leaves off the sidewalk. You will feel an almost immediate change of state. Do this simple practice several times a day, and over time you will notice profound results.

Can You Control Your Thoughts?

Can you consistently think only positive thoughts? When you are worried about something, does it work to tell yourself to just stop worrying? Thoughts float through your mind the way clouds drift through the sky. You can no more control or quiet your thoughts in any lasting way than you can stop the weather.

Try something right now: Close this book and for the next two minutes—one hundred and twenty seconds—keep your eyes focused on the book's cover. Notice every detail you can, and *think of nothing at all* but the color and title, keeping all other thoughts out of your mind. Try that now, before reading further.

Welcome back. Were you able to will yourself not to think any thoughts for two minutes? One minute? For twenty seconds? In all likelihood, if you were paying close attention, you found that it was only a matter of a few seconds before thoughts drifted back into your field of awareness—vague impressions, images, or internal dialogue. Such thoughts are constantly bubbling up in the cauldron of the psyche. You notice them or not, depending on where your attention is otherwise focused.

While you *can* learn to direct your attention in a limited way, you will never control the thoughts themselves. Experienced meditators who let their attention rest on an internal sound can reach deep states of relaxation because their attention is not focused on the arising thoughts—but *the thoughts do not stop arising.*

A Zen riddle: If a thought falls in the forest of your mind, but you give it no attention, did it really fall?

Banishing Bad Thoughts

You have the ability to use your active imagination to picture a ripe, delicious apple instead of thinking about someone with whom you are angry. But for how long?

Thoughts are like bubbles in the sea—you may cup your hands and hold some underwater, but eventually they rise to the surface. Practices such as counting your breaths or reciting a particular prayer or mantra create a moment-to-moment concentration on one idea to the exclusion of others. But if your attention wavers for an instant, the thoughts rise to the surface.

Positive thinking strategies are, like methods for quieting the mind, based on wishful thinking rather than on a realistic understanding. You don't have to control your thoughts; you just have to stop letting them control you.

A Transcendental Solution

There is another, more radical solution to the problem of the mind: *Let it be.* Make peace with and accept it as it is. No need to fix or quiet it or do anything else about it. The mind is like a barking dog. You don't have to get rid of the dog. After all, dogs naturally bark. Focus instead on directing your attention to what you are doing and *let the dog bark.* Let your thoughts be whatever they are, positive or negative, and get on with life. Learn self-compassion; make peace with your mind.

This is the highest form of meditation.

Many of us feel the need to quiet our minds because we are afraid of them—afraid of what we might think; afraid of negative, fearful, unpleasant, erotic, forbidden, disgusting thoughts; afraid of mental impulses.

Freedom from such fear comes when you realize three things:

First, thoughts are only the play of light on a movie screen. While thoughts may, like a movie, stimulate laughter or tears, they have no intrinsic reality.

Second, although you can distract yourself or direct your attention elsewhere, you cannot control your thoughts.

Third, and most important, since you cannot control or stop them, *you are not responsible for your thoughts,* no matter how good or bad they may seem. How can you be responsible for thoughts or comets or sunspots or for anything else you cannot control? You cannot control thoughts, only your response to them.

The Direction of Attention

I recently went out for my Sunday morning bike ride. As I was pedaling through a winding road in the woods, I was thinking about a speaking engagement that I had recently decided to decline.

I let my attention drift to my thoughts, my inner world, and turned away from the lush scenery. I rode for a half mile before I realized what had happened and turned my attention back to the world around me. I saw the emerald-colored carpet of moss and the shimmering leaves stretching like a canopy overhead, then I heard the sound of a rushing stream. While lost in thought I had also missed the azure sky with sunlight sparkling down through the branches overhead. I had lost, then regained, some extraordinary moments of beauty.

This is the meditation practice of daily life: Let the world become your object of attention. Few of us have developed our ability to direct or maintain our attention on a given object or subject at a given time. We are all suffering from some degree of attention deficit disorder. How can we change that?

The Art of Directing Attention

Let's look at the analogy of the mind as a television receiver and thoughts as the images and sounds that play. Cosmically speaking, all the channels are playing simultaneously. Your receiver usually picks up one channel at a time—one moment a comedy, the next a drama, the next the Shopping Channel. To the extent that our programming influences our emotions and behavior, we are all a little crazy.

We cannot shut off the programs (that is, stop our thoughts), but by turning our attention elsewhere, we can go outside into the world and play. As we pay less attention to the television and more to the world around us, we begin to experience pure awareness. We *become* that awareness. Judgments, expectations, interpretations, and associations continue to arise within that field of awareness, along with every other kind of thought, but we see them for what they are rather than mistaking them for reality, for truth.

Daily Life as a Warrior's Meditation

I developed an ability to concentrate because, beginning at eleven years of age, I learned a type of warrior meditation. For nine years I practiced this meditation nearly every day for at least three hours a day. My particular meditation was called gymnastics. In gymnastics you put your life on the line. When you're swinging around the horizontal bar or flying through the air above the trampoline, the consequences of an attention lapse can be far worse than losing a game.

When I coached gymnastics at Stanford University, other coaches couldn't figure out how in a few years our team went from the bottom of the Pacific-8 Conference to being one of the nation's elite teams. During one gymnastics meet, a coach approached me and asked if our team members meditated before a competition. "No," I answered. "They meditate *during* the competition."

Beyond Meditation

If you meditate with sincere concentration, you may come to a time where you will grasp the nature of the mind and experience some distance and freedom from its content. At that point you are free to get on with your life. Even meditation can become a mindless habit; formal sitting practice does not need to become a lifelong commitment. As a natural, healthful part of a balanced lifestyle, you may wish to include a brief period of meditation in the rhythms of your everyday life. But sitting practice is a beginner's practice; once you have seen what you need to see, each moment of daily life becomes meditation practice.

Like playing the piano, meditation is a skill that you improve with practice, if you do it with attention and intention. Playing the piano provides a clear demand and clear feedback; meditation does not. Some of us sit down to meditate and then simply daydream. This is fine if you want to spend some quiet time in reverie—but you are practicing daydreaming, not meditation. Meditation practice requires vigilance, attention, and a commitment to gently but firmly release a thought the way you would release a fish, by tossing it back into the stream. Once you have meditated enough to see the discursive mind as it is, as a parade of illusion, you can then go about your day—and your life—with your eyes open, your attention free. You have tamed your mind by making peace with your thoughts and need fear it no more.

Return to the Present

Only now exists. Past and future are illusion and exist only as mental constructs. Your body lives here and now. *Not even your mind can stretch to the past or future.* When you are thinking about the past, you are in the *present* moment, thinking. It's just that the *content* of your thoughts is about a remembered (or imagined) past or anticipated (and imagined) future. The mind pretends to be a time machine, taking you from past to future, but the mind is a trickster.

> We are here and it is now.
> Further than that all human
> knowledge is moonshine.
> —H. L. Mencken

Living the Simple Life

As the pace of life has accelerated, the idea of living simply, like the idea of developing a quiet mind, has gained great appeal.

Every extreme breeds a yearning for its opposite. But complexity is a fact of life, and simplicity may not necessarily involve ease or relaxation. Scott and Helen Nearing, authors of *Living the Good Life,* have demonstrated that a simple life may involve labors of different kinds—immersion of attention in the moment, to the matter at hand, whatever needs doing, one thing at a time.

It is entirely possible to live a full, busy, and varied life in the city yet experience a sense of simplicity when your attention rests in the present moment. In my life as a husband, a father of two busy teenage daughters, a professional writer, and a lecturer who travels widely and receives much correspondence and many demands, I must attend to many things; yet my life is quite simple since I can do only one thing at a time. The same is true for you.

When you need to think about, remember, solve, or access something in your mind or memory, direct your attention there. Otherwise, keep your attention on what is happening in this moment, on what you are doing here and now. The following exercise enables you to do just that.

The Three-Question Wake-up Call: The moment you notice your attention has drifted, you can direct it back to the body, back to this moment, by asking yourself three internal questions: *Am I breathing?* (Take a conscious breath.) *Am I relaxed?* (Let go of any tension you notice.) *Am I doing whatever I am doing with refinement and grace?* (Allow yourself to do so.) These questions are signposts pointing back to present reality. And in this way, you begin to practice everyday enlightenment.

As you tame your mind by training your attention, life becomes simpler. *Let this moment become the object of your lifelong meditation,* your everyday enlightenment.

> If you let yourself be absorbed completely,
> if you surrender completely to the moments as they pass,
> you live more richly those moments.
>
> **—Anne Morrow Lindbergh**

Most of us have heard the saying *"Carpe diem"*—Seize the day. A valuable reminder to live fully, but not a realistic idea, since you cannot seize the day. You can seize only the moment—this moment.

The quality of your moments produces the quality of your life. So, as thoughts come and go and the waves of mind rush on, *Carpe punctum*—Seize this moment. It deserves your full attention, for it will not pass your way again.

Now, in this present moment, with deeper insight into the nature of your mind, you are ready to access and trust the quiet voice that guides you through the silent spaces between thought, to subtle signs and synchronicities that appear whenever you need them, when you pay attention.

THE

SIXTH GATEWAY

Trust
Your Intuition

*Below everyday awareness
is a shamanlike, childlike consciousness—
weaver of dreams, keeper of instinct.
Your subconscious holds keys to
a treasure house of intuitive wisdom,
clear sight, and untapped power.
All you have to do is to
look, listen, and trust,
paying attention to
dreams, feelings, instinct.
If you can't trust your own inner senses,
what can you trust?*

Accessing Inner Guidance

The great decisions of human life
usually have far more to do with the instincts
and other mysterious unconscious factors
than with conscious will
and well-meaning reasonableness.
The shoe that fits one person pinches another;
there is no universal recipe for living.
Each of us carries his own life-form within him—
an irrational form which no other can outbid.

—Carl Jung

Road Map: Another Way of Knowing

The routines of everyday life—driving the same streets to work or to school, the same rituals in the home—don't make big demands on our decision-making capacities. But when important choices or decisions arise about a career direction, change of residence, or pending marriage, many of us feel ill equipped to make the right choice. This is because for most of us, early education developed logic and reasoning skills—we learned only to think rather than feel our way through life. The intuition capacities of our right brain were left to languish—undervalued, unappreciated, and largely unused. So we navigate through life using only our logical left brains as a compass, weighing factors and juggling variables.

Few of us fully trust our own inner guidance system. We can trust what we know only when we know what we have. You will learn to trust your innate intuitive capacity once you grasp the powers of your subconscious mind and discover how it works, when it works, and why it works. Then you will know where to find the still voice within you. Then you will learn how to listen.

165

Trust Your Intuition opens doors to creativity, guidance, clarity, and instinctive action. This gateway concludes with a powerful exercise that can prove to you your innate intuitive abilities and open clairvoyant sight—showing you how to access and trust your intuition and fulfill the promise of this chapter. But first we prepare, by patiently providing a context, a new vision of the big picture.

Intuition Basics and Broad Strokes

Intuition is not what most people think it is; in fact, it is not what we *think* at all. Reason may complement or interfere with intuition, but it cannot substitute for it. In fact, intuition comes from a different side of the brain from that of logic. Everyday enlightenment requires full use of both sides of our brains, integrating the logical and the intuitive, the conscious and the subconscious, science and mysticism, to form a full representation of reality.

Intuitive feelings are related to but different from emotional feelings. Someone out of touch with their emotions is usually out of touch with their intuitive feelings as well. Intuition is feeling-impression or sensation that can also arise as what we call "funny feeling" or in the form of images, sounds, and (on rare occasions) taste or smell.

I sometimes use the terms "intuition" and "instinct" interchangeably, since they are related (but not identical). Where instinct is more closely identified as a gut-level sensation, intuition is often a nonlocalized impression. But instinct and intuition are both related to right-brain capacities.

This gateway will explore topics including the nature of intuition and primary intuitive senses; keys to understand the powers of your subconscious mind; ways to induce altered states; oracular tools to access inner guidance; an advanced method to open clairvoyant sight; and how intuition relates to faith. We begin, as in the other gateways, with an exercise in self-reflection.

An Intuitive Self-Assessment

You probably use your intuition on a regular basis without being fully aware of it. The following questions can clarify the degree to which you currently use and trust those intuitive faculties:

- When you have to make a decision or choice and weigh the pros and cons, do you still feel confused or uncertain? What would it take for you to feel more certain?
- Does your decision-making process change when the decision involves what you feel is a major crossroads?
- Recall an important time when you followed your intuition.
- Recall an important time when you didn't.
- Do you tend to place more faith in the guidance of others than in your own instincts? If someone offers guidance that doesn't fit with your intuition, which do you trust more?
- If you could fully access your intuitive abilities, how might your life improve?

As in previous gateways, these few questions generate self-reflection that personalizes the principles that follow.

The Nature of Intuition

When you understand the ordinary rather than magical nature of intuition, you begin to trust your innate ability to know without knowing how. Socrates once advised me to "think less and feel more." He meant that there are times to ruminate, but the factors we weigh in making logical decisions are only the proverbial tip of the iceberg. Our subconscious mind also accesses what is below "see" level—variables of which we may not be aware. So intuitive decisions tend to be more aligned with our subconscious mission and destiny of which our reasoning mind is unaware.

In order to begin accessing and trusting your intuitive powers, you need to stop being so reasonable. Your intuitive capacities are fully intact but often hidden behind a screen of logic—you get an impression, but if it doesn't make sense to you at the time, you may discard it. Trusting your intuition may involve following some odd impressions without consciously understanding why.

I'll illustrate what I mean with an odd event that occurred to me some time ago. Before I wrote *The Life You Were Born to Live,* I used to send out life-purpose consultations on audiotape. On one occasion I opened about five envelopes, each with a check and request for an audiotape. But as I opened a particular envelope and looked at the check, I got a bad feeling—as though something were off. I checked the envelope; it did not strike me as unusual. I then looked at the check itself: bank imprint, phone number, signature—everything in order. Then I did something I had never done before (and have not done since). I called the bank to check on the account. They referred me to a second number. I could have dropped the whole thing, but the feeling remained, so out of curiosity I followed through. Eventually I learned that the account had been closed for two months. There had been no *reason* to follow through on my intuitive impression, but I did.

Trust your instinct and intuition. By doing so, you can tap into the synchronous or even magical elements of reality, access inner guidance, and meet opportunities that might otherwise have remained hidden. You become the master of your own destiny.

> There is no need to run outside
> for better seeing, . . . Rather
> abide at the center of your being; . . .
> Search your heart and see . . .
>
> —Lao-tzu

The Primary Inner Senses

You are already aware that you take in impressions about the world through your five primary senses of sight, hearing, touch, taste, and smell. You also learned in *Tame Your Mind* that these impressions pass through your subjective filters and that one facet of waking up—of enlightenment—is cleaning these filters through which you sense the world so that you gain the ability to grasp reality directly and objectively, as it is, without distortion.

This insight prepares you to more easily understand, access, and trust your inner senses, which work in a similar fashion. Your intuitive (inner) sense impressions most often come to you through one of these five senses. And to the degree you become aware of your mental filters and learn to perceive reality objectively (without all your meanings and interpretations), your intuitive messages come in clearly, without distortion, and become *clairvoyance* (clear sight), *clairaudience* (clear voices or sounds), or *clairsentience* (clear sense or feeling).

In sensing the outer world, most of us rely first on the visual (sight) sense, then the auditory (hearing), then the tactile (touch) sense. This tends to be equally true in accessing intuitive impressions. The subconscious mind delivers symbolic images, pictures, and colors for most people but may instead also speak to us in words (our own or another's voice). Further subconscious impressions may come in the form of tactile or kinesthetic physical sensations (a felt sense or gut feeling).

You may also detect intuitive impressions through your senses of taste or smell—you may sense a deal going sour, get a bad taste in your mouth, sense a sweet opportunity, or realize a situation stinks. But because you use your senses of smell and taste less, we will dispense with these as intuitive channels so we can concentrate on the three predominant modalities.

How You Access Information—A Self-Assessment

Take this simple test in order to clarify your primary and secondary sensory-accessing channels. Right now, before reading further, please imagine a thunderstorm. Imagine it vividly with all your senses, before reading further.

Okay. You'll notice that I used a neutral word: imagine. I didn't say picture, hear, or feel. When you imagined the thunderstorm, which sense did you use to enter the scene? Did you first *picture* the dark clouds, the rain pouring down, perhaps flashes of lightning? Or did you find it easier to first *hear* the crash of thunder, *then* see the lightning or stormclouds? Or, less commonly, you may have *felt* the tactile sensation of the air, the water, the wind, before you were able to picture or hear the storm.

Just as you are somewhat limited in the world without the full use of all your senses, so are you better equipped if you develop and use all your inner-sense modalities when gathering intuitive impressions—what does it look like, sound like, feel like? Each serves as a check and cross-reference to confirm or correct your other impressions. Still, if one modality is weaker, you can refine others (just as a blind person may develop more acute hearing).

Finally, we have a sixth nonlocalized intuitive sense. It doesn't come as a picture, a sound, or even a distinct tactile sensation. You just know.

The Mysterious Source of Knowing

Because the scientific method (a useful tool of the conscious mind and left brain) has become a form of religion in the modern world, anything unscientific becomes what "un-American" used to be—highly suspect and bordering on heretical. It is ironic that most great scientific discoveries, from those of Archimedes to those of Einstein, came from the intuitive right brain while its discoverer was napping, dreaming, bathing, or in reverie. Only later were they validated through the scientific method. In this sense, our right brain's intuitive capacities are senior to the left brain's logical labors, but both sides of the brain (like science and intuition), when combined, form a whole greater than the sum of the two separate parts.

In the process of writing, I open up in a prayerful sense, to information that comes to me out of mystery—things I know but do not know *how* I know. Perhaps it is a gift from my muse or from what Carl Jung called "the universal unconscious." I know only that we all have access to the same vast and mysterious storehouse of wisdom. The mechanism and means of delivery stems from our creative, intuitive right brain through which flow subconscious impressions. Such information, the whispered wisdom, the subtle pictures and feelings, are available to anyone who has the free attention to notice them. We return again to the higher theme and purpose of the twelve gateways—freeing attention and energy to access higher levels of awareness and experience. You are now involved with this process as we proceed through the sixth gateway.

With a little practice, as you become attuned to your intuitive messages, you can switch channels in the same way you might put most attention on your physical sight while walking in the woods but, after darkness falls, put more attention on your hearing and tactile senses.

In any case, it begins by taking a moment to *stop, look, listen, and feel*. This is, in essence, the same exercise you learned in the last gateway—taking a time-out for one minute of prayerful repose. As Ram Dass observed, "The quieter you become the more you can hear." And see. And feel.

By listening respectfully, attentively, to the quiet voice of your subconscious inner child, you reconnect once again to the simple wisdom at the heart of life.

What About the Higher Self?

The Huna teachings of Hawaii propose that when the soul takes birth in a physical body, it arrives with three selves: a higher self (or guardian angel), a basic self (the subconscious mind and instinctive body wisdom), and a conscious self (or ego identity that develops as we grow out of infancy). The higher self can communicate to you only *through* your basic self (or subconscious)— through your body and senses. The better attuned you are to your physical senses and emotions, the better you can see, feel, or hear the whispered guidance of your higher self. Trusting your instinct and intuition is a way of listening to your highest wisdom.

> Except during the nine months
> before he draws his first breath,

no man manages his affairs
as well as a tree does.

—**George Bernard Shaw**

Learning to Trust Intuitive Messages

Ever since the initiation experience that I described in the pro-
logue, my intuitive capacities have expanded because my conscious mind has formed a close and trusting relationship with my
subconscious mind. Rather than my logical mind dominating or
devaluing these intuitive stirrings, my left and right hemispheres
have made contact, become friends, and, at times, embraced. (A
neurologist might express this as a neural opening in the *corpus
callosum,* which connects the left and right brain—but I prefer my
metaphor.)

This respectful and cooperative relationship between your
conscious and subconscious, your left and right brain, is central
to opening and trusting intuition. To access your intuitive capacities, you begin by paying attention to new radio frequencies you
hadn't noticed before.

Intuitive Powers of the Subconscious Mind

Although we cannot see subatomic particles, physicists know of
their existence because of their effects. Similarly, although we
cannot see the subconscious, we can observe its effects. The phenomena described in this section, taken together, strongly support the existence of a (sub)conscious intelligence working
through the autonomic nervous system, in charge of the body.

The Placebo Effect

This effect, an established medical phenomenon, happens to a
significant number of people whose symptoms are reduced or
eliminated when given sugar pills (with no active ingredients)
that they believe are effective medicine. Clearly the pill isn't ef-

fecting a cure; but your suggestible subconscious, in control of the body, increases white cells or whatever else it needs to heal the body. Many miraculous remissions and healings are attributed to so many sources, including restricted diet or fasting, high-level exercise, prayer and faith healing, special water (such as that found at Lourdes) or holy objects, chemotherapy or radiation, modalities such as massage, herbs, or acupuncture, or a combination of these. No single approach works for everyone. The secret is to find out which modality appeals to you—which inspires, interests, or captures your imagination—which one you most *believe in,* because it is that belief that empowers you to heal. (The confident manner and charisma of the healer may in some cases be more important than the modality of therapy.)

Hypnosis

Hypnosis is a simple process that induces a state of relaxed trust or drowsiness. In such a state (and also when you are ill or anesthetized) the skeptical conscious mind recedes as the processor of information, and the suggestible subconscious mind can be accessed directly. Suggestions go into the subconscious (and the right brain) that can influence the workings of the immune system, for example. A skillful hypnotist can briefly touch a subject's arm with an ice cube and suggest that it was the burning end of a cigarette, then watch as a red welt appears on the subject's arm. You cannot consciously *will* a welt to appear on your arm, a fact that again points to the power of your subconscious mind, which controls your body's functions.

Material can come forth from the subconscious as well, which is why hypnosis is sometimes used with witnesses to crimes, who can, while in a trance, sometimes recall levels of detail not consciously remembered (things they saw but didn't know they saw). Hypnosis is also a way to communicate directly with the autonomic nervous system and immune system through the subconscious mind's mediation—why physicians and others have had some good results with visualization techniques and other right-brain therapies in supporting or enhancing immune response.

Take, for example, the work of Dr. Bernie Siegel and the amazing phenomenon of Edgar Cayce.

Bernie Siegel, Respectful Healer

Bernie Siegel, M.D., surgeon and author of *Peace, Love, and Healing,* has respect for his patients' subconscious healing abilities while in surgery. Anesthetized patients (with their conscious mind asleep but their subconscious mind alert and aware) are in a particularly suggestible state; how they are spoken to and treated can make a difference in their outcomes. Recognizing the power of his suggestions, he talks to unconscious patients throughout the operation. Sometimes, when a patient's pulse rate is too high during an operation, Dr. Siegel will say something like "We'd like your pulse to be eighty-six." He'll pick a specific number because he wants everyone to see the pulse go down to that exact number. Dr. Siegel has said that *something* in the body hears these messages and knows how to respond to them.

The same "something" can wake you up each morning just before the alarm goes off. Sometimes it knows who is calling before you pick up the phone. That "something" may even access physical skills and abilities from past life memories or other sources we don't yet understand, such as in the case of Mozart and other child prodigies who demonstrate extraordinary capacities they have never consciously learned.

And you now know what that something is—your intuitive mind.

Edgar Cayce: The Sleeping Prophet

One of the most astonishing and well-documented testimonials to the intuitive powers of the subconscious mind is found in Thomas Sugrue's book, *There Is a River,* the biography of Edgar Cayce, one of the world's most famous channelers. Cayce was considered a relatively dull student and poor speller, until one day he put his head down on his spelling book and fell asleep. When he awoke the young Cayce could spell any word in his book. After Cayce finished his otherwise undistinguished scholastic career, he found work as a photographer. Soon after, it was discovered he would talk in his sleep and diagnose illnesses with uncanny accuracy, as well as recommend effective treatments. He needed only a person's name and address. When asleep, he would in some way visit the person's body, diagnose what he saw, and recommend sometimes traditional, sometimes unorthodox, remedies. Cayce had no conscious knowledge of medicine or healing.

Cayce never charged for his work. As a devout Christian, he felt it was a gift from God and didn't feel he could charge for whatever he said in his sleep. Volumes of Cayce's dictations have been meticulously documented and widely published.

Edgar Cayce's abilities demonstrate the sleeping potential within each of us. The fact that he could access his powerful intuitive capacities while asleep points to the immense powers of our subconscious minds, hidden within the folds and mysteries of our right brains.

Opening Channels to Your Subconscious

Relaxation (and hypnotic trance) is one way to set aside our everyday consciousness and call forth our subconscious mind, but there are many other methods as well. Since ancient times, humans have found doorways to altered or trance states of consciousness—shifts of perception and awareness different from our daily waking state. These doorways include meditation, psychoactive substances, deep breathwork, chanting, dancing, fasting, and extremes of endurance, sensory deprivation, and even painful initiation ceremonies. Such methods were used primarily by shamans, priests, and medicine healers as sacred forms of purification, healing, or vision journeys.

Not all of these methods are as appropriate or effective within our culture or time. Some of the methods just listed either are illegal (nonprescriptive use of drugs) or entail serious risks if done without the supervision of an experienced guide. I will summarize here only those methods suitable for modern-day life—methods that provide a vision quest and generate a deeper intuitive relationship with life. (These following methods provide entry into the shamanic world of the subconscious but are not necessarily designed to bring back specific intuitive information. We will address such methods later.)

- **Meditation:** As relaxation deepens in a meditative state, images and dreamlike symbols flow in and out of awareness, attuning you to finer, deeper currents of creativity.
- **Dream Yoga:** Also called lucid dreaming, in which the dreamers are awake within the dream and are aware that they are dreaming. Tibetan monks say that this exploration of the subconscious world is practice for moving through the *bardo,* the space between lives, after death and before rebirth.
- **Breathwork:** Various methods use conscious hyperventilation (as in holotropic breathwork or rebirthing) to achieve states similar to those induced by hypnosis, or psychotropic drugs, but without the potential side effects. Music played during the breathing sessions helps to call forth archetypal images and experiences from your subconscious. Should be done only under the guidance of a trained professional.
- **Chanting, Drumming, and Dancing:** Rhythmically repeating words, sounds, and movement over time will induce a trancelike state that allows the subconscious to step forward.

These and other methods have been used by native cultures in America and around the world in order to set aside everyday reality and enter the realm of the shamans, the subconscious otherworld in touch with past, future, and eternal present within the depths of the psyche. With proper guidance, meditation, dreamwork, breathwork, and chanting, drumming, and dancing are being used effectively in modern-day culture as well.

Oracles: Tools to Access Inner Guidance

Having explored ways to access your subconscious, we now turn to specific means, which may or may not involve altered or trance states, to access intuitive information as a tool of divination or decision making. Such methods are known collectively as *oracles.*

Sensitive people, such as shamans, psychics, mediums, certain priests, healers, or channelers, may serve as oracles by acting as a mediator between the conscious and subconscious realms. There are others who combine their own intuition with specific oracular methods such as astrology, numerology, the tarot, palmistry, crystal balls, or the Chinese I Ching, Nordic runes, or other tools. Such individuals may go into mild or deep trance states to access their subconscious but may also simply synthesize information gathered through their own respective tools.

Consulting intuitive advisers in the same way we might consult a specialist in health or psychology can be interesting and informative. But the purpose of the sixth gateway is trusting *your* intuition rather than relying solely on the intuitive skills of others. More and less skillful guides exist in every field. As our self-trust matures, we come to rely more on our own inner counsel as final authority over information we receive from others.

People who serve as oracles are no different from you or me. They have simply learned to trust their natural intuitive capacities and, through practice, have become highly attuned to their chosen methods. You and I can also learn how to use such methods in making decisions or finding direction. Oracular tools are training wheels we use until we no longer need them and can directly unlock our subconscious wisdom. In other words, the power, mystery, and magic is not in the tool, it is in *you.* With that understood, we take an appreciative look at the various means and methods used to access inner guidance.

Astrology, numerology, the I Ching, the runes, the tarot, crystal balls, palmistry, and other methods used for thousands of years are based on consistent intuitive principles derived from the workings of the human psyche and the nature of the world.

How Oracles Work

If everything in our world is energetically and spiritually connected, then a drop of rain or snowflake is a hologram of the entire universe. Thus we can take in information through methods that use our right brain, whose intuitive capacities operate much like a radio transmitter-receiver. For some years I myself served as an oracle, using a numerological method presented in *The Life You Were Born to Live.*

Such holistic and intuitive systems are, almost by definition, nonrational and have been mistakenly associated with occult practices and shunned by both science and religion. Yet these systems have lasted, and will continue to last, throughout time—not because they can (or should) unerringly guide your life (no system or method should take the place of your own inner guidance), but because they remind us of the mystery and interconnectedness of the universe.

I now present the Rorschach effect and the pendulum effect, two phenomena that explain the workings of most oracular methods. We will then explore some of these methods.

The Rorschach Effect: Named after the nineteenth-century psychiatrist who devised it, this psychological test consists of a series of mirrored inkblot images and random designs that are shown to psychiatric patients, who then are asked to describe what these pictures look like to determine their degree of psychological integration. Since the pictures don't actually look like any one thing, we project our own subconscious imagery, content, and meaning onto what we see.

This mechanism—projecting our own subconscious meaning and interpretation—is the same one used to intuitively read meanings in tea leaves, crystal balls, the tarot, runes, the I Ching, and other oracular tools.

The Pendulum Effect: This second phenomenon is based upon *ideomotor action,* which refers to a phenomenon that demonstrates how your subconscious mind can have an impact on and deliver simple "yes" or "no" messages through your body. It works to receive input from the symbolic subconscious mind by translating it into simple physical signs in the same way one might communicate with paralyzed stroke patients by having them blink once for "yes" and twice for "no." To access messages from your subconscious, try this simple experiment:

- Attach a ring or earring or small weight to a six- to eight-inch piece of thread or string.
- Hold the end of the string, letting the weight hang freely.
- Now, keep your hand still until the weight is relatively motionless.
- Next, think or imagine that the weight has begun to move back and forth, back and forth, in a straight line; just gaze at the weight and think "back and forth," "back and forth," without in any way consciously intending to move your hand. Watch what happens.
- Think or imagine, next, that the weight is moving in a circle. Just think "circle" and notice what happens to the back-and-forth motion. You will notice that thoughts create movement without your conscious intention.

Now it gets even more interesting.

- To determine which direction your subconscious mind prefers to use for "yes" and for "no," first think "yes" and wait to see which way the pendulum moves. Then, to check, think "no" and see how it moves. These "set" the yes and no signals. Find out what works in your own case.
- Next, in a relaxed state, visualize questions or decisions about which you would like subconscious input. Remember—the questions need to be phrased so that they can be answered by a simple "yes" or "no" sign. Hold the weight steady, relax, and wait.

Using a pendulum is one of the most effective ways to access your own body wisdom, especially for questions about your own health, but also including any aspect of life about which you may have subconscious knowledge. This phenomenon of ideomotor action also operates for physical-intuitive guidance methods such as dowsing for water or minerals.

Now that you recognize the subconscious mind as a primary source or channel of your intuitive capacities, it is time to learn how to access it. One of the most important methods involves using your dreams as an oracle.

Dreams: When the conscious mind sleeps, your subconscious steps forward to rebalance your psyche in its own mysterious way by weaving a rich and varied tapestry of symbols, metaphors, and archetypes, upon which you can project or find meaning. Some dreams may reveal only that you ate too much pizza the night before, but others convey oracular lessons, cautions, opportunities, and guidance. Dreams are the royal road to the subconscious and a fascinating tool of intuitive insight.

Many of us remember dreams only on occasion, and then only in nonsensical fragments. I hadn't given much energy or attention to dreams until I visited with a Jungian therapist who said, "Bring me your dreams next week." Committed to this enterprise, and willing to wake up during the night and write down what I remembered, I ended up with five pages of dream imagery by the following week. You can remember your dreams when you clearly intend to do so, and it becomes easier over time (especially if you practice meditation, which serves to break through the barriers between waking and dreaming awareness). Keeping a dream journal, a diary of your dream time, your dream life, provides a rich source of intuitive information.

Intuitive Problem Solving in the Dream State

You may have had the experience of going to bed with a problem or a dilemma—or struggling with a decision—and when you awaken, the problem is resolved or clarified. Carl Jung's *Memories, Dreams and Reflections* is one of the best all-time texts about the mystical process of dreaming. And Stanford professor Stephen Laberge, in his classic work, *Lucid Dreaming,* offers guidance for modern dream yoga, to actively enter into the dream world as it unfolds.

Your subconscious mind can solve problems or riddles seemingly out of reach of our conscious mind. Dr. William Dement of

Stanford University, a world-renowned expert in the field of sleep and dreams, gave the following riddle to his students: *H I J K L M N O*—eight letters of the alphabet. The riddle made no sense, but he asked the students to think about it before bed, then sleep on it and write down their dreams to see if their subconscious mind could come up with the answer.

Ted, one of the gymnasts I coached at Stanford during this time, told me about the riddle the next morning but said he still hadn't solved it. "All I remember dreaming about," he said, "was a storm at sea. I was on an old schooner, and the waves were rolling and crashing around me, and the rain was pouring down. I have no idea what the dream meant."

Later that afternoon in class, Ted discovered that he had solved the riddle without consciously knowing it. H I J K L M N O are the letters of the alphabet from H to O. Get it? H_2O—water. And he had dreamt about pouring rainstorms, the ocean, rolling waves.

Dreams do more than solve riddles. They also represent who you are and reveal much about your shadow, hidden aspects of yourself that you will meet in the next gateway.

Prayer: Like dreams, the sacred practice of prayer can also help you to access intuitive wisdom. Prayer is a sincere, humble, yet fervent request for higher guidance. This practice is nondenominational; prayer is not limited to any particular religious tradition. Prayer may be the highest, most personal and powerful form of accessing intuitive wisdom, because traditionally you are asking God, or Spirit, or your higher self for help or clarity. As such, prayer works best when asked with the attitude "Thy will be done"—in other words, with a willingness to follow whatever guidance comes.

Sometimes prayer asks for a sign in the body or in the world. The help you pray for may be delivered during the prayer or some time afterward. This method can be practiced (improving with your own openness over time), tested, and *verified*. It brings clarity, insight, and answers to crucial questions, increasing our sensitivity to the quiet voice of our inner guidance.

To find desired answers, you have to ask the right questions.

Many of us never think to consciously ask questions because it feels silly or pointless or because we don't believe answers will come. But this is one meaning of the biblical injunction "Ask and it will be given you . . . knock, and the door will be opened for you." The method of asking, whether in a prayerful attitude or nonsecular state of openness, as in a trance or reverie, involves a clear and focused request, followed by a state of relaxed receptivity and trust in your intuitive channels to hidden realms of shadow and the highest realms of light.

Travel: Although travel hardly strikes most of us as an oracular method, leaving your everyday environment to explore new territory has a stimulating or tonic effect on your subconscious mind—you feel awake, aware, and alert. And it is quite common, almost universal, to achieve new perspective, clarity, and intuitive insight into yourself and your life while traveling—literally getting some distance from an issue or problem. Thus travel can provide a good opportunity to make intuitive decisions. You don't need to spend a great deal of money or necessarily travel to exotic locations. Even going for a walk in an unfamiliar locale can inspire new and creative ideas.

The Heart of Intuition

As I have already noted, even if psychics, astrologers, or other oracles are truly gifted, intuition is at best a do-it-yourself project. Other people's perspectives can be helpful at times, but ultimately the sixth gateway is about trusting your *own* inner guidance, doing your *own* readings, rather than searching for wisdom outside yourself. The goal is to take responsibility for guiding your own life and trusting your own intuitive capacities to do so.

You are an oracle. You can read the signs in your own body, in your dreams and waking reveries, in the reflections you see in rain puddles and in your heart's whisperings. You are the expert on your life and destiny. When you are paying attention, no one knows you better than you can know yourself.

The world is an oracle. You can access intuitive wisdom in any moment while watching a supple tree, bending in the wind;

you can make meaning out of the shapes of clouds; the changing seasons or a stream winding down a mountainside can lend life-changing insights.

Having explored the pathways of intuitive guidance, appreciate this: Just as you can drive a car or watch television without understanding all the mechanisms of internal combustion or electronic wave transmission, so can you trust and use your intuition without knowing precisely how it works. Trust is the key that opens the gateway. Now it's time to apply what you have learned in making and trusting your choices and decisions.

Intuitive Decision Making

Life confronts you with many decisions, options, and choices during the day. Do you turn left or right, do this or that, say yes or no?

> When you come to a fork in the road, take it.
>
> **—Yogi Berra**

Logic and reason alone (using half your brain) doesn't necessarily work well no matter how much analysis you perform. You can weigh variables and compare pros and cons, benefits and liabilities, until your mind starts chasing its own tail and you experience paralysis by analysis.

You may have difficulty making important decisions because you are afraid of making the wrong decision; you may confuse what truly attracts you with what you (or others) think you *should* do; you may try to make the decision too early, long before it is necessary or relevant (which is like trying to figure out which foot to use to step off a curb that's halfway down the block); or you may still rely only on your conscious mind and get lost weighing variables.

The left brain has knowledge, but without the intuitive wisdom of the right brain every decision comes out half-baked. There are two sides to every issue (and every brain). The key is finding a blend and balance of the right and left, inside and out, East and West, logic and intuition.

The following guidelines will help you to open to and trust your intuitive decision making powers:

- **Ask yourself, "What if I knew?"** When you feel uncertain, doubtful, or wavering, ask yourself the magic words "What if I knew?" and see what appears.
- **Stay relaxed and play it like a game.** The more relaxed you are (as in hypnosis or sleep), the more your usually dominant, logical, left-brain conscious mind steps back and quiets and your intuitive capacities come forward. And keep it light; when you aren't attached to whether you win or lose, you often play the best.
- **Let go of logic.** Logic interferes with intuition. Use them both, but not at the same time. Ignorance is bliss: assume nothing and wait. See what appears.
- **Trust your innate abilities.** When I competed in the finals of the World Trampoline Championships years ago, I made up my routine in midair. As I somersaulted through the air, my body made an instant decision about the next move. My conscious mind simply couldn't have done this. I opened up and trusted my body to do whatever it would, just staying present. As I trusted my instincts, you can trust your intuition.

Even applying the preceding guidelines, you may sometimes lack sufficient perspective to make a clear decision. After all, how can you know the consequences of a decision ten years from now? You cannot know, not for certain. But you can gain perspective by using your intuitive imagination.

Timelining: Using Your Intuitive Imagination

Projecting your imagination into the future provides an intuitive perspective far deeper than looking only from the temporal viewpoint of the present. It also enables you to apply intuitive wisdom to a decision by anticipating the future consequences of that decision. The process is quite simple and takes only a few minutes, affording you more intuitive data on which to base a decision. (Using the fork-in-the-road metaphor, it allows you to project your imagination up each path, to sense what awaits you.)

Let's say you have to decide between choice A, B, or C:

1. First you assume, for the moment, that you have committed to choice A.
2. Having done so, sit quietly, with your eyes open or closed, take a deep breath, and relax; then ask yourself the following question and see what appears in your mind's eye:
   - Having chosen A, what will I look like, feel like, and be doing one *hour* from now? (Wait and allow your intuitive imagination to create a picture.)
   - Having chosen A, what will I look like, feel like, and be doing one *day* from now? (Again, wait and see.)
   - Having chosen A, what will I look like, feel like, and be doing one *week* from now? (Wait and see.)
   - Having chosen A, what will I look like, feel like, and be doing one *month* from now? (Wait.)
   - Having chosen A, what will I look like, feel like, and be doing one *year* from now? (Wait.)
   - Having chosen A, what will I look like, feel like, and be doing *ten years* from now? (Wait.)
3. Next go through the same list for choices B and C. At the end of this process, which takes only a few minutes, you will have more perspective than before, having accessed your intuitive imagination.

Perhaps you're wondering if you only *imagine* how you might look and feel and what you may be doing, how do you know it's accurate? What if you merely *invent* a better scenario because that's the option you really prefer? To answer those questions, consider: Why did your imagination (or subconscious) deliver those specific images and not others? And if you made up a nice scenario because you really prefer one choice over the others, hasn't your decision been made?

Intuition and Faith

Ultimately you put away the tools and methods and go directly to the source of inner guidance—Spirit or God or your higher self whispering within you. Trusting your intuition is really the same as trusting God. Intuition must ultimately rely on faith, because your inner guidance system does not necessarily lead to risk-free decisions. Sometimes your choices may take you where you *think* you want to go, but on other occasions you may trust your intuition, make a decision, and find the going very tough for a while. That doesn't mean you made the wrong decision.

Conventional truth tells you that you can make mistakes.

Transcendental truth informs you that you cannot ultimately make the wrong decision.

Intuition is not about certainty. It is about trust and faith. Faith is the courage to treat everything that happens as exactly what you need for your highest good and learning.

Sometimes your intuition guides you directly onto a difficult path to test you, temper you, and teach you to deal with difficulties and evolve in the process.

Life won't always give you what you want, but it will consistently give you what you need. It won't always tell you what you want to hear, but it will tell you where you need to go, what you need to do, and whom you can trust. This faith awakens intuition—an expanded way of knowing, seeing, and doing in the world.

THE

SEVENTH GATEWAY

Accept
Your Emotions

Emotions are like waves on the sea
or weather in the skies,
rising and passing of their own accord.
You cannot control your feelings
by an act of intention or will.
So you are not responsible for your feelings;
only for your response to them.
Accept emotions completely,
let your feelings be;
just don't let them run your life.

The Center of the Cyclone

The key is to not resist or rebel against emotions
or to try to get around them by devising all sorts of tricks;
but to accept them directly, as they are.

—Takahisa Kora, M.D.

Road Map: Emotional Riddles

In polite society we rarely show strong or spontaneous emotions, almost as if we don't feel them. Yet most of our lives are driven by emotion—seeking pleasant feelings and avoiding unpleasant ones. We pursue whatever we hope will make us feel good. In fact, for many people, the entire quest for enlightenment is a search for permanently pleasurable emotions.

If your life is a journey, then emotions are the natural weather fronts you pass through (and that pass through you) along the way. You will find this metaphor of "emotions as weather" often in this chapter, because emotions and feelings—two words I use interchangeably—do behave much like the weather.

Imagine what your life would be like if you spent much of your time and energy struggling to fix the weather every time it stormed, snowed, or grew windy or hot. Yet most of us attempt to do just that when storms arise inside us. We seek the help of professionals, looking for strategies to fix our feelings. But, as logical as it may seem, seeking to improve our emotional state by working directly on our emotions isn't realistic (or as useful as working on our behavior), as you will see.

Having gained a deeper awareness of the issues of worth, will, energy, money, and mind in the first six gateways, you now stand at the threshold of a fresh, radical, and above all realistic approach to emotions and how to deal with them in everyday life. Accepting your emotions (and the emotions of others) serves to heal and rejuvenate all your relationships, from acquaintances to intimates.

Accept Your Emotions is not a recipe for feeling better or experiencing only positive feelings, but rather a realistic approach that involves accepting your feelings as natural, learning from them, letting them pass through you, then getting on with your life. In this gateway you learn to change your relationship to your feelings. This requires vigilance and an open mind, because you are going to confront unexamined assumptions accepted by most of us almost from birth.

In this gateway you will explore the source and primary causes of emotional difficulties; why feelings are natural; how negative emotions have positive lessons; why therapy aimed at fixing feelings doesn't work; seven ways to influence your moods; acceptance and healing; and, finally, an emotional meditation to rise above the storms.

Those of us who are the least interested in exploring this gateway may benefit from it the most. (This principle also applies to the other gateways.)

The Birth of Emotions

Most children begin life in an emotional Garden of Eden. If you were a normal healthy baby, your natural state, when rested and fed and freshly diapered, was bliss. (For confirmation of this, look into a baby's eyes.) Of course, you also had at times intense (and quite natural) emotional ups and downs. You arrived with instinctive fears and startle reflexes and soon learned frustration and anger, and when you were sad, you let the entire house know about it. Emotions moved through you in waves; you let them flow, then let them go. You felt your emotions intensely and expressed them without inhibition. Then, when your relatively simple needs were met (diapers changed, held and cuddled, fed), you returned once again to your resting state of ignorance and bliss.

As you grew, you left that garden of childhood innocence, and began to anticipate, grow anxious, form expectations and judgments about yourself and the world. I don't need to elaborate on this theme; you are quite aware of your present emotional (or completely nonemotional) state. Still, as in the previous gateways, the following self-assessment brings focus to your relationship with the emotions in your life.

An Emotional Self-Assessment

Everyone, East or West, experiences emotional storms and doldrums. The only real difference is that for some of us the clouds blow over more quickly than for others. When you take the following emotional inventory, note that we are not going to address positive emotions much here, because few of us feel that happiness or joy or excitement is a problem. But let's consider the following questions:

- How do you tend to behave when you feel upset?
- Do you wish your spouse, partner, parents, children, or friends would be less—or more—emotional?
- Would you be described as "an emotional person"? (What does that mean to you?)
- How do you respond when someone around you is critical or negative toward you?
- Are you ever embarrassed by your own or others' emotions?
- Is fear, sorrow, or anger more of a problem for you?
- Do you wish you could feel happier, motivated, or peaceful more of the time?
- When you feel happy and loving, why can't you hold on to those feelings?
- How long do negative emotions last (when you are angry, fearful, or sad)?
- How long do positive emotions last (when you are excited, inspired, or happy)?
- Do you wait for positive feeling-states (like motivation, inspiration, commitment, or dedication) before doing whatever needs to be done?

These questions set the stage for a new approach to accepting, even welcoming, all kinds of emotions into your life so that you can begin to experience life and Spirit in living color rather than black and white.

The Roots of Feeling

A meteorologist might be able to tell you complex reasons why it rained today, involving the interaction of temperature inversions, the jet stream, and marine air hitting warming mountains. Psychologists, who serve as emotional meteorologists, may offer explanations for your internal weather. But no matter what the reasons, if it's still raining, you need to ride out the storms, accept them as natural, and get on with your life.

There's a story about a man who wrote the Department of Agriculture to complain about the crabgrass spoiling his lawn. The department wrote back with a number of suggestions. He tried all the remedies but could not completely eliminate the crabgrass. Exasperated, he wrote back and said that every suggestion had failed. He received a short note that said, "We suggest you learn to love it."

Of course, we don't love painful feelings like anxiety or depression. We don't have to love or even like them, but we do have to accept them, as difficult as that can seem at times. Emotions, no matter how painful, are not the problem. The problem is dropping out of school or work, putting your family or duties or life on hold until such time as you can work out your emotional issues. Would you rather feel depressed while sitting alone in your room trying to figure it all out or feel depressed while getting your house cleaned or your project completed? (You may still feel depressed, but you have a cleaner house.)

The heart of accepting your emotions (and, as you've seen, of reclaiming your will) is to do what you need to do despite what you are feeling. Accept and learn from your feelings, but don't let them run your life. By remaining productive during difficult emotional episodes, you are more likely to improve your emotional state than if you do nothing but ruminate and wait for sunny skies.

To understand why relaxed acceptance may be the most realistic approach to emotions, let's begin our exploration by examining where emotions come from. This insight doesn't help you control emotions, but it does generate perspective and compassion for yourself and others. So let's look at some common emotion generators. Welcome to Emotional Meteorology 101.

Mind and Meaning: While I was strolling with a friend in Europe, a gang of youths walked past us and one of them gestured toward us. I smiled at what I thought was a friendly gesture and was about to wave, but my friend was angry. Apparently the gesture, which I didn't understand, was considered both rude and obscene. But it had no meaning for me, so it aroused no emotion. Many emotions begin from our mental interpretation of what occurred.

Diet: What you eat and drink affects your moods. Sometimes negative emotional states come not from your heart, but from your intestines. Lightening up your diet, as described in the third gateway, can help to brighten your moods.

Fatigue: Most of us feel more dour or irritable at the end of a long day when we are too tired to deal with a problem—usually the easiest but not the best time to get into an argument. The impact of fatigue on your emotions depends upon whether it stems from stress and burnout or from, for example, completing a good workout or satisfying task.

Intoxication: Anything that produces an intoxicated state may elevate or depress your emotions by reducing inhibitions. If you feel good, you may get happier; sad people get sadder; angry people get ugly.

Hormones: Whether you are male or female, hormones tend to affect your moods and emotions, and like any emotional factor, they tend to, but do not have to, affect your behavior.

Tension/Stress: As in the case of illness or pain, tension or stress may produce stress, reactive emotions, or hypersensitivity.

Illness and Pain: Some chronically moody or temperamental people may be suffering from chronic illness or pain. Few of us are at our best when feeling ill or out of sorts. It takes courage to behave with kindness when in pain.

Circumstances and Environment: Clearly your emotional tone tends to vary depending upon whether you just learned you were accepted to the college of your choice or were laid off from your job. Pleasant circumstances stimulate more expansive emotions than painful ones. Most people arriving in Las Vegas tend to be in better moods than those leaving.

Other Factors: Emotions are affected by anything from astrological transits to biorhythms—and from childhood memories, old associations, even songs or scents from the past.

The point of the preceding list of factors that generate emotions is that you cannot, and need not, analyze or understand all the factors that produce your emotional peaks or valleys. It's enough to know that the interaction of mind and circumstance contributes to your emotional lows and highs. The key question is not where your emotions come from, but what, if anything, shall you do with them?

One way most of us deal with feelings is to ignore them or pretend they don't exist—to deny them. Then, as the pressure builds, we occasionally experience emotional episodes such as arguments or explosions (and we may later berate ourselves for having "lost control").

The Denial of Feeling

The day you were told that big boys (or girls) don't cry, the first time someone asked you *why* you were upset, the day you learned that you upset others when you expressed your anger, you began to cut yourself off from accepting (or even recognizing) your own feelings. You learned to intellectualize your emotions and started to analyze, suppress, justify, and deny them. Your exile from the Garden of Emotional Authenticity had begun.

Symptoms of Emotional Denial

Why would any rational person want to get in touch with his or her emotions? Didn't we get past that kind of thing in the sixties and seventies?

Facts of life:

- Emotions will no more be denied than stormclouds.
- You need to accept emotions before you can transcend them.
- Before you can accept your emotions you have to know what you are feeling—to know and appreciate and be able to express that feeling.
- You don't transcend emotions in the way you might imagine.

When we devalue or deny our emotional energies, we pay a physical price. Chronic emotional tension can generate or aggravate symptoms such as headaches, backaches, arthritis, hypertension and high blood pressure, dyspepsia, colitis, aggravating conditions such as ulcers and insomnia, and other psychosomatic ailments. And as we age, tension produced from holding in unexpressed emotions tends to produce physical stiffness, muscle aches and pains, and reduced flexibility. Movement becomes more painful, so we move less, thereby reducing our range of movement, our range of life. In some elderly people you can see the cumulative effect of denied emotions stored as chronic tension. Such restriction can even create a mental condition called "psychosclerosis"—hardening of the attitudes. Psychologist Wilhelm Reich would remind his clients that unexpected emotions are stored in the flexor muscles of the body, and the organs weep the tears that the eyes refuse to shed.

> One of my problems is that
> I internalize everything.
> I can't express anger;
> I grow a tumor instead.
>
> **—Woody Allen**

Those of us most out of touch with our emotions are usually also out of touch with our bodies. When athletes ignore physical pain, this may have short-term benefits but long-term liabilities. The same is true for tuning out our feelings. When we lose emotional sensitivity we also lose touch with our intuitive capacities.

In losing touch with our feelings, we also lose touch with the feelings of others. It can come to the point that we live in a kind of benumbed state, feeling disconnected or dissociated from life. In fact, what some of us have experienced as a spiritual problem (a sense of disconnection from God) is actually an emotional problem (a disconnection from feeling).

A Simple Practice

If you are no longer sure what you feel anymore—whether you are afraid or hurt or angry—the following exercise can help attune your emotional awareness and, in the process, improve your intuitive capacities and empathy in relationships.

- When you think you may be upset but aren't clear about what you feel, ask yourself, "If I felt something right now, would it be closer to fear, sorrow, or anger?"
- You may respond, "I don't know how I feel." So persist with yourself: "Fine, I don't know what I'm feeling. But *if* I knew—if I suddenly had an insight, or if the feeling became so strong it was obvious—would it be closer to fear, sorrow, or anger?"
- Then make a statement to yourself or to another. "I feel _____." This is a first step toward reintegrating your feelings into your body and your life and opening deeper levels of authenticity.

Expressing Your Feelings: Upside and Downside

Again, to accept your emotions, you have to know them. Of the two levels of emotional authenticity—knowing your feelings and expressing them—knowing is the most important. You always want to know what you feel, but you don't always have to express yourself. Sometimes we feel better when we get something off our chest—and sometimes we don't. That's why there is no hard-and-fast rule about expressing what you feel.

Expressing your feelings can be an act of courage and honesty that provides valuable feedback to others who may not realize the impact of their words or deeds. Remaining silent out of politeness, stoicism, or discomfort does others and yourself a disservice. But it is a disservice, and only creates more turmoil, if you express yourself in a blaming manner: "You messed up again! You make me so angry, you jerk!"

Expressing your truth in a respectful way makes it more likely to be heard.

Skillful expression means using "I" words rather than "you" words. Fill in the blank: "When you say [or do] that, I feel _____." Or, "I would appreciate it if you would [or would not] say [or do] that." If necessary, you may add, "I have a hard time being around you when you act like that." That way you've defined your boundaries, expressed your feelings. Leave it at that. No need to criticize, patronize, or ostracize.

You can deliver any message if it's in the right envelope—and has a return address. If you get a response, just listen.

The ability to express feelings is an important life skill. But forever expressing upset feelings tends to restimulate them. Learn to stand up for yourself and define clear boundaries. But don't center your life around the never-ending cycle of feel and express or constantly checking out your sensitivities, looking to see if anyone has offended you. Other people do not need to hear about every feeling you have. Find a constructive balance.

Fixing Feelings

When you are in physical pain you may see a physician, a chiropractor, or other health professional. If your emotions are painful, you may seek out a psychotherapist. Many therapists focus on what their clients came to them for: to feel better. Generally this is done by working on feelings—getting in touch with, expressing, improving mental attitudes and emotional states by analyzing the causes, working through childhood issues, letting feelings out, or working with the mind and feelings to develop better self-esteem and more confidence and achieve authenticity and emotional honesty.

There may be value in pursuing these goals, especially when the alternative is sitting alone in your room and stewing. It's good to have someone listen to your problems. But all this can become a fascinating, and potentially endless, self-analysis adventure in which we spend part of our day analyzing our problems and other parts of the day dramatizing them.

We are like bottomless archaeological sites. Dreams furnish endless content, as do the vagaries of relationship, work, and fortunes of everyday life. We end up getting very good at being in therapy. But when all is said and done, you have three primary options in how you respond to painful or upsetting emotions:

- You can *deny* (suppress or repress) them.
- You can *dramatize* them (let them drive your behavior).
- You can *observe* and learn from them without acting upon them.

Observation is the central point of the seventh gateway: to accept your feelings completely, as natural, then spend your time, energy, and attention on constructive activity rather than centered on fixing the feelings.

Freedom from Self-Centered Emotion

If you become overly preoccupied with yourself and your feelings, your attention becomes trapped within a self-focus. In contrast, when you are absorbed by what you are doing as you are engaged in activity, you are rarely anxious. But as soon as you try to analyze, understand, fix, or resolve your feelings or internal state, you heighten your self-focus.

> Patient: "When I raise my left arm while biting down on tinfoil, I feel a tingling at the base of my spine. What's the matter with me, Doctor?"
>
> Doctor: "I'd say you have too much free time."

The more you pay attention to such emotional symptoms as

anxiety, the more you end up focusing your energy and effort on the symptoms instead of on what you want to accomplish in spite of the unpleasant feelings.

Accepting your emotions does not mean you ignore, devalue, or pretend they don't exist. It involves fully acknowledging your feelings, letting them be just as they are, then continuing to act constructively in line with your goals.

You attain emotional freedom not by alleviating the discomfort or by attaining a permanent, pleasurable feeling state (an impossible goal), but by taking constructive action, which helps you to live a full and meaningful existence free of the domination of your quixotic emotions.

Feelings Are Natural

Once you appreciate that emotions are natural (whether you happen to like all of them or not), it becomes easier to accept them as you would accept, but don't have to like, drizzles or snow flurries. For instance, if you learn that you have been promoted, you're likely to feel excited and happy; if you learn of the death of a friend, you'll experience grief. Such feelings are natural responses to your circumstances, and you need not try to fix or change them. Being in conflict with your emotions is far more exhausting than the emotions themselves.

It's easy to accept your feelings when they're positive, but who wants to accept emotional pain? The answer: Almost nobody. Still, it seems more realistic to accept what we cannot control than to try in vain to make the feelings go away. Since you have no more direct control over your feelings than you have over the weather, the best you can do is to act as constructively as you can despite your feelings—they will pass soon enough, in any case. In the meantime, you can accomplish what you set out to do.

Silver Linings in Emotional Clouds

Just as physical pain alerts you to attend to a problem, painful emotions also serve a useful purpose. Within every feeling is a germ of valuable information; every emotional charge contains a lesson, and every lesson is positive, even if the emotion is not.

> If there were no desires,
> there would be no satisfaction.
> —**Shoma Morita, M.D.**

Anxiety indicates a strong desire to succeed. Fear generates alertness and caution and reminds you to prepare well and to protect yourself when necessary. You don't worry unless you care. Concern reveals thoughtfulness and sensitivity. Insecurity reflects a desire to do well and to prove yourself. Shyness reminds you that you want to be liked and to make a good impression. Anger indicates passionate involvement or desire to be involved. Depression may indicate a sensitive soul, grieving for the world. Accepting your emotions sometimes means appreciating the positive lessons contained in negative emotions.

The Changing Climate of Emotions

Recently, after I completed a lecture, someone approached me and said, "I feel so inspired!"

"Don't worry," I responded, "it will pass."

Like the weather, emotions are always changing. All feelings, whether positive or negative, fade over time, unless they are re-stimulated. Love and hate both pass; so do grief, excitement, rage, joy, and fear. If you want love to last in your relationship, you need to cultivate and restimulate it; if you want grief to fade, avoid restimulating it with reminders and associations.

Feeling-Behavior Journal

To test the premise that feelings change constantly, try the following: Set your watch to beep at, say, twenty minutes after the hour, every hour, for one day. Make three columns on a sheet of paper and note down the following three factors each time your watch beeps: the time of day, what you were doing when, and what emotion you were feeling.

Here's a sample journal:

Time	Behavior	Feeling(s)
8:20 A.M.	Driving child to school	Rushed, preoccupied
9:20 A.M.	Speaking with client	Enthusiastic, hopeful
10:20 A.M.	At desk eating snack	Neutral
11:20 A.M.	Making phone call	Irritated

When you look over your completed journal, you'll note that many different feelings arise during the course of even one day or even in the space of a few hours. Each of us experiences a fascinating set of changing weather patterns. Sometimes the feelings are related to what you are doing at that moment, and sometimes they arise from thoughts or associations that have drifted through your mind.

The important point is that if you live and act on the basis of your changeable emotions, then you live an unstable, stop-and-go existence. You will act when you happen to feel motivated, stop when you feel self-doubt, start again when you feel inspired, then stop when you feel discouraged. This gateway teaches you to accept your emotions, but not base your life on following, fighting, or fixing them.

Emotional Realities at the Control Tower

In *Taming Your Mind* you learned how little control you have over the thoughts that pass through your awareness. The same is true for your emotions. If you could will yourself to change your feelings when you are sad or afraid or worried—just wish or will the feeling away and replace it with a more pleasant feeling—then there would be no need to accept emotions; you could just change them. But close observation of your life will reveal that you have even less control over your emotions than you do over your thoughts.

In the preceding "Feeling-Behavior Journal" exercise, you observed how feelings come and go whether or not you wish or intend them to do so. Consider this carefully, because it is one of life's central truths: You cannot make yourself feel what you want to feel. You can't make yourself fall in love with someone or feel grateful to someone else who has just hurt you. You can't willfully and reliably stop feeling depressed or lonely.

Equally true is that you cannot be responsible for what you can't control. So accepting feelings goes hand in hand with shifting attention to what you *can* do to improve your situation (rather than trying to instantly improve your feelings, which you can't do). By taking constructive action to improve your situation, you are likely to influence your emotional state.

Seven Ways to Indirectly Influence Your Emotional State

Although you cannot directly control or change your emotional state by intention alone, you can influence your emotions through breathing, posture, relaxation, changing your environment, distraction and humor, and taking appropriate action.

If you feel depressed, you may tend to sit alone, slouched over, perhaps staring at the floor or into space; your breathing is shallow as you reflect on the ways you've messed up your life. A good way to get *out* of depression is to stand straight and tall, breathing fully and deeply, as you walk through a beautiful meadow or a stimulating and brightly lit shopping mall, and reflect on what you've done right in your life. Do this whether you feel like it or not. I don't guarantee that it will lift your spirits, but it's a good start.

Let's overview some of the things you can do to influence your emotional state:

Rebalance your breathing. When you feel anger, sorrow, or fear, your breathing becomes inhibited or thrown out of balance. By consciously breathing evenly and deeply into your belly, you won't make the feelings go away, but you will rebalance your body and psyche so that you can speak or act more effectively.

Attend to your posture. Body, mind, and emotions interpenetrate and influence one another. Since you have more direct control over your body, start there. Since emotions influence your posture, your posture can also influence emotions. To increase the likelihood that you will feel more expansive, sit and stand straight and tall. Hold your arms out to your side with your palms up toward the sky. You can also use the muscles of your face to lift the corners of your mouth upward while relaxing your mouth and letting your teeth show. (It's called a smile.)

Remember to relax. Try this simple experiment: Relax your body now, as deeply as you can in a few breaths, breathing in the belly, releasing tension you may have been holding in your chest, shoulders, neck, or abdomen. When you feel fully relaxed and at ease, imagine how difficult it would be to feel angry or fearful in this state. When you relax, you can do much to release the tension associated with fear or anger. Relaxation short-circuits the harmful effects of emotional tension, allowing the flow of energy to remain unobstructed so that you continue to act and move effectively.

Change your environment. The moment you change your environment, you change who you are, in both subtle and dramatic ways. Put me in my office and I feel one way; put me on a beach in Hawaii and I can almost guarantee I'll feel differently. Your boundaries aren't nearly as solid as you imagine; in a sense, you become part of your environment and it becomes part of you. But the change doesn't even have to be a major one. Notice how your feelings change from one room of a house to another or when you step outdoors. To change habits or emotions, a change of environment—even if it's getting out of the house and going for a walk—can do wonders. A change of scene opens you up to different facets of yourself.

Distract yourself. In *Tame Your Mind,* you learned how you had some control over where you direct your attention. Although

you can't make your feelings go away, you can distract yourself
by shifting your attention to something constructive.

> No man is lonely while eating spaghetti;
> it requires so much attention.
> **—Christopher Morley**

Distraction differs from denial because you clearly know what
you are feeling but consciously direct your attention elsewhere.
Let's say that you are terribly afraid of riding in elevators and
experience all the unpleasant symptoms of that phobia. Nevertheless you have a very important business presentation to make on
the fifty-second story. You step inside the elevator, feeling terrible,
but manage to distract yourself from your feelings by mentally
going over all the key points in your presentation, completing
them just as the elevator door opens at your floor.

The police often use distraction when responding to domestic
disputes. An officer may show up in plain clothes and a delivery
hat, carrying a pizza. Instead of asking, "What's the problem?"
he says, "Here's the pizza you ordered." This gambit interrupts
the emotional pattern of the domestic scene. In everyday life, distraction can be something as simple as changing the subject. Or
ordering pizza.

Apply humor. Lightening up lends perspective to any situation. The following story, sent to me on the Internet, provides a
good example of humor diffusing a tense situation:

An irate crowd of air travelers stood in a long line at a United
Airlines ticket counter after their flight had been canceled, when
an angry man walked to the front of the line, threw his ticket on
the counter, and yelled, "I want a first-class seat on the next flight
out, now!"

The harried ticket agent, brushing back a lock of hair, replied,
"I'll be glad to help you, sir, as soon as I take care of the people
in line."

"You want me to wait in *line?*" he yelled even louder. *"Do you
know who I am?"*

The ticket agent hesitated only a moment before picking up

the microphone, turning up the PA system, and announcing to the waiting area, "Ladies and gentlemen, there is a man at gate seventeen *who does not know who he is.* If anyone can help him find his identity—"

"Screw you, lady!" the man yelled, storming off.

In a parting shot she added, "Sir, I'm afraid you'll have to wait in line for that, too."

Her humor didn't help improve his emotions, but it helped hers. And the previously irate people waiting in the line were now smiling or laughing. No one else complained.

Take appropriate action. The most constructive way to influence your emotions is to *do* something. For example, if I'm filled with self-doubt and overwhelmed with worry about an upcoming exam, hitting the books is the most effective way I can influence my emotions. Even if the worry and self-doubt remain, I will have studied for the exam. In the same way, mountain climbers focus on climbing the mountain instead of getting rid of the fear of falling.

A man I'll call George told me how he hated feeling guilty because he didn't visit his elderly mother more often. He wanted to know how to reduce his guilt. "Go visit your mother," I suggested.

There are many constructive ways to indirectly influence your emotional state. As you learn to accept your emotions fully, however, without allowing them to drive or limit your behavior, you'll find it less necessary to change or fix them.

Reviewing Key Emotional Principles

Because some of these ideas may go against the grain of what you have assumed or believed, it may take some time to settle in. Please review these key points.

Feelings fade over time. Sometimes feelings fade slowly and sometimes quickly, but they do fade unless restimulated. You may be devastated by grief, depression, anxiety, or disappointment, but in time you experience such feelings less intensely. If you continue to restimulate these feelings, you will continue to suffer from the emotional states associated with past experiences.

Life is a series of moments. No one feels the same way all the time. Even if you are angry, depressed, crazy, afraid, or grieving, you'll have moments when you are distracted. There are no enlightened people, no nice, bad, smart, neurotic, or stupid people, either—only people with more (or less) enlightened, nice, bad, smart, neurotic, or stupid moments.

You cannot directly control your feelings. When you're depressed can you just snap out of it? Can you will yourself to fall in or out of love? Actors struggle with this challenge all the time, since many believe they need to somehow conjure up emotions they aren't feeling in order to be authentic in the role. But actors don't have to feel a given set of emotions; they only have to *act* them. (That's why they are called "actors" rather than "feelers.")

You are not responsible for your feelings. You cannot take responsibility for that which you cannot control—not even if you feel hatred; not even if you feel lust; not even if you have the worst possible, most perverted, bizarre thoughts and feelings passing through your awareness. (If you have altruistic, compassionate, kind, courageous, feelings, you are not responsible for these, either.) You *are* responsible for what you *do* with your feelings—how you respond to them—but not for what you feel.

Jean, a nun, was a participant in a residential training that I presented several years ago. She came to the training with the hope that it would resolve the terrible guilt that had haunted her for years. (The guilt, like any feeling, would have passed, but Jean restimulated it every time she had an unacceptable thought or feeling.) Like many of us, she had been raised in a tradition that held her responsible for every thought or feeling that passed through her awareness, especially lustful thoughts and feelings.

Accept lustful thoughts or feelings as you would accept any other thoughts or feelings. This will not open the floodgates to even more forbidden thoughts or emotions; on the contrary, it allows you to accept whatever you feel as natural. As you stop trying *not* to think or feel something, you free your energy and attention for higher orders of experience.

Even those of us who experience chronic depression, anxiety, or anger—possibly as a result of a biochemical imbalance that may require medical treatment—can benefit by accepting both positive and negative feelings while focusing on acting constructively and walking through the storms toward our destination.

Freeing yourself from the impossible burden of responsibility for your emotions—with all the accompanying guilt—may stimulate feelings of happiness and relief. But the happiness will pass, as will the relief, and so will the lust, or hatred, or envy, or sorrow, or joy, or any other feelings that rise and fall, like waves on the ocean.

Accepting Others' Emotions

Some of us center our lives around other people's feelings; we try to make them happy. But since you can't control your feelings, how can you possibly fix the feelings of others? The plain truth is that feeling responsible for someone else's unhappiness (or happiness) is simply not realistic.

No longer feeling responsible for the feelings of others, you can come to fully accept them rather than react *to* them. If you are to accept your own emotions as natural, you need to accept everyone else's emotions as well. Their emotions, whether calm or stormy, are their affair.

Just as you may need to express yourself, others will feel the need, on occasion, to express themselves to you, sometimes gently, sometimes in an outburst. Few things are more healing in a relationship than to let others express their anger or hurt and to accept that as their present reality, to validate their truth (which doesn't have to be *the* truth). After listening, you can even ask if there's anything more they would like to say. This opens the way to a far closer and more intimate relationship with that person.

This does not mean, however, that you have to listen to someone who habitually, chronically, or endlessly criticizes you. Accepting others' emotions is not the same as becoming a psychological toxic waste dump. Remember your boundaries.

Transcendence

If your goal is to carry a child home to its mother, and you are walking through a storm, you may notice the weather around you, but you remain attentive to carrying out your purpose— getting the child home. This is how you can carry on with your life in all kinds of emotional weather. And as you mature in the seventh gateway, a time will come when you transcend emotions—not because they have gone away, but because you have made peace with your feelings, letting them pass through you like wind through a forest. You will continue to know and honor what you feel. But rather than resist or struggle against the tides of emotion, you'll persist through all kinds of weather.

In a kind of meditation on emotion, you can have an angry thought or feeling without automatically acting angry. And when you do this, you experience a self-mastery so powerful and inspiring, it is like walking through a storm without getting wet. The inspiration passes, of course, just like the anger.

Emotional Enlightenment

The following might be considered enlightened, or at least unconventional, ways to respond to emotions. Let's say your spouse or partner is complaining about something you didn't do or should have done. You might tend to yell, or mope, or walk away, angry or defensive. Instead be outrageous. Say, "I love you," and give your spouse or partner a hug and a kiss.

Suppose you were passed over for a promotion you expected and feel frustrated, discouraged, unappreciated. Barge into your employer's office, express your appreciation for the feedback, state that you respect his or her judgment and intend to improve your performance in the future.

What if you ask someone out and that person declines? You may feel disappointed and disheartened. You smile, offer thanks for considering your invitation, and wish that person all the best in finding the person of his or her dreams. Then go make a list of people to ask and ask until someone accepts.

Late for an appointment, I ran into a hardware store because it was right on the way. I quickly found the item I needed, but the clerk was new on the job and very slow as he wrote out a receipt. I said, "Excuse me, but I'm late for an appointment and really in a hurry—" He looked up at me as I continued, "So I'd appreciate it if you would take all the time you need and go *especially* slowly. It will be good for me." He did a double take and laughed.

Notice that in these examples, the behaviors were not consistent with the emotions. Such emotional nonattachment is a practice in emotional freedom, since your behaviors are no longer at the mercy of your feelings, which rise and fall, come and go, appear and fade, as feelings do, like thoughts, like clouds in the sky.

Consider how much your life has been pushed and pulled and driven by your changeable emotional weather. Imagine the freedom of accepting your emotions, and the emotions of others, as a natural part of life—and, instead of trying to fix what isn't broken, focusing your attention and energy on constructive activity. You have already done this so many times; the teachings of this gateway enable you to do it consciously, clearly, deliberately. This liberates your attention to ascend higher, from accepting emotions to facing your fears.

THE

EIGHTH GATEWAY

Face Your Fears

❧

Fear is a wonderful servant,
but a terrible master.
Like pain, it can alert and advise you,
but may also cloud or limit your life.
Fear appears in many disguises, such as
"I'm not really interested in doing that"
or "Why bother?" or "I can't."
You face fear every day—
fear of failure, of rejection,
even the fear of being yourself.
Your fears are not walls, but hurdles.
Courage is not the absence of fear,
but the conquering of it.

Living as Peaceful Warriors

*Many of our fears are tissue-paper-thin,
and a single courageous step
would carry us clear through them.*

—Brendan Francis

Road Map: Exploring the Forest of Fear

You now begin your final ascent toward the summit, through a forest of fears and the shadow-land beyond, up toward the prize of an awakened heart and the call to service that is the perfect expression of everyday enlightenment.

How often are you aware of being afraid? Most of us would report feeling afraid only in dramatic moments—the sudden growl of a dog, a screech of brakes on the highway, the moments before we make an important presentation. But fear is with us every day in little ways. Our souls may be immortal, but we are also physical beings who can suffer pain, injury, or death, suffer embarrassment, failure, shame, or rejection. Thus primal fear gnaws at the foundation of nearly every endeavor. This gateway could have come first, but fear can be so intimidating an adversary, you need the power of the previous gateways to prepare for this confrontation.

In the previous gateway you learned to accept emotions, including fear, as natural. But because fear can have such an inhibiting (or even devastating) impact on our lives, and because that impact is often hidden to our conscious awareness, we need to independently address how to face and overcome our fears in this gateway.

Fear is not only your adversary; it is also your guide and adviser. It is natural and even appropriate—even a sign of sanity—to let fear guide you in physically dangerous situations where a lack of attention or care could mean injury or death.

Such moments of physical risk are rare. Your major battles with fear are not outside you; they lurk inside, in the caverns of the psyche, in the arena of psychological survival and dark imaginings, where fear shape-shifts into subtle guises such as self-doubt, insecurity, lack of confidence, shyness, inhibition, timidity—a reluctance to assert, express, or even *be* yourself. Whatever form fear takes, your willingness to face it squarely will determine your fate in the high country of human potential. Whether fear is your friend or foe depends upon whether you become its master or its servant. Here, in this gateway, you can take a stand and step forward resolutely into the life you were born to live.

The content of some previous gateways centered around awareness, understanding, and perspective. But the primary way to face your fears is by taking *action*. Therefore this gateway centers around specific exercises—things to do.

A single courageous act calls forth others. Such moments, little decisions, shape your life and inspire other people to do the same. Welcome to the eighth gateway, your initiation into the realm of the peaceful warrior.

In this gateway you will explore the location of fear, have a chance to face your personal moment of truth in the pin test, confront and overcome self-doubt, and learn a direct method to free the body of fears stored as specific zones of tension.

Understanding the Adversary

My friend Walter called to tell me he had failed a test of courage. It involved a challenge course in which he was to climb to the top of a telephone pole, stand on the top, and leap off to a trapeze about five feet away. Even though he was on a safety tether, this task was imposing.

"You say you failed. Didn't you make it all the way up?" I asked.

"I climbed all the way," he replied.

"But you weren't able to stand up on top—you fell?" I guessed.

"No, I didn't fall."

"So you missed the trapeze?"

"Oh, I grabbed the trapeze all right," Walter replied.

"I'm missing something here, Walt. You told me you'd failed."

"Yes, I did," he assured me. "You see, I was trying to beat fear, *but I was scared the whole time.*"

Walt was suffering from a basic misunderstanding of how we face our fears. You cannot control your fear by willing it away. You conquer this adversary only by making it your servant and adviser and *never* allowing it to become your master. Fear cannot take your power; the danger is that you may surrender your power without a fight.

A Stuntman's Secret

Dar and I were childhood friends who met at a trampoline school. One day we climbed a ladder up to a billboard, high above the roof of the school, and dove off, landing on a soft pad below. I climbed to the fifth rung; Dar just kept climbing. Ten years later he was one of the most daring and successful stuntmen of modern times.

For one of his stunts, Dar had to run full-tilt forward, spin around backward, crash through a glass window, fall *sixteen stories,* and then do a somersault with a half twist, before dropping into an airbag. Any miscalculation or mistake would have cost him his life. Dar's stunts included diving off the top of the Capitol Records building in Los Angeles, leaping from a helicopter hovering at three hundred feet to land on an airbag (that looked the size of a postage stamp below), and driving a car off the rim of the Grand Canyon, whereupon he climbed out in midair and pulled his parachute. Dar once jokingly reminded me, "When skydiving, if you pull your chute when the people below look like ants, that's good; if the ants look like people, that's bad."

Every time Dar prepared himself for a new aerial stunt, he

would recite a prejump mantra, louder and faster, getting ready: "Owah tajer kayam . . . ohwha tajerkayam . . . OHWHATAJER-KIAM . . . OH WHAT A JERK I AM!"

Some people believed that Dar was as crazy as he was fearless, but he was neither. He just had a secret that he had learned long ago on that ladder above the trampoline center: Dar Robinson, one of the greatest modern-day daredevils, was terrified—practically scared to death—with each and every stunt. His heart leaped from his chest; he had to consciously control his rapid breathing; he sweated, he trembled, just like the rest of us—then he did what he had set out to do. This is what you and I can do in everyday life.

Ralph Waldo Emerson once wrote, "Do the thing you fear and the death of fear is certain." Wise words. But dead wrong. Fear does not die; it may not even go away. Or if it does vanish, it may resurrect itself, moving to greet you farther down the road. Your task, then, is not waiting for fear to die, but to face it while you live.

Anatomy of Fear

Understanding the symptoms of fear—how you physically feel when you are afraid—helps to manage it, much like knowledge of the physical process of childbirth helps many women to weather its powerful waves and rhythms. Knowledge doesn't calm the seas, but it does help us take steps to trim the sails and batten down the hatches and ride out the storm.

When you feel low-level fear—a vague anxiety, concern, or nervousness—your symptoms are likely to be subtle: a slight change in breathing, imperceptible or unnoticed increase in muscle tension in all or part of your body, a knitted brow, nervous mannerisms like biting your lip or clenching your jaw. But when you perceive something as acutely dangerous or threatening, chemical messengers like adrenaline and glucose flood into your bloodstream to energize your muscles and ready you to face, fight, or flee from danger. Your mouth may become dry. Your heart beats faster. Your breathing may become rapid and shallow or stop momentarily. Fear is psychologically uncomfortable. It's supposed to be, just as pain is physically uncomfortable—designed to get your attention. But sometimes you need to bear what is painful, and sometimes you need to do what is fearful.

The Layers of Fear

You are not actually afraid of the act of public speaking, or singing, or taking tests, or letting a tarantula crawl across your arm, or even leaping out of airplanes. Rather, you fear your own imaginings of what *might* go wrong—that you may forget your speech, sing off-key, fail the exam, get bitten by the spider, or forget to pull your ripcord. And the truth is, you are not even afraid of these things in themselves, but rather of the emotional or physical consequences—embarrassment, shame, mediocrity, pain, or death—all worst-case scenarios.

Mention an ocean cruise and some of us envision formal meals, deckside shuffleboard, or beautiful sunsets, while the more fearful of us visualize the *Titanic*. The same is true of camping in the woods—some of us picture panoramic vistas, cozy campfires, and starry skies, while others imagine snakes, insects, and bears. As you have learned, expectations tend to shape your experience of life, and fearful expectations create a fearful life. One key to facing your fears, then, is to consciously begin to visualize positive outcomes—to form the pictures you want rather than focus on images you fear.

When to Listen and When to Overcome

People have asked me how they can determine when to listen to fear's counsel and when to push through the fear. As a general rule, when the danger is physical, let fear guide you to take care and prepare well or even choose not to take foolish risks. But when the fear is psychological, as in the fear of embarrassment, shame, rejection, and so forth, that is the time to push through it.

Physical fears are direct, objective, and realistic. In the unlikely event that something goes wrong when you are skydiving, you may receive an injury or may even die. Fear advises you to take precautions.

Psychological fears are indirect, subjective, and symbolic. The sky doesn't fall if you forget a speech or sing off-key or fail an exam—there is no risk of physical injury or death. If you go deeper into your psyche, you'll find that you are afraid not of failure, but of what it represents: issues of psychological survival, primal fears of losing face, of rejection, abandonment, ostracism, worthlessness, and mediocrity, of being a charlatan and a fool.

Assessing Your Relationship to Fear

The ancient warriors knew that we must understand the enemy in order to vanquish it. Take the following inventory of the fears in your life and how they might relate to your needs and goals:

- Are you a risk taker?
- Might you ever describe yourself as timid, shy, insecure, or suffering from self-doubt?
- Have you noticed how you deal with subtle fears every day?
- Recall an incident when you let fear stop you from doing something you wanted to do.
- Recall an incident when you accomplished something you feared.
- Do you have any phobias?
- What are your five worst fears? Failure? Losing face (shame, embarrassment, ridicule)? Rejection? Inadequacy or mediocrity? Public speaking? Pain? Heights? Insects? Animal(s)? Enclosed spaces? People?
- If you could save the life of a child by doing what you most fear, would you?
- As you overcome your fears, in what specific ways might your life change?

The deeper your understanding, the greater your power. As awareness penetrates a fear, it starts to dissolve fear at its core. Many of us misunderstand the nature of fear and of courage.

How You May Let Fear Limit Your Life

Whatever the sources of fear, if you run from it (the way many of us avoid emotional confrontations rather than staying present and resolving them), you limit your life in the following ways:

- You may become your own jailer, imprisoning your experience in a cage that's meant to keep the dangers out, but ends up locking you in.
- You may avoid trying anything new because you don't want to feel incompetent or appear foolish or silly.
- You may not ever fully commit to an effort so that you can console yourself with thoughts such as "If I had really tried, I could have done it."
- You may avoid, whenever possible, any situation in which you don't have control, because of the fear of being out of control.
- You may hold yourself back from achieving success out of the fear that success will leave you unfulfilled or with nothing left to do.
- You may avoid expressing your true feelings out of fear that the feelings may come back to you and cause discomfort.
- You may give yourself a label that becomes both explanation and excuse: "I can't do that because I have a phobia. I'm a phobic personality."

Phobias and Other Labels

Phobia is a fancy psychological name for a big fear. Little fears generate subtle physiological reactions; big fears generate dramatic ones. When our physiological reactions to elevators, closets, wide-open spaces, dog, cats, snakes, spiders, mice, moths or other insects, or heights become unpleasant enough, we call them phobias.

Avoiding danger
is no safer in the long run
than outright exposure.

The fearful are caught
as often as the bold.

—Helen Keller

We often say "I can't" when we really mean "I don't want to" or "I won't." We truly cannot do some things such as leap up to rooftops or outrun a race car, but we *can* overcome any fear. It may feel unpleasant—we may tremble, faint, sweat, and have flulike symptoms—but we can do it anyway. I have a friend named David who is afraid of flying (well, actually afraid of crashing). His palms sweat, his heart beats fast, he trembles, and his knuckles turn white as he grips the armrests. He would likely be diagnosed as phobic by some psychologists. Despite these symptoms, David flies many thousands of miles around the world every year because it is necessary in his work. The fear (phobia) has not gone away. He has not tried to make it go away. Those who say they can't fly because of their fear actually cannot fly because they don't buy a ticket and get on the airplane. David buys a ticket and gets on the plane. This is how he faces his fear.

I have not ceased being fearful,
but I have ceased
to let fear control me.

—Erica Jong

Fear Is Not the Problem

Fear is like a little garden spider that makes us jump back or the poor lost bee on the steering wheel that we blame for our automobile wreck. The problem in fear is our *response*—the way we treat animals or insects that frighten us. Fear is the cornered animal within us, baring its teeth, the lowest common denominator of human experience. Fear crushes the delicate spider or slender wasp. Fear is also the universal scapegoat we blame when we take flight from intimacy or shrink up inside ourselves in a thousand little ways.

Nevertheless, let's appreciate fear for its whispered or shouted warnings. Fear calls to you like an overprotective mother to whom you should always listen but not always heed. Show more respect but less obedience to the frightened child inside you who, after all, may be wise or foolish, helpful or disabling. Appreciate fear as a voice of caution, but view it as a wall to scale, a hurdle to leap, a challenge to meet, a call to action.

You cannot control your fear. You *can* control your response: You can slow your breathing. You can shake loose and relax your muscles. You can feel the fear and do it anyway.

Those of us with the strongest fears gain the most from our passage through the eighth gateway.

Using Anger to Overcome Fear: An Exercise

Have you ever been afraid, but then got angry? What happened? If you don't remember such a time, imagine what might happen. You may conclude that anger is stronger than fear and can be used to move through fear into action. And you would be right. The following visualization exercise conveys a clear metaphor to your subconscious mind about how anger overcomes fear. By following the process precisely, you will form a template deep within your psyche that you can draw upon any time you need it in everyday life.

- Imagine that you have spent your life in a dimly lit room. Outside, a new free, open life awaits you. You would like very much to go outside and step more fully into life.
- You walk to the entrance and are about to step outside, when a figure appears. Mr. (or Ms.) Fear blocks the doorway. Imagine who or what Mr. or Ms. Fear might look like. A parent? A teacher? A stranger? An apparition, monster, alien, or clown? Visualize this figure.
- Now you walk to the entrance, desiring to step outside, but just as you reach it, Mr. or Ms. Fear steps in front of you and says, "Stop! You can't, you mustn't, you will fail, it's too dangerous, it won't work." *Stop* at the entrance, even though you deeply want to go outside into the light. Feel

what it is like to let fear stop you. Imagine Mr. or Ms. Fear blocking your way, intimidating, discouraging, paralyzing you. What does this feel like?

- Now, repeat this process in exactly the same way. Replay the movie of your wanting to go outside but letting fear stop you. Run this scenario again and again—three times, six times, ten times—each time letting fear hold you back. Do this as many times as necessary until you become angry. Not just a little sad or discouraged, or frustrated, or peeved, or irritated, but *angry*. At this point you are ready to do something different.

- Take that anger and turn it into resolve. Take a deep breath, and this time replay the movie and walk to the entrance. Mr. or Ms. Fear hasn't gone away. He or she is still standing there, telling you to stop. But this time, giving fear no more attention, walk out of the door—step outside into the sunshine, into a new life.

- Now bring this experience into your everyday life. Having learned the process, pick a specific fear in your life that has stopped or inhibited you. This fear may range from expressing your feelings to bungee jumping. As before, imagine fear stopping you again and again until you grow weary, then irritated, then angry, and, in your mind's eye, change the outcome as you walk through the fear. Then go out and do it.

The lesson and moral of this exercise is that when you meet fear on the road and need to get past it, get angry or get stopped. The choice is yours.

Courage 101

The fears that give us the most trouble in daily life are more often psychological than physical. We may routinely race down the roads and highways at death-defying speeds, but get weak in the knees if we have to speak in front of a group of people or ask a special person for a date.

Facing high-adrenaline (but relatively safe) activities such as white-water rafting, skydiving, rock climbing, ropes courses, bungee jumping, or fire walking may appear to be the ultimate ways to overcome fear, but are actually Courage 101—symbolic ways that may prepare you for truly terrifying challenges of everyday life—like expressing your feelings, admitting you were wrong, risking embarrassment, ridicule, or rejection—or just being yourself.

The following activities can, for anyone, serve as sound preparation and safe practice in facing your fears.

Movies: Suspense thrillers, horror films, science fiction, or similar tension-release genres provide a chance to vicariously face murderers, lunatics, and monsters and become heroes and courageous adventurers.

Virtual Reality: Far more than film, today's virtual reality rides closely duplicate the visceral experience of racing along in vehicles, flying through the air, or even diving into the sea, so that you can safely engage adventures and challenges that would otherwise be death defying.

Amusement Park Rides: Roller coasters and other thrilling rides offer maximum fear with minimum risk. Unlike film or virtual reality, such rides entail real-life somersaults, speeds, physical forces, and visceral experience.

Challenge Courses: "If I did that, I can do anything!" For those of us who want such an exhilarating experience, some personal growth seminars provide opportunities to face your fears through such activities as

- fire walking: Once limited to yogis and shamans, now experienced by thousands of people who have walked across red-hot coals as a metaphor of facing their fears.
- skydiving: Today's tandem jumps and new parachutes create a relatively safe experience leaping out into the void.
- white-water rafting: Depending upon the rating of the rapids, this experience ranges from a pleasant paddle to white-knuckled white-water rafting.
- bungee jumping: Why would you leap from a tower with

elastic cables attached to your harness or ankles? For cheap thrills, it's hard to beat.

- rock climbing and high ropes courses: While safely tethered, participants climb, balance, and perch on trees, poles, or cables up to fifty feet high. Puts you right up against the "I can't possibly do this" feeling. Then you do it.

Then there is performance and competition. Anyone who has done stand-up comedy (including telling jokes at family gatherings), acted in a drama production, given a speech, played a musical instrument, sung in concert before an audience, or participated in an important sports competition knows the fear associated with performance. This, certainly no less than skydiving, requires that you face your fears square on. In fact, many people rate the fear of public speaking as slightly higher than the fear of death.

The key point here is that you don't need to leap from airplanes to demonstrate courage. If you really want a scary challenge, take a date to a local restaurant and sing a few lines of a love song over dinner. (I have many friends who, if given the choice of singing in public or skydiving, would head straight for the airport.)

Each of us has our own pet fears. Those of everyday life are the most challenging and most significant. Take a few moments to reflect on your everyday fears.

Just Doing It: An Exercise in Facing Fear

- Choose one challenging activity or task (such as speaking or singing in public, asking for a date or a raise, expressing a fantasy)—something that you would truly like to do but haven't because you might fail, or be rejected, or feel foolish.
- Commit to doing it within the next six weeks.
- Tell a friend about your commitment and your reasons for doing it; alternately, write a letter describing your plans or draw up a contract with yourself and sign it.

- Make whatever preparations or arrangements you need in order to follow through.
- As the date and time draws near to confront and overcome the fear, remember to stay in the present moment. When you think about the action you'll likely feel nervous, anxious, or maybe just excited. It may not turn out to be as frightening as you had imagined. Or it may. By directing your attention to the present moment, you restrict your fear to when it is natural and appropriate—when you are about to do what you fear, rather than hours or days before.
- After you do it, draw or paint a picture of what the experience meant to you. You can also write a few paragraphs about it, but drawing more appropriately expresses the experience of your subconscious mind. You don't need to understand what you draw or paint; just see what comes.
- As a follow-up, you might pick one action each month that you would like to do but haven't done, at least partially from fear, and go through the same process of commitment, preparation, then action. It might be one of the challenges on previous pages, such as going on a virtual reality or amusement park ride or even white-water rafting or skydiving, or it might be something immediate and practical you face in everyday life.

Action Overcomes Fear

Far more important, however, are the fears that come up in your everyday life and interactions. When you notice yourself avoiding taking action because you feel nervous or reluctant, that is your moment of truth. What will you do?

Anyone who has faced a moment of truth—who has felt the fear and leaped from the airplane, walked onto the stage and sat down to the piano or begun speaking to an audience, or otherwise walked to the raw edge and leaped—knows something that more timid souls do not. That once you are fully engaged, immersed in the activity, the fear either vanishes or fades, because your attention is no longer focused on what might happen; you are absorbed by what *is happening*. Fear may remain, but you don't notice it.

No matter how committed you may say or think you are, it is only an intention, a plan, or a fantasy. You cannot know your degree of commitment or courage until you test it in the fires of action, in the moment of truth, when it's all or nothing, do or die. The following test is one practical way to develop, discover, and demonstrate courage and commitment. It serves as a metaphor for any moment in life you need to break through your fears.

The Pin Test: Commitment in the Moment of Truth

What if one day a car suddenly swerved into your lane or someone on the street began to shout curses at you or attack you? Would you freeze, panic, or take committed, decisive action? The following exercise—the pin test—serves as a lesson and metaphor for showing courage in your personal moments of truth.

In preparation, you need to find a wooden surface, such as a tabletop, and several ordinary straight pins—the kind of sewing pins used in hemming pants or keeping new shirts folded neatly in the stores.

The first step in this exercise is to stick the point of a straight pin down into a tabletop or other wooden surface so that it stands up vertically by itself. Then you slap your flat, open palm down onto the tabletop, directly over the pin, so that you bend the pin.

This pin becomes a symbol of the fears that stand between you and your goal. Going through it—slapping the tabletop and crushing the pin—represents the committed action you need to break through fear to reach your goal. With this in mind, do the following:

- On a flat wooden surface, such as a tabletop, slap your open palm so it stings slightly and makes a resounding noise. This is your rehearsal of the same movement you will make as you slap your palm directly down onto the vertical straight pin with its point stuck into the wooden surface.
- First, test your pins by carefully holding one and bending

it. You may even wish to push the point of one pin down into the tabletop so that it stands vertically and drop a hardback book on it to see how it bends. Then you're ready.

- Focus on the pin and form the commitment to slap your palm down onto the pin and tabletop as if the pin weren't even there. Don't think *to* the pin; think *through* the pin the way martial artists must think through the board in order to break it.
- When you are ready, simply do it. This is your moment of truth.
- If you fully and forcefully bring your flat palm down on the table with a loud slapping sound, you won't even know the pin was there. The pin will simply bend in half, leaving your palm unmarked and completely intact. (The only discomfort you may feel is the sting of your palm slapping the table.)
- No halfhearted attempts. Almost enough isn't nearly enough. If you hold back—if you let fear interfere with your resolve and cup your palm or slow down—you are far less likely to meet your objective, and you might even nick your hand.
- Either choose not to take this challenge or go for it with the full force of your being. It's natural to *feel* reservations, doubts, or fear. Just don't let those feelings interfere with what you have chosen to do.
- When you accomplish it, notice how it feels to do what you set out to do despite your fear or doubt.

If you choose not to try the pin test, honor your clear choice in the matter. At the same time, note that this challenge is an opportunity. You can benefit only from what you actually do.

Self-Doubt: The Great Impostor

As you've seen, not all fears are as specific and defined as facing the pin test or jumping off a high diving board or giving a speech.

Just as some of us don't recognize when we are being manipulated or exploited or seduced until we are hit over the head, so we may not recognize the subtle and insidious workings of fear when it appears as a vague, barely discernible sense of discomfort or doubt. We often don't realize that we are facing fear when it appears as nervousness, hesitation, procrastination, reluctance, lack of interest, or (the most insidious form fear takes) self-doubt.

When you were an infant, it never occurred to you to doubt yourself. Whoever came up with the proverb "If you fall down seven times, get up eight times" must have been watching infants try and fail and try again as they learned to stand or walk.

As you grew and began to compare yourself with others, you started to form beliefs about your capacity. Nearly all our beliefs about our competence or capacity stems from believing that we lack talent when we lack only experience.

Here is how it happened in my case: I began kindergarten two weeks late, so by the time I started painting trees, the other kids had been doing it nearly every day for a week, but I didn't know this. I only knew, when I started to compare my trees with the other children's, that their trees had branches and leaves while my first effort looked like a green lollipop. I assumed that they had more talent. So when given the choice to paint or to play in the sandbox (I was really *good* at sandbox), what do you think I chose?

Each of us carries within us a short (or long) list of things we sincerely don't believe we are very good at. We may be able to justify those beliefs with examples from our own experience. But what appeared to be true then may no longer be true now. Ugly ducklings have a way of turning into swans. Albert Einstein flunked math in his early school years, and Babe Ruth was the strikeout king before he was the home run king.

Doing the Impossible

You are now about to face a task guaranteed to raise significant doubts about your ability to accomplish it. Your past experience will tell you "I can't do this." Your powers of logic will also say "nay."

The following challenge will prove to you that you can do more than you believe:

- First, read the following list of twenty objects: a table, a bunny, a telephone, an automobile, an orange, blue jeans, a lit cigar, a small fishbowl, a television set, a handbag, an old alarm clock, a motorcycle, a refrigerator, running shoes, a mountain, yellow paint, a waterfall, underwear, a tennis ball, and an elderly physicist.
- What if I told you that within the next four minutes you will be able to memorize that list of twenty objects—not only forward, but backward. And that's not all. If I name any object on that list, you'll be able to remember which object came just before it and which came after.
- Based on past experience, you may have strong doubts about your ability to accomplish this. Please rate your doubt on a 1–10 scale, 1 (very little doubt) to 10 (strong doubt). Write that number here ____ or say it aloud.
- Now, use your natural powers of imagination to visualize a movie. First, picture a small *table*. Reach out with your arms and imagine yourself holding the table legs. Feel the table moving up and down. Why? Because a pink *bunny* is bouncing on that table as on a trampoline; it's bouncing up to grab the ringing *telephone* on the ceiling. See the bunny grabbing the phone on the ceiling? Then a big *automobile* comes crashing down through the ceiling and lands on a gigantic, brightly colored *orange* in the living room, squashing the orange and spraying orange juice all over the *blue jeans* hanging on the walls. Of course, when you soak blue jeans with orange juice, the fly unzips and a lit *cigar* falls out, tumbling down into a small *fishbowl* with a hiss, magically transforming the fishbowl into a *television* screen. What's on television? The Shopping Channel—featuring a glittering *handbag*. The handbag opens, and out pops a spinning, jangling *alarm clock*, then another. The two spin-

ning clocks become the wheels of a *motorcycle*, which bursts through the television screen and slams into the *refrigerator*. The refrigerator door opens and out come several pairs of *running shoes*, which run right up a *mountain*, and at the top they kick over a huge can of *yellow paint*. As the yellow paint pours down the mountain, it becomes clear and pure water, turning to a huge *waterfall* like the Niagara Falls, pouring down to soak many pair of *underwear* hanging on a clothesline. A bright yellow *tennis ball* falls out of the underwear and lands on the head of an *elderly physicist* who, in that moment, has a bright idea.

- Let's run through the movie. The first object you held in your hands was a ____; on it bounced a ____, which grabbed a ____ from the ceiling, which collapsed as an ____ crashed through, landing on the gigantic ____; the juice then soaked the ____ hanging on the wall; the zipper opened and the ____ fell into the ____, which turned into a ____, which showed a ____, out of which popped a spinning ____, becoming two, which turned into the wheels of a ____, which burst out of the TV screen and crashed into a ____ out of which came many ____, which ran up a ____, spilling ____, which turned into a huge ____, which soaked the ____ on the line, out of which fell a ____, landing on the head of a ____ who had a great idea.
- Now close your eyes and run the movie backward, starting with physicist and ending with table. Have fun with it!
- Finally, if I were to name, say, the *orange*, which object came before it? ____ And which came after? ____ How about the refrigerator? What came before and after?

Note that you just did something—maybe not perfectly, but respectably well—that you seriously doubted you could do. You could do this, and you can also overcome the next doubt you encounter.

Practicing Courage: As the proverb goes, "Those who bravely dare must sometimes risk a fall." As a gymnast I used to fall twenty or thirty times a day when attempting to learn new elements. When failure is a typical daily occurrence, it takes the edge off the fear.

There's great value in experiencing failure, rejection, embarrassment, shame. We discover that the sky doesn't fall. Life goes on. And if we keep trying, we continue to improve.

Competence as the Key to Diminished Fear: It's said that we are all ignorant—only about different subjects. Similarly, we are all afraid, only in different circumstances. You or I might feel frightened standing on the edge of a ten-meter diving tower, contemplating a swan dive. Experienced platform divers, however, feel little or no fear in this situation, because such a basic dive no longer represents a risk for them. But when they performed their first swan dive from the platform, or when they attempted a new element they'd never done before, they also felt fear.

Fears diminish as skills improve. As you develop competence, you gain confidence.

Do you doubt that you are a good cook? Do you believe you lack physical coordination or sports talent? Do you think that you are not very good with numbers because of a difficulty with word problems in the fifth grade? Do you believe you lack a gene for hooking up electronic equipment?

Then take this final challenge:

- Find something—anything—that you would like to be good at but doubt that you are (and probably can give reasons why).
- Make a clear and specific goal, such as "I will unplug and disconnect all my electronics equipment, then put it all back together" or "I'll learn a cartwheel" (or other physical skill) or "I'll cook a five-course gourmet meal."
- Then, once you have your goal, set a realistic, specific time frame. "One of these days" is not quite specific enough.
- Then make a list of things you can do to *prepare* yourself—a step-by-step plan to learn how to do what you intend to do. This may start with making some phone calls, calling your library for a reference book, getting lessons, or consulting with a friend who is experienced at what you want to learn.

● In other words, pick a goal, take your shot, doubt it if you will, then do it because you can.

Picking goals we doubt, then doing them, is one of the most invigorating, rejuvenating, inspiring things I know of. Remember Bob Dylan's words: "Those who are not busy being born are busy dying."

Freeing the Body of Fear

Fear begins as a thought, feeling, belief, or expectation, but it ends up stored in your body as physical tension and inhibited or shallow breathing. One way of dealing with fear is to work directly with the body, to clear the fear, which is stored as tension.

Professor Oscar Ichazo, founder of the Arica School, proposed that the body has different zones of fear—areas where different fears are stored. By working with your hands to massage these areas, literally right down to the bone, you release both tension and fear from the body.

Chronic fear-produced muscular tension limits movement patterns, causing physical pain or even biological anesthesia (blocked sensation). We begin to restrict ways of moving and thinking, losing degrees of awareness, cleverness, spontaneity, and other cerebral functions. Self-massage enables us to take direct responsibility for clearing the fear-produced tension in our own bodies. By working gently, deeply, respectfully, into each area of stored tension, we produce a more vital, elastic, and youthful body.

Following is a summary of the different zones of fear in the body. Whether or not each zone of fear listed applies in your case, *feeling* that you are clearing out a particular fear as you work deeply along the muscles and bone surfaces—doing this work as a ritual of purification—has a profound effect. Trust that good instincts will guide your hands to use the right pressure.

You can set aside several hours to do the whole body or do a little bit each day in your free time. (If you spend even five minutes on a single zone each day, by the end of one year you would have spent over thirty hours freeing your body of stored fears and tension.)

You will need a partner to work areas of the back. Use a small amount of massage oil and be sure your fingernails are trimmed. Work slowly and patiently, gently, yet deeply, with an attitude of respect for the body. Begin with a light caress before pressing more deeply.

The Zones of Fear

- **Feet (fear of being oneself):** Pull, twist, and bend each toe; work the tops of the feet, around the ankle bones, and deeply on bottom of the feet.
- **Calves and shins (fear of action):** Smooth along the top and edges and each side of the shins; deeply work the upper and lower calves.
- **Knees (fear of death):** Free the inside/rear of the knee; move the kneecap around and work deeply into the back of the knee.
- **Thighs (fear of insufficient capacity):** Work around the upper thigh and groin, all muscles around pelvic bones, and deeply into the thigh.
- **Genitals, including sitting bones and tailbone (fear of sexuality):** Work out all tenderness around genitals, anus, and tailbone.
- **Pelvis, from pubic bone to top of sacrum in back (fear of life, shyness):** Work deeply around the upper pelvis from spine to pubic bone.
- **Diaphragm, bottom ribs down to the pelvic bone (fear of assimilation, eating, breathing, taking one's space in the world):** Work under rib cage at the spine around to the solar plexus (below the sternum).
- **Rib cage to collarbone (fear of anger, shown as sadness and sighing):** Work under the collarbone, the chest muscles, and between each rib.
- **Hands, to the top of the wrist bones (fear of doing):**

Work between all fingers and into the point between thumb bone and index finger.

- **Forearm and elbow (fear of punishment):** Work the channel between two bones in the elbow joint and from the pit of the elbow to the wrist.
- **Shoulder, deltoids, and armpit to elbows (fear of disappointment):** Work around muscles at the top of shoulder, then the biceps and armpit.
- **Upper back, trapezius, and rhomboids (fear of losing control, inability to delegate puts the weight of the world on one's shoulders):** Work under partner's shoulder blades and along all the muscles of the upper back.
- **Lower back, from pelvis to shoulder blades (fear of losing):** Work along sides of your partner's spine and shoulder blades.
- **Base of skull to upper back, trapezius (fear of social blunders):** Define all fibers at base of partner's skull down to the upper back muscles.

The Head and Face (done alone or with a partner): Work gently and slowly along all bone surfaces, pressing deeper where tolerable and softer where more sensitive. Smooth forehead from middle to sides. Press your forefinger between the brows and smooth along the bony ridges. Massage temples, cheekbones, around nose, lips, and chin. Work deeply under the jawbones. Massage external ear, twisting and turning. Vigorously rub scalp.

- **Fear of Misunderstanding:** Ears, neck area, and mastoid bone
- **Worries and Wondering:** Forehead from eyebrows to hairline
- **Anger:** Eyebrow ridges and space between eyebrows
- **Prejudices and Judgments:** Eye socket ridges and muscle attachments
- **Shame:** Cheekbones
- **Fear of External Control:** Nose
- **Fear of Being Disappointed:** Lines from base of nose to the mouth

- **Fear of Being Disgusted:** Mouth, lips, and muscles around the mouth
- **Fear of Inferiority:** Chin
- **Fear of Revulsion (sights, smells, circumstances):** Jawbone

This intensive bodywork is designed to clear away the residual tensions associated with past and current fears. It does not make *fear* go away, only the tension that accompanies it. By eliminating the tension, you'll learn to keep your body relaxed and your mind flexible, so that you can act effectively, decisively, and courageously in the face of fear.

Farewell to Fear

You may have discovered that the more fear you feel in the face of a challenge, the greater your sense of elation when you have conquered it. There are few words in life more satisfying than "I did it!" Each time you face your fear by doing whatever it is you want or need to do, you practice everyday enlightenment. As it turns out, fear is not a wall, but a doorway of opportunity; not the end of the world, but only the beginning. Sometimes we have to make a leap of faith and grow our wings on the way down.

The end of one path brings another. Having delved into the core issues of fear in your everyday life, you are ready to enter the next gateway, the shadow-land of your psyche, meeting and illuminating the abandoned and disowned parts of your personality and, in doing so, finding the opportunity of becoming whole.

THE

NINTH GATEWAY

Illuminate Your Shadow

*As an infant, you were pure potential,
full and whole, open and authentic,
yielding and powerful, good and bad,
disciplined and spontaneous,
a container of possibilities.
In growing up,
you disowned parts of your being
that conflicted with emerging values.
Creating false self-images,
you became "this" but not "that."
Hidden opposites will have their day;
it's what you don't see that can hurt you.
By illuminating your shadow,
you become whole again, and real.
Releasing energy once bound
in defense of self-image,
you find energy, understanding,
humility, and compassion.*

Cultivating Compassion and Authenticity

I went to the woods because
I wished to live deliberately,
to front only the essential facts of life,
and see if I could not learn what it had to teach,
and not, when I came to die,
discover that I had not lived.

—Henry David Thoreau

Road Map: The Quest for Authenticity

The ancient Greek sage Socrates advised, above all, "Know thyself." His most famous student, Plato, wrote in his *Dialogues:* "The life which is unexamined is not worth living." These are strong words.

A modern sage named Harry Palmer put it this way:

> From the time of the ancient Brahmins of India, through the Greek and Roman civilizations, up to the modern deans of the human potential movement, one doctrine, though worded differently, has remained unchanged. It weaves its way in and out of every spiritual practice, every philosophy, and every self-help program. It is, *know thyself.*

> Is this merely an extraordinary piece of good advice that has been passed from generation to generation for ten millenniums or is it something with roots that go deeper? Is it the expression of some essential purpose that inhabits the human soul?

> Even the proverbial abandoned child, raised in complete isolation on a deserted island without recognizable language or cus-

239

tom, will one day come to the entrance of this inner path. Who am I? Why do I exist? What is life? These are questions that cannot be satisfied by worldly things. They reveal a path of inquiry that leads inward, through the uncharted turbulence of the mind, into the region of the soul.

In *Face Your Fears,* you learned of our primal fears of mediocrity—of being unmasked as a charlatan and a fool. These fears do not go away by reassuring ourselves or by playing roles that deceive no one but ourselves. Rather, they are healed as we look deeply into our own shadow to discover that we *are* fools and charlatans after all—and to find that we are also heroes and knaves, thieves and lovers, wicked imps and holy sages. We are each a diamond of many facets and flaws.

> Everyone is a moon,
> and has a dark side
> which he never shows to anybody.
> **—Mark Twain**

You are aware of some of your qualities—the tip of the proverbial iceberg. Other aspects you have denied, and with them, you have cut away a part of your power, your creativity, and brilliance. Now is the time to illuminate your shadow, become whole and real, with nothing left to deny or defend.

Having taken an appreciative look at the hidden treasures of the subconscious, you are now prepared to delve deeper, into the shadow realm, where parts of your identity, disowned and abandoned, wait to be reclaimed like lost children.

Why you have rejected aspects of your character, qualities that make up the rich blend of personality and power, will soon be clear. The shadow realm is a realm of fallen angels and fears, where self-image dies and illusion gives way to a new and integrated reality, humility, compassion, and sense of authenticity. You may feel older yet undoubtedly wiser.

Remember that the higher purpose of your explorations in each gateway—and the specific reason that you might want to acknowledge hidden or secret parts of yourself—is to elevate your awareness and attention so that you can experience life more fully and liberate the energy previously used to defend your self-image.

On this exploration you will encounter topics that include contemplations on darkness, light, and becoming whole. You will also shed light on your own shadow as you clarify its meaning and power and consider why you would want to illuminate your shadow in the first place. Then, after exploring time-tested ways of expressing your shadow side in constructive ways, you'll come to the three-question reality check—perhaps the most constructive means ever devised to meet and embrace your shadow and become real and whole.

Darkness and Light

One night, walking along the street and seeing two menacing figures approach, Socrates told me, "Sometimes you've got to deal with the darkness before you can see the light." His words are prophetic for all of us.

Where there is light, there is shadow; every outside has an inside; every high has a low; for everything revealed, something remains hidden. Nations, organizations, spiritual groups, religions, and cultures all have their collective shadows. But it is the *personal* shadow you must embrace to pass through the ninth gateway.

> There is no light without shadow
> and no psychic wholeness without imperfection.
>
> **—Carl Jung**

In James Barrie's enchanting tale, Peter Pan loses his shadow at the Darling household, where he had been eavesdropping on Wendy as she told bedtime stories. Peter is forced to risk being discovered—seen for who he is—because he *must* find his shadow at all costs. And so must we all.

Without his shadow Peter doesn't feel complete, and in fact, he isn't. Whether Barrie understood the deeper significance of his tale or whether it simply flowed from his creative unconscious is less important than the truths his story reveals about all our lives—that we must all find our shadow.

A Self-Assessment

As in previous gateways, it may be useful to reflect upon the following:

- If someone offends you, calls you a name, or accuses you of something, do you automatically defend yourself?
- How many times have you stolen and lied? Are you certain?
- Do you sometimes feel resentful when you give more than you receive?
- Are you getting your fair share of life's bounty?
- Do you have some resentments about the mistakes your parents made?
- Do you feel you do more for your spouse or partner than he or she does for you?
- Do you know yourself?
- Are you a good person? Are you also a bad person?
- Name two or three of other people's traits or behaviors that bother you the most. Is there a part of you that would like to behave that way?

As you explore this gateway, you may experience some enlightening insights, for in illuminating your shadow, you realize that in each of us lives a little of all of us, and find within yourself greater authenticity and compassion.

Shedding Light on Your Shadow

To paraphrase Carl Jung, the shadow is the sum of those aspects of your being that you denied, devalued, and disowned. In other words, your shadow is what you insist you are not.

Imagine a great wolf-dog you bring home one day, whom others in your household disapprove of, so that you come to disapprove of him yourself and lock him down in the basement. The wolf-dog has qualities of loyalty, courage, sensitivity, but can also be powerful, even ferocious. You tell the others he is gone; you deny he lives there anymore. After a while you begin to forget he exists. But he is there, growing more ferocious and menacing. If only you brought him out into the sunlight, stood up for him, let him run and play and use his power to pull your sled through the snow, to protect the household. In denying him, you lose his power and positive qualities. One day he may even break free from the basement, a ravening and destructive beast, or so a part of you fears. But he is only an abandoned wolf-dog of many qualities, locked in the basement.

Your personal shadow consists of all those qualities you deny, repress, suppress—the dust you sweep under the rug of your awareness. These rejected aspects of your personality are not necessarily evil, immoral, or negative. Yet they may seem so, which is why you have disowned them. If you are raised in a pacifist household, you may reject your assertive, aggressive side. In contrast, if you are raised in a highly competitive household, you may reject your gentle, sensitive side. What you reject, for whatever reason, becomes part of your shadow.

In fact, your shadow also contains potentially positive qualities. Many men, rejecting fear, push their sensitive, nourishing, childlike qualities into their shadow; many women, rejecting anger, push assertive, powerful warrior qualities into their shadow. Antisocial individuals act out qualities society rejects, while denying their fearful, confused, vulnerable, even compassionate qualities, believing they represent weaknesses.

Reality, Light, and Shadow

Everything contains its opposite. Clowns and comedians have a sad, cynical side; sweet people have a sour shadow; inside a pessimist you find a hopeful optimist; scratch a puritan and just beneath the surface there's a raving hedonist, begging for sex and chocolate. The truth of the shadow is this: You contain all things—highs and lows, saint and sinner, moralist and libertine. And what is wrong with that? Shouldn't we embrace the positive and avoid the negative, cling to goodness and shun evil?

Illuminating your shadow is not about inviting the devil to dinner or allowing your negative qualities or impulses to influence your behavior. When you have seen your dark side, you can make a clearer choice about how you will behave. Knowing that I have a lazy side helps me to consciously apply myself to my work rather than give in to my tendency to avoid exertion.

The Search for Authenticity, Self-Knowledge, and Self-Esteem

For some of us, personal growth has become a never-ending self-improvement program—working to develop a nicer, happier, more secure personality. Many of us with low self-esteem feel insecure because we have based our esteem upon an artfully constructed mask; the result is not self-esteem, but *self-image-esteem*. Even talented, wealthy, successful people remain restless, anxious, and insecure if they hide behind a social mask. We find self-esteem through authenticity and self-compassion, which comes when we see and accept both our light and our shadow. Embracing the shadow is one of the most powerful shifts a human being can make.

> No one can become conscious of the shadow
> without considerable moral effort. . . .
> it involves recognizing the dark aspects of the personality
> as present and real.
> —Carl Jung

You cannot become or even accept yourself until you know yourself. Once you know, accept, and become yourself, you accept and live in harmony with others in your world.

As you come to accept yourself as you are, you will discover the compassion to accept your partner, parents, children, and friends as they are. The world becomes a come-as-you-are party.

Paradoxically, as you embrace your shadow and your world, this acceptance opens the way to change. You come to realize how exhausting the social facade can be. With that realization, life becomes a relaxed opportunity for growth, not a flight from inferiority; you continue to improve without having anything to prove. You become more of who you are.

Why Illuminate Your Shadow?

Reality is a dance of dualities—night and day, light and darkness, high and low. Of course, it is far more pleasant to contemplate our light, our hopes and dreams, than to explore our dark side. So why open Pandora's box? If there are parts of yourself you don't like, why not just let sleeping dogs lie? Since your shadow is, by definition, what you would rather not look at, the idea of embracing it may seem like a task you would rather do later. Much later.

Light has always been more popular than shadow. Even though the ninth gateway is not one of the easiest or most pleasant to explore, it may ultimately be one of the most transformational, leading to self-knowledge, compassion, forgiveness, freedom, and authenticity. The reasons for embracing, accepting, and illuminating your darker side are many:

You become whole. By embracing your shadow qualities, you draw upon an expanded repertoire of feelings, tendencies, drives, and qualities—the entire range of human possibility, high and low. As you become complete in yourself, you bring a self-contained whole to any relationship and will therefore seek a whole and balanced partner.

You become authentic. You might acknowledge, in a general sense, "I'm no angel—I can be pretty rude sometimes. I make mistakes a lot. In fact, I'm too self-critical. I don't need to see my shadow, I need to appreciate my light." Most of us have trouble appreciating either our shadow or our light. This gateway is not about focusing on our good or bad points; it is about getting real. By illuminating your shadow, you also reclaim your light. Until you embrace the full scope of your humanity, your wisdom and foolishness, you remain burdened by a subtle sense that you don't fully exist, that you dare reveal only a part of yourself to the world. Most of us carry the fear that if people really knew us, they would reject us. So we show ourselves to the world in bits and pieces. But once you see and accept your shadow, there is nothing left to hide. You regain the authenticity, appeal, and charm of childhood.

You regain control of your life. Your shadow is, by definition, what you have not yet seen. It's what you don't see that can hurt or control you, because what you deny can emerge in destructive ways. Here is one example.

Some time ago an article appeared in the press about a reputable literary agent I had never met who prepared to auction a novel to four major publishers bidding. At the last moment three of the four publishers dropped out, leaving only one publisher. As the literary agent later put it, "From a part of me *that I didn't know existed before,*" she decided not to tell the lone publisher that the others had dropped out. The lone publisher bought the book for a sizable advance—then learned the others had dropped out and withdrew its offer. Had she known there was a part of her capable of such dishonesty, the agent might have examined her behavior more closely and handled the situation—and herself—differently.

That part she "didn't know existed" is also familiar to those spiritual teachers whose acquisitive shadow side ran off with the ashram's money or televangelists whose libertine shadow side had sex with prostitutes.

You illuminate your shadow by allowing rejected traits such as aggression or violence constructive expression and release, such as in sports or martial arts. A highly honest person with a dishonest shadow can make up fantastical stories for children or become a writer or actor. We don't have to deny or repress parts of us that are dishonest or sexual in order to be good citizens; we only have to not animate them. You don't have to deny your unkind side; acknowledge it, and act kindly. In contrast, those who make an exaggerated point of being good, or only peaceful, in denying any fragment of their opposite, are likely to experience that opposite emerging in troubling ways.

You experience greater compassion. When I came to know my own irresponsible, lazy, immature, selfish, dishonest, weak, fearful, ruthless, manipulative selves, it became more difficult to condemn others. Many of us avoid, poke fun at, or otherwise think poorly of those who pretend to be something they are not, until we discover that we share many of the same pretenses and fears.

Shadow work is not about self-criticism—catching yourself as you would a criminal in the night. Judgments only drive your hidden qualities deeper into the cave of denial, like a frightened wolf-dog. Rather, welcome your shadow into the house of your spirit. Explore your dark forest, illuminate it not by chopping through it with a sword of judgment, but by shining a beacon of compassion.

> I think that one must finally
> take one's life into one's arms.
>
> —Arthur Miller

You free energy and attention previously bound up in defending an idealized self-image. Do you already know yourself? Have you illuminated your shadow? Have you explored beneath the veneer of personality and self-image through the mirror of relationship? If so, then you can confess, even to yourself, "I am a puritan, a libertine, arrogant, selfish, stupid, hypocritical, greedy, ruthless, pretentious, prejudiced, racist, and sexist. They are not all I am, but they *are* a part of who I am." Having met and embraced your shadow, you will have less to defend in yourself or to condemn in others.

You clear the path to the gateways that follow. Until you have seen your own dark places, you are like someone at a masked ball, falling in love with one another's masks, never touching heart to heart. In turning from your shadow, you also turn from your light. Once you have seen what there is to see, and know your reality, you are better prepared to embrace your sexuality, awaken your heart, and serve your world.

Ways to Find Your Shadow

If your persona shadow is, by definition, unknown by your conscious mind, hidden within the labyrinthine maze of your subconscious, how can you find, much less embrace, it?

Dreams

Dreams are the playground of the shadow. In the dreamscape, your shadow resides and reveals itself with your own rich storehouse of encoded, symbolic images. When you search your memories for clues to your shadow, bear in mind that every symbol and every character appearing in a dream is an aspect of the dreamer. The mother, father, stranger, saint, vampire, clown, witch, wolf, snake, criminal, princess, and other archetypal images are all aspects of your shadow, your self.

Meditation

Meditation is not only a good way to gain insight into your own mind; it also serves as one of the primary ways to become acquainted with your shadow. In sitting meditation, as in dreams, content from your subconscious that you hide from the world and from your own awareness reveals itself. Confession is good for the soul, and meditation is yet another form of confession and catharsis. In meditation, shadow thoughts rise up from places of darkness and light to the surface of our awareness, to be noticed and released without attachment. The truth you feared might destroy you is the truth that can set you free.

Observing Yourself in Relationship with Others

Your relationships and interactions with others—particularly those relationships that carry an emotional charge—reveal much about your shadow side. By observing what most bothers or irritates you about other people—those very qualities you would most strongly deny if accused of having—you will discover the forms of your own shadow.

> If you hate a person,
> you hate something in him
> that is part of yourself.
> What isn't part of ourselves
> doesn't disturb us.
>
> **—Hermann Hesse**

Your shadow lives a secret life, animating forces, urges, unseen feelings, stifled roles that cry out for expression. When you illuminate these parts, you can channel their expression in positive and constructive ways.

Writing, Acting, and Painting

When you write in a journal, paint on a canvas, or act on a stage, you can express all that you think or feel freely, opening channels of rapport between the conscious and subconscious minds. You become your own multifaceted characters in the novel or theater of your life.

Finding Your Balance

Each of us is of two minds, like two people in a rowboat—one a scientist and the other a mystic; one a Republican, the other a Democrat; one rich and the other poor; one male and the other female; one an idealist and the other a pragmatist. The double nature of human consciousness creates a tug-of-war between opposing values. Nonetheless, these aspects have to learn to cooperate if you are going to reach the other shore. As Ben Franklin said as he signed the Declaration of Independence, "We must indeed all hang together, or most assuredly, we shall all hang separately."

Using Insight Lenses or Tools

One way to access your shadow is to use a lens to observe your-self. In the play of polar opposites, we tend to value one side over the other, so that its opposing value becomes part of our shadow. The model of the following nine polarities was first revealed by Professor Oscar Ichazo, a brilliant spiritual teacher of the modern world.

Examine the following polarities closely; they provide keys to an illumined understanding of the shadows of your psyche:

- Inside every puritan is a hedonist; inside every hedonist is a puritan; each denies the other.
- Inside every confident peacock is an insecure chicken; inside every chicken is a peacock; each devalues the other.
- Inside every workhorse is a lazybones; inside every lazybones is a workhorse; each secretly envies the other.
- Inside each social butterfly is a lone wolf; inside each lone wolf is a social butterfly; each disdains the other.
- Inside every know-it-all is a questioner; inside each questioner is a know-it-all; each is impatient with the other.
- Inside each skillful person is a bluffer; inside each bluffer is a skillful person; each argues with the other.
- Inside each team player is a rebel; inside each rebel is a team player; each resents the other.
- Inside each rigid person is a sentimentalist; inside each sentimentalist is a rigid person; each disavows the other.
- Inside each believer is a doubter; inside each doubter is a believer; each rejects the other.

Few of us are entirely one-sided. You may act more callous at work but more sentimental at home (or vice versa). You may be puritanical with food and a hedonist with sex. You may spend your waking hours a social butterfly and your dreaming time a lone wolf. Or, like author Leo Tolstoy or Saint Teresa of Avila, you may even spend the first part of your life as a hedonist, then become more puritanical later in life.

As you reintegrate those values and aspects of your character that you previously rejected, you find greater balance in your life. Balance, perspective, and wisdom come when you embrace your shadow and become whole.

Contemplation and Reflection

It is difficult to gain self-knowledge, because nearly all of us selectively attend to that which serves to build a positive and acceptable self-image. Over time we relegate those memories that do not support our idealized self-image to a storage locker we call the shadow. We clearly remember the difficulty others have caused us and forget the troubles we have caused others, put a positive spin on our shining moments, and rewrite our history. This process is not usually conscious or deliberate, but it is universal.

The more idealized our self-image, the more we begin to believe the world owes us something, and so the more our frustration when life does not meet our expectations. In contrast, the more realistically we see our shadow, the more humble, compassionate, and grateful we may feel for life's unearned gifts.

The question becomes: How can we effectively reflect upon our lives and come to know our shadow side so that we see ourselves more realistically, as a whole and authentic being rather than a smiling cardboard cutout? How can we see beyond and through the self-serving distortions to achieve real self-knowledge?

Contemplation is one way to do this. Unlike meditation, which involves detached observation of whatever arises in our awareness, contemplation entails deliberate and focused reflection on a particular question or topic, leading to insight and self-knowledge. Following is a powerful contemplation to illuminate your everyday shadow.

The Three-Question Reality Check

Originally developed by Ishin Yoshimoto, who was both a successful businessman and a lay Buddhist priest, this form of self-reflection has been used successfully in mental health counseling, addiction treatment, and rehabilitation of prisoners, as well as in schools and business environments. Yoshimoto named this method *naikan,* which means "looking inward." Its primary purpose is to develop a more expanded, realistic view of oneself.

Pick a person you know. Consider your relationship with this person over a finite period of time—it could be for that day, or for the past month, or year, or three years. Then ask yourself:

- What have I received from _____?
- What have I given to _____?
- What troubles or difficulties have I caused _____?

Write down your answers briefly but specifically.

You may want to reflect on your relationship to your spouse or partner, a brother or sister, a friend or business associate—but traditionally one begins by applying the three-question reality check to one's parents, beginning with one's mother. In the illustrations that follow I consider my relationship to my mother during my middle school years:

What have I received? The benefits derived from the first question depend on how well you can retrieve specific memories rather than such generalizations as "She always worked hard to help me." Specific memories might include "My mother prepared more than a thousand dinners for me. She drove me to school every day. She spent many hours reading my school papers. She washed my clothes and folded them neatly." (Beware of discounting someone's labors because you view it as her job or duty. The intent or motive behind these gifts is less important than the fact that you benefited from another's efforts.)

What have I given? Again, be very specific here. It is not effective for me to write, "I made her proud by getting good grades" (which benefited you). Instead I need to specify, "I painted her room. I earned money on a summer job and bought her flowers and earrings on her birthday."

What troubles or difficulties have I caused? Acknowledging the troubles and difficulties we cause is vital and necessary if we are to live an examined life. That is why Yoshimoto recommended spending most of our time on this third question; it is the most important and difficult of all.

Notice that it does not include the question "What troubles has _____ caused me?" I was, like most people, already a master at noticing how other people cause me inconvenience or difficulty. But when I began to notice how many times *I* had been a source of worry, trouble, and inconvenience (which I had previously dismissed or forgotten), it transformed my attitude and actions in a way that no personal growth seminar I had ever taken had touched. In reflecting upon the difficulties I had caused my mother, I was overwhelmed with memories of the specific times I woke her and kept her up whenever I was ill without ever considering that she had to get up early to go to work; of worrying her with my too fast driving habits; of a noisy school party that went late into the night; and of when I complained about her not having the right kind of potato chips. These memories went on and on in painful detail.

As I contemplated my interactions—what I received, what I gave, and what troubles or difficulties I caused—I began to see a reality far less self-serving than the memories I usually retained. I found my attitude shifting from vague resentment to gratitude and my desires moving from getting what I felt was owed me to a heartfelt desire to repay debts of which I was previously unaware. I began to illuminate my shadow; I started to become whole.

The Three-Minute End-of-Day Debrief

Taking a few minutes at the end of the day to do the three-question reality check is, besides its other benefits, the most effective means of conflict resolution I've yet experienced. Seeing yourself realistically, including the troubles you have caused, awakens compassion that heals conflict. If you are feeling angry toward a spouse, partner, associate, or neighbor, apply the three questions—What have I received? What have I given? What troubles have I caused? You may find that even a brief reflection replaces resentment with gratitude, criticism with kindness, and self-image with perspective. Such self-reflection, you may discover, can evolve into a form of prayer.

Some time ago, when my wife and I had just returned home from a trip, we were both tired and irritable and got into an argument. I went into my office, my mind filled with anger. Still, I spent a few minutes reflecting on the day, starting with what I had received from her. I was surprised to remember that she had kept the air tickets for me, waited in line and bought me lunch while I read in an airport lounge, and done other things for me I had taken for granted and forgotten. Then I tried to recall what I had given her; other than putting her luggage into the rental car and driving us both to the airport, I came up with nothing. When I turned my attention to what troubles or difficulties I had caused her, I felt flooded with remorse as I recalled my hurtful words to her and how I had carelessly spilled some juice on her dress and a letter she was writing, all of which I had dismissed and forgotten. I went upstairs that night wanting only to apologize, very specifically, for the difficulties I had caused, to show her kindness, and to ask for her forgiveness. Which she gave with a kiss.

It's a funny thing: I used to practice forgiving others for their omissions and mistakes. Now I realize that my work is not about forgiving others, but rather about asking others' forgiveness.

This is what my shadow has taught me.

Self-reflection, Self-Image, and Self-Worth

We leave the ninth gateway—*Illuminate Your Shadow*—by revisiting the issue of self-worth. This is relevant here, because exploring your shadow, especially through the three-question reality check, tends to lower your sense of self-worth to the degree it was based upon an illusory, self-serving self-image. At the same time, this process provides a more complete, balanced, realistic view of our conduct and relations with others. Ultimately it's a great relief to finally realize that I'm not okay, and you're not okay, and that's okay.

I don't deserve this award,
but I have arthritis
and I don't deserve
that either.

—**Jack Benny**

Illuminating your shadow reveals that you do not deserve life's blessings by virtue of having earned them with all your good works, but that Spirit continually supports and blesses you whether or not you happen to feel deserving. The sun and the air and the song of the bird, the support and love of family or friends, remain. The blessings of Spirit shower upon you in a hundred forms each day. This is not merely a sentimental platitude, but a moment-to-moment reality you notice when your attention is free to do so.

Having seen yourself as you are, accepted both your light and shadow, you will find that your dependence on a feeling of self-worth is replaced by a reliance on the innate and unconditional worth of all reality, which includes all creatures, things, and people, *and* you. In finding your own wholeness, you transcend the need for self-worth and simply become willing to accept life's blessings and opportunities whether or not you feel worthy.

When I focus on getting my share,
I'll always be disappointed,
but by noticing what I am already receiving
and then working to repay those around me,
I find a genuine opportunity for fulfillment.

—**David K. Reynolds, Ph.D.**

The fact is, sometimes we act kindly and sometimes callously, sometimes honestly and sometimes less so, sometimes we are givers, but more often takers. Illuminating your shadow, you find compassion for the foibles, illusions, and shadows of others.

Now, having opened the door to your personal shadow, you are ready to embrace and illuminate the shadows of your sexuality.

THE

TENTH GATEWAY

Embrace Your Sexuality

*Hungers and appetites
—for sexual release, for food, for life—
are as natural to you
as clouds are to the sky or waves to the sea.
If you suppress or exploit
the surging power of your drives,
you create obsessions, compulsions,
and guilty secrets.
Life is not a matter of
indulging or denying
the energies of life,
but observing, accepting,
and wisely channeling them.
Embracing your sexuality
celebrates your humanity.*

Celebrating Life

All of the animals except man
know that the principal business of life
is to enjoy it.

—Samuel Butler

Road Map: Liberating the Energies of Life

Enlightened sexuality has less to do with your skills of foreplay than your capacity for intimacy and joy in *every* aspect of life. In the context of spiritual practice, sexuality is your fundamental relationship to pleasure, your connection to creativity's fountain of rising energies, your passionate intercourse with life, your communion with Spirit through the arms of your lover.

Fulfilling pure desire, fueling the erotic fire through mindless, throbbing, sexual stimulation, certainly has its place and time within the sacred circle of an established relationship. But the scope and purpose of *Embrace Your Sexuality* extends beyond erotic play to open the possibility of truly *making* love, creating joy, blending heart and heat, sex and spirit, riding the ragged edge of ecstasy to the soul's domain.

Lofty words, perhaps, considering that most of our sexual lives until now have been something less than enlightening. What we call having sex often consists of a somewhat satisfying routine of rutting—getting it on, doing the horizontal mambo, genital stimulation as a distraction, a release, a search for solace, or a way of rocking ourselves to sleep.

Although most of us consider ourselves sexually aware, if not sophisticated, our sexual sophistication is often a pose or illusion. Freeing our libidos, cutting loose cultural baggage, antilife pro-

259

gramming, is not as easy as it may appear. *Embracing your sexuality is not about having more or less sex; it is about the enlightened expression of sexuality in context of personal and spiritual growth.* For without growth, where is satisfaction? Despite many orgasms and numerous cycles of desire and satiation, we still may not feel whole. This feeling of discontent derives from the fact that few of us approach sexuality as a spiritual practice.

But some of the more sexually active or creative souls among us imagine ourselves liberated yet remain spiritually dissatisfied without knowing why, as we sail the salty seas of carnal passion while dying of emotional thirst.

Then there are those of us, female and male, whose sensitive sexual natures are hidden like a rose within a box within a room within a fortress tower or cave of ice, secretly fearing our animalistic nature, the loss of control and loss of face that sexual intimacy requires.

Only when you fully accept your sexuality can you accept your humanity and finally feel whole. The same sexual drive that urges us to union with a partner can lead us to communion with God.

Clearly, embracing your sexuality does not imply license to sexually exploit yourself or others, but rather to express who you are (as long as it does not harm others) and to fully acknowledge that you are worthy of love. You already know this—but do you fully appreciate it? Do you fully accept yourself as you are? Do you love yourself? Perhaps you have problems and issues to work out—have not yet found wholeness or balance in the arena of relationship and sexuality. Embracing yourself as you are and releasing all judgments about your lack of perfection heals you through your stuck places and allows your trapped life energy to flow.

Fortunately, after gathering nine arrows in your quiver, one from each gateway, you are ready to embrace your soul's sensuality in a way you might not have previously imagined. You will be able to engage your partner in a more genuine, playful, expressive, vibrant, attentive manner. You may not do this every time you make love—sometimes you're just tired or out of sorts—but over time, trusting your mind, body, and life itself, you will increasingly animate the full possibilities of sexual communion.

As you pass through the tenth gateway, you will encounter topics that include the illusion of sexual sophistication; the collision of desire and society; common sense and sexual shadows; sexual identity and the two-sided brain (a possibility of balance and wholeness); realism and idealism; the puritan-hedonist dilemma (between indulgence and denial); sex and spiritual life (a cultural experiment); and, finally, sexual practices to unify flesh and spirit.

Before we begin, pause to take an emotional-sexual inventory.

A Sexual Self-Assessment

Exploring these questions can begin a process of self-reflection and help you benefit from the material that follows.

- Do you have any personal sexual issues, fantasies, desires, or concerns that you haven't shared with your spouse or partner? (You aren't obliged to share every thought, but if you haven't, what has held you back?)
- Do you sometimes have sexual fantasies about someone of the same gender? Does that feel okay to you?
- Have you ever wondered or worried that you might not be male enough or female enough?
- Would you describe yourself sexually as more puritanical or hedonistic? (Do you go with the rules or with your impulses?) Is one superior? Why?
- Might your spouse or partner prefer you to be different sexually?
- Might you prefer your spouse or partner to be different sexually?
- Do you think these differences are more physical, emotional, or mental?
- Are you sometimes bored with sex? What might you do to make it more fulfilling?
- Would you describe yourself as heterosexual, homosexual,

or bisexual? (Do you say this on the basis of experience or fantasies and feelings?)

- Do you have sexual guilt or shame? In what area?
- What sexual acts do you especially like, and why?
- What sexual acts would you not do, and why?
- Do you have a greater or lesser desire for orgasms than your spouse or partner?
- Do you masturbate? Why or why not?
- If you are married or in a committed relationship, have you ever been sexually intimate with someone else while you were married? What did you learn from this? Would you do it again?
- If you are single, have you been sexually intimate with someone who was married at the time? What did you learn from this? Would you do it again?
- What, if anything, holds you back from *completely* honoring who you are sexually, including your thoughts, desires, fantasies, and expression?

Initially, consider these questions privately. But since sexuality is (generally) a form of intimate expression between two people, you may decide to discuss some of these or related issues with your mate.

Opening Up and Getting Real

The first hurdle to connecting with your full sexual potential is overcoming the stigmas and (often hidden) shame attached to sexuality, which make honest, open, and explicit discussions extremely difficult for many of us.

When I raise questions about diet, money, or religion in lecture halls, people seem comfortable talking about such things. But when the topic turns to sexuality—if I ask about masturbation or sexual fantasies, I can feel the energy shift in the room. Everyone can feel it. The uncomfortable hush is broken only by nervous laughter. This is because powerful emotional charges converge around our sexual lives—even around our fantasies—making us afraid or wary of talking openly about sexuality, sometimes even with our partners.

Let us say that a married, heterosexual public figure, a high-ranking politician, told his therapist that he had fantasies about having sex with other men, or underage girls or boys, or even animals. And let us say that a report of this conversation was released to the media. His political career, which may have been built upon years of public service, would be irreparably damaged on the basis of a few fantasies, which are in themselves harmless.

You may doubt that the consequences would be so dire. But recall what happened to former surgeon general Jocelyn Elders, who had the temerity to suggest that masturbation had some positive attributes in terms of safe sex and that children ought to understand this. And recall the front-page headlines and ridicule when former president Jimmy Carter, probably one of the kindest and most moral presidents in recent memory, was open enough to confess that he had lust in his heart. His political image never fully recovered from this personal revelation shared by many.

More than food or money, the arena of sexuality is haunted by the ghost of morality pointing its bony finger, as if we become moral by virtue of engaging (or not engaging) in sexuality approved by others. But how do we become so constrained by our views of sex? The answers rest with the way we are socialized during adolescence.

When we are very young we touch our genitals (and anywhere else that feels good) with natural pleasure. Shame, guilt, and embarrassment are unknown to us until we learn such feelings from our parents or others who are socialized in much the same way. As we grow older, our sexual identities are further confused by a host of sources, including religion (on the one hand) and television (on the other) and society's official standards of normal and abnormal behavior.

> Sex is something I really don't understand. . . .
> I keep making up these sex rules for myself,
> and then I break them right away.
>
> —J. D. Salinger

Sexuality and Socialization

Death may be a difficult transition, but it couldn't be much harder than puberty. When you hit puberty (and when puberty hits you), the sexual innocence of childhood turns to the dilemmas and contradictions of adolescence. Trapped on a runaway hormonal express train careening into adulthood, two realities collide.

The first reality is society's insistence—through parents, church, temple, or tradition—that you control, abstain, sublimate, and suppress your surging sexuality, pacing within you like a caged animal. The second reality is the rising energies of life, of sexual desire, blossomed like a spring flower or raging like a forest fire. You become a casualty in the war between body and belief, desire and morality, lust and remorse and shame.

This conflict still exists in civilized men and women everywhere, but in the flash flood of adolescence it assaults us when we are least prepared. Some of us receive guidance, but most of us receive only rules; still, the body has its day. So we end up feeling bad about feeling good.

Religion, Sexuality, and You

Not a single one of us, whether or not we are directly involved in a religious tradition, has escaped the influence of religious traditions on our attitudes. Some of our shame or guilt over sexuality—our contradictory feelings about sexuality and spirituality—stem from religious traditions whose tenets and teachings emphasize spirit over flesh, penance over pleasure, and idealism over realism.

Religious dogma is not wrong; it is just not realistic. Nor is it supposed to be. The purpose of religion is to awaken our highest ideals and possibilities, make demands, stretch our souls, draw forth the highest and best within us. Religion calls us to our human maturity.

Ultimately it may well be best, from a religious or spiritual perspective, to practice abstinence and direct our sexual energies into other creative pursuits until married. But this is not what most imperfect humans actually do. Even many priests and nuns, who have dedicated their lives to their calling, have problems living up to the ideals of the church.

> Give me chastity and
> self-restraint,
> but do not give it yet.
>
> **—St. Augustine**

Whatever faith we practice, we need to realize that sexuality has no inherent morality or immorality. Such ideas are a human invention. No absolute, sexual guidelines exist. Every culture and era has its own beliefs and ideas of sexual right and wrong. As Bertrand Russell insightfully observed, "Sin is geographical." According to one anthropological study I read years ago, the Trobriand Islands natives engage in sexual play and intercourse in public without any sense of self-consciousness. Yet they consider it inappropriate and shameful to be seen eating in public.

Even when we have overcome the restraints of religious dogma, doctrinal sins, and shame, we still face another arena of resistance to natural and balanced, sacred sexuality—our own brains.

Sexual Identity and the Two-Sided Brain

The great cosmological truth and symbol of China, and specifically Taoist thinking, is the concept of yin and yang, the dynamic balance of opposites. Yin is the receptive (female) principle, and yang the active (male) principle. This understanding of life was based upon close observation of the world and the cosmos—the operation of natural law. No matter what your gender, the left hemisphere of your brain is often associated with traditional masculine qualities of hardness, extroversion, activity, assertive-aggressiveness, the linear, logical, deductive. No matter what your gender, the right hemisphere of your brain is often associated with feminine qualities of softness, introversion, receptiveness, passivity, stillness, and the emotional-intuitive.

Wholeness and Balance—The Best of Both Genders

Clearly both men and women embody capacities reflecting both the right and left hemispheres. Still, left-brain qualities tend to be masculine and right-brain qualities tend to be feminine. About this there is almost universal agreement. Gender stereotyping? Perhaps. A sensitive and provocative area? Undoubtedly. Do these qualities apply universally to all men and women? Hardly. But when you begin to unify and balance both hemispheres of your brain, you expand and even transcend your gender role so that you can animate at will both yin and yang qualities. You become balanced and whole—capable of hardness or softness, able to turn outward or inward. You can be active or receptive as the moment demands. You may act assertive in one circumstance and become receptive the next. You reason logically and clearly but bring forth sensitive emotional and intuitive qualities when needed.

As you integrate right and left sides and become whole, you remain anatomically a male or female, but your character and qualities evolve to a state of inclusive androgyny. *Webster's American Heritage Dictionary* defines androgyny as "being neither distinctly masculine nor feminine, as in dress, appearance, or behavior." Inclusive androgyny entails the ability to access and embody both masculine and feminine qualities and capacities.

> I'm just a person trapped inside a
> woman's body.
> **—Elayne Boosler**

Clearly the battle of the sexes reflects the battle inside each of us, men and women in conflict with our opposite gender shadows. When the male and female sides of our own brains reach a state of harmony and balance, we can truly embrace others, not only as mates and sexual partners, but as brothers, sisters, and fellow human beings in spiritual communion.

> Bisexuality immediately doubles
> your chances for a
> date on Saturday night.
> —**Woody Allen**

Sexual Differentiation and Doubt

In most societies of the past, when men's bulk and strength led them to the hunt and to war, and women's unique ability to bear children led them to child-rearing and caring for home and hearth, a strong active-receptive, male-female polarity was necessary and natural. Today, those of us still striving to behave and appear as the ultimate male or ultra-female only invite unnecessary worries and insecurities.

The old questions or criteria about what makes a real man and a feminine woman persist beyond their usefulness. To reassure ourselves of our genders, we have only to glance inside our underwear. Unfortunately, many cultures deride those who express traits of the opposite sex, as evidenced by our society's persistent fear and denigration of homosexuality. In order to completely accept your own unique sexuality rather than fitting popular stereotypes of behavior, you need the strength to face these issues without flinching.

Common Sense and Sexual Orientation

It's quite common for heterosexuals to have masturbatory fantasies about the same gender and for homosexuals to fantasize about opposite genders—that is, if we have an imagination. Our fantasies do not make us homosexual, or bisexual, or heterosexual; they only make us sexual. As we prepare to enter a new millennium, it seems that we have more important things to worry about than other people's sexual orientation. How or with whom someone expresses their sexuality seems less important than whether they are loving, sensitive, committed, able to give and receive. Any form of sexual expression can be intimate, even sacred—or can become a promiscuous, casual, uncommitted, recreational sport or even an exploitative and loveless form of suffering, an addiction to erotic endorphins, a quick fix of sexual adrenaline.

Due to the nature of our socialization, we may harbor many sexual secrets—hidden impulses, desires, or fantasies—our sexual shadows. Many of us hide sexual secrets even (or especially) from our intimates. These secrets often concern private fantasies, desires, or fears. One important facet of sexual illumination involves bringing your sexual shadows into the light of awareness in a spirit of compassionate acceptance of who you are.

A Self-Examination of Sexual Secrets

To examine your hidden sexual life, find one or more fantasies that you would feel awkward or reluctant to share with anyone. Now explore the following questions:

- Why would you want or need to keep your sexual fantasies a secret?
- What do you fear others might think? Is it possible, even likely, that other people have the same fantasies or desires?
- Can your fantasy hurt anyone? If so, who, why, and how?
- Do you think there is anything inherently wrong with any fantasy? If so, what? If not, why not?
- If you told your partner, what do you think he or she would do? Would your partner be troubled by your fantasy? Why? What would you gain by sharing it? And what would you lose?
- Do you feel any tension or loss of freedom by keeping this hidden? Does it represent an obstruction to intimacy?

The preceding questions are not meant to imply that you should or need to share every fantasy that passes through your mind or that you must confess your inner sexual life. Rather, this self-reflection helps you understand what is involved in the dynamics of keeping sexual secrets because of fear or shame.

The same consideration holds true for your outer sexual life, including secrets you may hide from your mate, ranging from the harmless (secret masturbation) to the serious (adultery). Consider what you gain and lose by not telling or by telling—and what your partner might gain or lose. Make sure you understand both sides.

Now that you have explored some effects of cultural conditioning, religious socialization, and other factors on your sexuality, you may find it timely to openly consider and illuminate your sexual secrets. We begin the process with two common secrets: masturbation and fantasies.

Masturbation in the 1990s—Sin or Godsend?

We know from books and magazines on sexuality that masturbation is common and natural, even for married men and women. Then why do many of us still feel awkward or embarrassed about it? Do you masturbate? (Aha! Caught you!) If not, is it because you were told not to? Because you don't feel comfortable doing it? Because you believe God will punish or reject you? If you do masturbate, and if you have a partner or are married, are you comfortable discussing it with your mate, or is it something you prefer to keep to yourself?

When mainstream religions forbid the practice to millions of people around the world—a practice both pleasurable, readily available, and safe—it may be worth a paragraph or two.

In the film *L.A. Story*, the character played by Steve Martin says, as he admires a girlfriend's breasts, "If I had breasts like that, I'd stay home all day and play with them." Then there's the age-old question "Why do dogs lick themselves?" The answer is, "Because they can." (Wouldn't you?) Self-stimulation feels good. That doesn't mean we sit around and do nothing else, but we need to examine why we are so conflicted about something clearly harmless that feels so good.

Where once masturbation (or homosexuality) was condemned for wasting the sperm that might otherwise help a woman be fruitful, in today's world of AIDS, unwanted pregnancies, abortions, affairs, and undesired population growth, you have to consider masturbation as a harmless and pleasurable way to discharge pent-up sexual energy. And in a marriage where one partner has a strong sexual urge and desires an orgasm daily, while the other partner feels desire only once a week, it serves a purpose.

For singles (or married persons away from home) masturbation is certainly more desirable than seeking someone in a bar and risking problematic, even dangerous, complications. Obviously masturbation is no substitute for a loving, committed bond with another human being, but at certain times it can be a godsend.

Some truths are universal and eternal. Others are conditional, arbitrary dogmas appropriate within their time but no longer relevant in the changing tides of history. Ultimately each of us must live our own lives, free of idealism, shame, or dogmas that do not serve our wholeness or our realities. Never be afraid to ask, why? Never be afraid to answer, why not?

Sexual Fantasies

For those of us, male or female, with high sex drives or promiscuous impulses, it may be more desirable to visualize sex with numerous others while masturbating than actually attempting it. Since your subconscious mind doesn't readily differentiate between experiencing something with your physical senses and imagining it, fantasizing while masturbating fulfills your desires and creates no complications or pain for anyone.

The church might declare such fantasies tantamount to adultery, but given the choice, I recommend fantasies. If I imagine murdering someone, that does not make me a murderer; if I imagine myself a Nobel Prize–winning physicist, that does not make me a scientist; and if I imagine having sex with a gorilla, that does not make me a pervert. It may be preferable to fantasize only positive, happy, wholesome thoughts. But wholesome by whose standards? And how does one control one's thoughts?

Fantasies cannot harm us unless we become concerned, guilty, or obsessive about them—or unless we confuse, or substitute, fantasy for reality. The following letter and response, one of many oddities sent to me via e-mail, bears relevance to the arena of sexual fantasies in particular:

> I am a married middle-aged woman, fairly conservative in my thinking and sexual activity with my husband. I'm concerned about a fantasy I've been having, about being forced into having sex with several men at the same time. This would be horrifying if it ever happened in real life, but in my fantasy, it's a really powerful turn-on. Is this normal?
> Concerned.

Dear Concerned:

> There is no such thing as a wrong fantasy. If you are finding pleasure in a forced sex fantasy (and many women do), it does not mean you actually want to participate in this activity. Many women write scenarios in their minds to create an erotic mood leading toward orgasm. Whether yours involves group forced sex, a football team, or just the coach, know that whatever is turning you on is O.K. Fantasy is a healthy way to exercise your erotic imagination. The more comfortable you are with your erotic side, the better your sex life.

The preceding concern and response only point out how we mistake fantasies for behavior, then feel concerned whether we are normal (as if being normal made us safe and virtuous). *Behaviors* can certainly become aberrant, perverse, inappropriate, or even harmful, but in the realm of fantasy, anything goes. Those of us who judge our own or others' fantasies as wrong need to look closely at where that idea came from and whether it holds up under close examination.

> Of all the sexual aberrations,
> perhaps the most peculiar
> is chastity.
> **—Remy de Gourmont**

Even when we recognize our sexual secrets, achieving an enlightened sexual balance may be difficult simply because we have certain inborn tendencies. In the arena of conduct and morality many of us lean more toward either a puritanical or hedonistic disposition—toward self-denial or self-indulgence. Until we find balance in this arena, sexual enlightenment remains out of reach.

The Puritan-Hedonist Dilemma

Of all the dualities that exist within your mind, the puritan and hedonist seem to stand in most dramatic opposition. Yet neither is superior to the other.

> Puritanism—the haunting fear that
> someone, somewhere, may be happy.
> —H. L. Mencken

If you lean toward puritan behavior, you sacrifice, work, deny pleasure for long-term goals, and are fastidious and moral; you go with the rules. You achieve health through effort, but you may not be much fun at parties—if you attend at all.

If you lean toward hedonistic behavior, you live for the moment, for the pleasure, and go with your impulses and tendencies. Your motto is "Life is short; eat dessert first." You might say of puritans, "When they give up sex, meat, sugar, tobacco, alcohol, and dancing, they don't actually live longer—it just feels that way."

Are you more of a hedonist or puritan? It is possible to be balanced in the sense of valuing both qualities in different situations. Reflecting on this question in relation to embracing your sexuality is the beginning of finding your balance. In the interest of that awareness, try the following exercise:

Role Playing: The Puritan/Hedonist Game

The following role-playing game, besides providing amusement, will help you clarify on which side of the puritan-hedonist scale you generally reside and will give you a chance to role-play the other side. You'll need a partner willing to spend four to five minutes doing the following:

- **The Scenario:** You and your friend are to imagine that you are walking through a residential neighborhood when someone calls to you from the upstairs window of a mansion and invites you both to a full-blown orgy in progress, replete with gorgeous, enthusiastic, fun-loving people. Upstairs you will find uninhibited, lusty people with little or no clothing on (you see some underwear fly out the upstairs window); you hear laughter, whoops, and moans of pleasure. Not only that, but they are enjoying the world's finest liqueurs, cigars, pastries, chocolates and other sweets, and every other sensory indulgence.
- You and your partner then discuss whether you should attend the orgy or not. (They want both of you to join in or neither. This ups the stakes for you to convince your partner of your viewpoint.)
- For about two minutes you play the role of a strict puritan, while your partner plays the role of a raving hedonist. Each of you have the job of convincing your partner of your views regarding whether or not to attend. Play your role to the hilt. Really get into it!
- After two minutes switch roles, again trying to convince one another of your perspectives.

Someone of a puritan disposition might raise the specter of AIDS or other venereal disease and invoke the rules of morality, health, and good judgment. Someone of more hedonist tendencies would certainly vow to practice safe sex while praising to the skies the virtues of passion, love, and fun. You will certainly come up with creative arguments on both sides.

This exercise gives you a good sense of which role you are more comfortable arguing. (If you tend to agree with your partner, you know where you stand.) Of course, you may be a hedonist in the sexual arena but a puritan in the arenas of food and health—or vice versa. In any case, insight brings illumination. The solution is to find a state of natural balance where you can relax into uninhibited (healthful) fun and sexual celebration at times and apply your self-discipline and will when appropriate.

In terms of your own sexual behaviors and values, do you behave more as a puritan or hedonist?

There are both healthy and unhealthy puritans and hedonists. If you appreciate your innate worth, you tend to be a healthy hedonist or a healthy puritan. If you are a *healthy* hedonist, you enjoy but do not abuse; you are open to pleasure and fun and savor the fruits of life. If you are a *healthy* puritan, you have learned to delay gratification, apply your strong work ethic to achieve goals, and believe in business before pleasure. As such, you are likely to reap the fruits of your labors and discipline; you are good to yourself in the long run and don't judge those who choose a hedonistic path. If you have a low sense of self-worth, you tend to be an unhealthy hedonist or an unhealthy puritan. If you are an *unhealthy* hedonist, you overindulge in food, promiscuous or indiscriminate, high-risk sexuality, alcohol, tobacco, or other drugs, and engage in self-destructive or ultimately debilitating activities. If you are an *unhealthy* puritan, you deny yourself the pleasures of life (such as dancing, occasional desserts, an intimate, uninhibited sexual life with one's companion) and may be self-righteous about your own purity.

Some of us approach sexuality and pleasure in general like the country preacher who every time he made love to his wife thought about praying—and every time he was praying thought about making love to his wife. He never succeeded as a puritan *or* as a hedonist. (And God didn't know *what* the hell was going on.) This applies to most of us; very few indeed are complete pleasure-loving, guilt-free hedonists or totally disciplined, nonobsessive, nonfantasizing puritans. So the pendulum swings.

Awareness of your puritanical and hedonistic aspects helps you to balance and reconcile them. In doing so, and in finding a balance between self-indulgence and self-denial, you come closer to embracing your sexuality resolutely, lovingly, and responsibly.

The answer to the perceived dilemmas of sexuality is not the either-or choice between flesh and spirit, but the healing embrace and integration of both. This takes you yet another step closer to completing the tenth gateway and practicing everyday enlightenment.

Unifying Flesh and Spirit: The Ultimate Sexual Practice

A culminating phase in our sexual evolution involves connecting your body and physical senses to your emotional and spiritual being. One method for this sexual union is the use of tantric practices.

Spiritualizing Sexuality—Connecting Genitals to the Heart

Most of us associate kung fu with the martial arts, but the words actually mean "skillful practice" and apply to any activity. Just so, many of us associate tantra solely with sexual techniques. But tantric practices are not limited to sexuality. Tantra involves an approach to spiritual practice that embraces vital life, sexuality, food, physical exercise, and all the senses in a sacred manner. Rather than practicing indulgence or denial, it teaches right and balanced use of sensory experience under the dominion of our higher selves.

In the following tantric practice, you learn the essence of tantric yoga by using your attention to create a bridge of awareness between your genitals, heart, and whole body. This act of conscious remembrance not only enhances and enriches, deepens and dimensionalizes, the pleasure of sexual embrace; it also transfigures human sexuality into an act of communion and worship. You not only hold your lover in your arms; you embrace the Divine.

Practice the heart of tantra yoga in your sexual relationship as follows:

The next time you make love (or masturbate, if you currently have no partner), rather than focusing attention exclusively on genital pleasure, place equal attention on your heart, your genitals, and your whole body.

We all have the capacity to do this simple act, but our attention must be free to do so. Consciousness of self is blocked by self-consciousness. You cannot attend fully to integrating genitals, heart, and whole body while you are paying attention to pictures in your mind or wondering how you are doing, how you look, what your partner thinks of you, and so forth. In order to be mindful, you first need to be mindless. Embracing your sexuality both requires and develops the ability to lose your mind and come to your senses.

Embracing this tantric practice of connecting genitals and heart during sexual intimacy serves as one important facet of everyday enlightenment. In order to integrate this practice even occasionally into your life, you need to engage your will. Will and feeling-attention (or attention with an emotional, even devotional aspect) serves to awaken your heart, the eleventh gateway waiting just ahead.

Sex, Love, and Will

If you or your partner are rarely in the mood for making love, or if you lack energy to do so, there is something in the way of intimacy—something out of sorts or out of balance that you need to air out and explore together in the spirit of love and understanding. But before you get caught up in endless psychological discussions and analyses (a process that might end up reinforcing the very relationship problem you are working on), perhaps what you need to do is commit yourselves—*will* yourselves—to make love a little more often even if one or both of you aren't in the mood.

In the Orthodox Jewish tradition, Friday evening, the beginning of *Shabbat* (Sabbath), is the occasion where a man is expected to give sexual pleasure to his wife. If there are problems in the way of this, they are to be worked through. Although this tradition may seem to lack spontaneity, there may be great and practical wisdom in it, where loving partners come together at the end of the work week to celebrate their intimacy and their loving bond. Contrast this with having sex only when you happen to feel like it.

Normally you think of applying your will in order to *not* engage in sexual activity—not act on desire, but instead practice self-control, self-restraint, abstinence, or celibacy. But you can also apply your will as a tantric practice in order to engage fully in sexual activity even when you don't happen to be in the mood. Sexual intimacy takes many forms and represents many states, from lust to reassurance to comfort to communion. Sexual intimacy is also a way of making love, of creating love, of restimulating and acting out mutual caring.

Sometimes you feel tired or a little irritated about something your partner said or did, so you turn away physically. Whether your partner's reasons are ideal, if he or she turns to you needing love, affection, or simply physical satisfaction, instead of rejecting your partner, you can apply your will and turn to your partner with kindness, compassion, and understanding, remembering why you first joined together. This loving touch may or may not lead to intercourse, but it can heal an emotional rift and offer needed reassurances of love and caring. Many of us may report that we have on many occasions made love when we weren't really in the mood but because our partner expected or wanted it. But how often have we done so as an act of both heart and will, giving, healing, surrendering in service and devotion to Spirit in the form of our partner?

Love may lead to sexual intimacy, but sexual intimacy may also stir the embers of love. So even though you may not feel like sexual engagement in the moment your partner does, in responding to him or her, you discover why it is called *making* love. Sometimes we need to make love not with the idea of getting our share of pleasure, but as a form of healing we offer to our partner. This is a spiritual act of tantra and of service.

Argue when you need to. But always make up, and touch one another, and embrace, in whatever form that takes, even if you need to apply your will to do so at times, to create a more perfect union. Soul mates aren't found; they are made.

Love, Desire, and Sexual Communion

There are times you eat when you are not hungry. If a loved one has made you something special, you may eat it as an act of kindness even though you don't have much appetite. (You may or may not end up enjoying the food, but the kindness remains.)

There are times when you engage in sexual activity when you do not desire it. If a loved one wants to have sex, you may make love as an act of kindness even though you don't have much appetite. (You may or may not end up enjoying the sex, but the kindness remains.)

In everyday life it is better to eat when you are hungry and better to engage in sexuality (leading to orgasm) when you feel desire. Natural hunger expresses your body's need for calories and nutrients. Similarly, natural desire (for orgasm) expresses your body's need for sexual release. But embracing sexuality also involves surrendering this activity to the dominion of your higher self.

Some sexual moments center solely around one's own pleasure; other sexual moments center solely around another's pleasure. As most of us have experienced, the best sex combines an interplay of both, a dance of self and other until separate selves merge. The giving is receiving, and the receiving is giving, so that at some point in your union it becomes less important, even irrelevant, who is giving or receiving. This circle of energy is created when two people make love, exchanging gifts of touch, sensitivity, and caring. In the end, what more can one give?

Tantric Practices of Love in Everyday Life

It's one thing to read about the benefits of enjoying life and feeling pleasure, and to talk about the importance of loving yourself, but can you give yourself permission to do so? The following exercise involves taking yourself out for a night on the town. Take an entire day, or as much time as you are willing to give, to enjoy your own company and do what you enjoy (even if you normally do it with someone else):

Solo Tantra

- Go to a movie. Or shopping. Or a fair or other event.
- Treat yourself, as you would a good friend or lover, to a lavish lunch or dinner.
- Satisfy every feasible desire on this date.
- End the day with an intimate evening of solo sexual bliss.
- If you have a partner who is interested in engaging in this exercise, you might suggest that he or she go on the same solo date.
- The following week, if you are in a relationship, go on a nearly identical date with your partner and lavish the same attention on him or her (whether or not you are sexually active together, as appropriate).

Tantra for Two

If you are sexually active, try this simple yet powerful tantric exercise. If you have children, you will want to do this after bedtime or, better still, on an overnight vacation:

- Shower together, then do fifteen minutes of yoga or stretching and breathing.
- Meditate together (preferably by candlelight) for ten minutes. Put on soft music you both enjoy.
- Embrace and touch for at least ten minutes before intercourse, while caressing each other's arms, legs, back, face, and feet—a loving massage.
- During intercourse by candlelight, be still for at least five

minutes and simply gaze deeply into each other's eyes. Consider your love for your partner.

- Acknowledge to yourself and let go of any levels of self-consciousness that may arise, and surrender with love into your partner's eyes. Feel and release whatever comes up, and return to love.
- Feel the mystery behind your partner's eyes.
- At some point, if you do this, you may see and feel your partner as a divine being and experience the profound love you feel, both personal and transpersonal, that often goes unnoticed in the stress of day-to-day living.
- Notice if key issues or insights arise in this exercise, and share them verbally afterward.

You can learn much about your present priorities, your relationship to pleasure, your self-worth, and your intimacy comfort level if you do not do these exercises and then ask yourself, deeply and respectfully, why not?

Final Words

Given the emotionally and morally charged nature of sexuality, you may have felt offended if my words trod on your beliefs. If so, and you continued to read this far, I congratulate you and honor your beliefs and values. I deeply believe that each of us needs to find our own way, our own religion, and our own sexuality. In the realm of sexuality, as in politics, religion, and ice-cream flavors, what is ultimately best is a matter for each individual to decide on his or her own. In the meantime, explore the reality of how you actually live, honor your ongoing process, and learn the lessons of experience.

As you leave this gateway, remember its title: *Embrace Your Sexuality.* Honor who you are, a unique expression in the world. Continue your journey with a lightened heart, trusting that your thoughts and fantasies are part of what makes you unique. And remember that at its highest human expression, sexuality becomes a practice of everyday enlightenment.

Look back now through the ten gateways through which you have passed and the broader view you have earned from where you now stand. Having explored the challenges and wonders of making love with your partner and your world, you are ready to explore the depths of your heart.

THE
ELEVENTH GATEWAY

Awaken Your Heart

*Love is life's great secret.
It transcends fear and isolation,
guiding you beyond the shallows of sentiment,
to the shores of boundless being.
Love endures not from words or feelings alone,
but from actions that carry you
beyond the interests of separate self,
beyond reason or motive,
to embrace all people, things, and circumstances.
Loving-kindness begins in little ways,
in moments of insight and humility,
in your soul's longing for love's communion,
which waits just on the other side
of your heart's doorway.
You are not here to contact your higher self;
you are here to become it.*

The Healing Power of Love

Love doesn't just sit there,
like a stone; it has to be
made, like bread,
remade all the time,
made new.

—Ursula K. LeGuin

Road Map: Preview of Coming Attractions

Our spiritual evolution has an element of mystery in that it occurs from a blend of effort, time, and grace. Still, this much is clear: To fulfill the promise of your human potential, your heart must awaken. But what does it mean to awaken your heart? If love is found naturally at the heart, what will you find at the heart of love? What is love's essence and source—God? Spirit? Mystery? A figment of imagination? A bit of cerebral chemistry? Brian Swimme, heartful cosmologist, has proposed that love is gravity—the universal force of attraction that every single body in the universe has for every other body, the unifying glue that holds the cosmos together and draws us all inexorably back to the Source of all being.

This poet's picture, this transcendent vision of love, is a good place to begin, because without this larger view we are fooled by love's pretenders—seduced by soap-opera sentiment and romantic desire, bedazzled by fading roses and fickle phantoms of lust or infatuation.

Awakening your heart entails moving from conditional feelings to unconditional kindness—awakening the healing powers of the heart that can lift you beyond yourself to love without fear, limit, or reason.

285

In this gateway we explore new ways of understanding love and living it. To the degree you have understood the principles of the first ten gateways—including reclaiming your will, taming your mind, accepting your emotions, facing your fears, and embracing your sexuality—you have prepared yourself for the great leap into the heart, the place where flesh and spirit meet. The mythic Lover's Leap is a leap not downward, but upward, into a heightened experience of life. As songwriter David Roth reminds us, "We're not falling at all, we are rising in love."

To the degree you have embodied the lessons of the gateways leading to the heart, you are now prepared to embody a new way of loving, founded upon enduring behavior rather than changeable feelings. You have cultivated the garden of your psyche, preparing the soil and sowing the seeds so that love can blossom naturally. No one can teach love or learn it, for the mind has no heart and the heart has no reason. All I can offer here is a love note to you, my readers and friends, sharing what I have found to be true at the heart of life. I am no saint, except as you are in moments of loving, but caring compels me to share ways to bring love into the world as a midwife welcomes a newborn.

When we speak of love, it may manifest as romantic love or as love for a child, a brother, sister, parent, friend, for humanity, for God. Ultimately, the highest wisdom of the ages tells us to love, serve, and remember God in, as, and through everyone and everything. Love unconditionally with all your heart—this is all you ever need to learn, to do, to become—in this gateway, in this book, in this life. Whatever the question, love is the answer. But loving, as your life has revealed, is not so simple. Countless poets, philosophers, psychologists, and romantics have rhapsodized, discussed, eulogized, and analyzed love. But until our hearts awaken, love remains a word, a puzzle, a desirable goal rather than a living reality. Bill Moyers once observed, "Even the Bible is a closed book unless we approach it with an open heart."

How do we awaken our hearts? How indeed. Welcome to the eleventh gateway. The summit is in sight.

In this gateway we'll consider why it takes courage to love in this world as well as examine how and when love blossoms naturally; and, based upon what you have already learned, we will explore ways of keeping love alive—the keys to long-term loving relationships. The heart of this chapter involves how to apply your will to create a new way of loving that transcends how loving you feel; includes methods to awaken your heart and bring more love into the world; and, finally, as our hearts awaken, a preview of coming shifts in global consciousness that will affect every facet of society.

Love as Courage

This is the bittersweet truth of human life: The path to love is strewn not only with rose petals, but with thorns. By journey's end you will lose everyone and everything you have ever loved; that is why it takes courage to love anyone in this world. You will seek love in safety until you discover there is no safety in love, and none needed. Only when you are willing to risk the pain and sorrow of loss will you trust enough to open your heart to joy.

Some of us believe we want a soul mate, an intimate relationship, yet another part of us wants to remain safe in the citadel of isolation. Loners can remain detached and dissociated, hitchhiking through relationships and then walking away at the first sign of trouble. It takes courage to persist through the rocky roads of relationship; it takes courage to have and to love children. We suffer every one of our loved ones' illnesses, injuries, and disappointments. We lose sleep over our children's dilemmas and know their pain.

It is far safer never to love, for your heart is a sleeping giant filled with passion and pain, joy and fear. It is safer to remain within the armor of solitude, like a turtle in its shell. The only price you pay is your humanity.

No matter how successful, powerful, or wealthy one may be, life without love is a realm of shadow. When psychologists began to study violent criminals, they found that almost without exception, none of these offenders had experienced parental love or ever had a pet to take care of as a child. Without love we wither like a flower without water. Whether or not you are married, whether you live with others or live alone, you need someone to love in your life in order to fulfill the promise of the eleventh gateway. Whether that someone is your spouse, friend, children, parents, pets, or others, they serve as a means of awakening your heart.

Looking into Your Heart—A Self-Assessment

Reflect upon the following questions to shed light on the practice of love in your life:

- If you had to choose, would you rather love or be loved?
- Think of five people you have loved in your life. Rank these five people in your degree of loving. If you have trouble doing this, why? If you do not have trouble doing this, why did you rank them as you did?
- Can you be angry with and love someone at the same time? Argue in favor of this, then against it.
- If there were no sex in the world, whom would you love, and how might you demonstrate that love?
- Does this gateway interest you more, or less, than the others? Why?
- When was the last time you said the words "I love you"?
- When was the last time you *demonstrated* your love through your actions?
- What would it be like if you loved everyone you met—the clerk at the market, the bus driver or bank teller, male or female, young or old?
- Is there a difference between love and kindness?
- What might you do today to bring more love into your world?

There are no right or wrong answers here. We are all humans-in-training, learning the art of loving. As in any of the gateways, self-reflection serves as a reality check to dissolve illusions, enhance awareness, expand self-knowledge, and turn deserts into gardens. The transformation begins with intending but needs courage, self-sacrifice, and patience to bloom. (The awakened heart may not be heaven, but you can see it from there.)

Awakening and Attention

In the ancient spiritual traditions of India and China, attention is said to rise through seven ascending levels of experience and awareness. In the lowest level of experience, attention is preoccupied with issues of survival, safety, and fear. In the second level, once survival issues are resolved, attention turns to relationship, pleasure, and sorrow. When attention rises to the third level of experience, it focuses on matters of power, self-control, and anger. The dramas of our daily lives, reflected in film and literature, center around these three levels of experience—survival (fear), relationship (sorrow), and power (anger). Only when these three arenas are resolved can your attention rise to the fourth level of human experience—love and service—and to the mystical realms beyond.

When attention is centered in the lower level of survival and fear, love manifests as lust, obsessive desire, and exploitation. When attention is centered in the second level of relationship and sorrow, love manifests as romantic sentiment and sensitivity, as bouts of pleasure and pain, fighting and making up—the stuff of romance novels and soap operas. When attention is centered in the third level of power and anger, love manifests as duty and fidelity—but also as control issues, struggles with self-discipline. You have at times probably experienced all three of these forms of love.

In rare moments of free attention, your awareness may rise into the heart, manifesting as selfless giving—the kind of unconditional love sometimes experienced by parents for their children. It is so rare for attention to establish itself firmly in the heart (without being pulled back to the issues of the lower three centers) that those who demonstrate such unconditional love over time are called "saints." This ascension of attention from the lower three centers into the heart is what it means to *awaken your heart.* Such awakening manifests a gradual process of illumination as the light of attention enlightens the heart, resulting in more frequent waves of love.

Remembering to Love

The wisdom, the power, the courage, the love, the kingdom of heaven—are inside us. It's just that we forget. We forget to trust ourselves; we forget to listen; we forget to pay attention to the highest and best inside us. We forget because we've been sleeping, slumbering, dreaming, wishing, hoping, while love has been waking us, shaking us, calling us to open the shades and let in the light of awareness. It's time to take hold of our lives, time to accept ourselves, our world, and our present reality even as we aspire to our highest ideals.

Awakening your heart produces a natural, graceful, expansive state of unconditional love—no strings attached. That means you cannot help but love, even when others do not love you back. It does *not* mean that you always *feel* an emotion of love or that you love every personality; it means that you have found the will to treat others with kindness and compassion irrespective of feelings.

In your higher moments, you may indeed feel deep and profound compassion, but you can't wait for or depend upon changeable feelings, which may appear and then disappear like long-lost lovers. Romance fades like the bloom of a flower, unless you cultivate it carefully through loving actions, so that it blooms anew.

Love Begins with You

One of the strangest delusions believed by many of us is that it is good to love other people but bad to love yourself. I suggest that the more you are able to see, love, and accept the one facet of Spirit gazing at you from the mirror, the more you will be able to love Spirit within others. If we are the same awareness shining through a billion separate forms, then all love begins with self-love. For the heart to awaken, it cannot exclude a single soul, including yourself. If you do not love yourself, how can you find the space to love others?

Self-love is a beginning practice of love. From self-love we learn to love another—a parent, a pet, a friend, a partner—from family to friends, to associates, to the larger world. There's no place like home to begin the practice of love. Home is where the heart is, and home is generally where the hassles are, too. What better place to practice loving without reason than that place where we cannot always find a reason to love?

If practicing love is not yet a priority at this point in time—if you have other gateways to attend to that seem more immediate and pressing—then attend to them. This, too, is the work of consciousness. Love yourself enough to forgive your humanity, and let yourself be. This allows love to grow. Love enough to trust the process of your life unfolding.

Keeping Love Alive

Some moments we love; some moments we don't. Since life is a series of moments, each appearing and disappearing, no one can truly promise, "I will love you forever." Feelings come and go, change and fade—even the feeling of commitment. You may feel grief or rage, then momentarily forget as you laugh or wonder at something you see or hear. Acknowledge the reality of our moment-to-moment existence. Recognize that feelings fade unless restimulated, and use this to your advantage. Avoid restimulating undesired feelings. If someone leaves you, it may be wise to remove that smiling photograph from the desk or wall, at least until time heals the raw wound.

It makes sense to study successful people to find what qualities and behaviors they have in common and to model or duplicate their actions. After all, as you learned in *Reclaim Your Will*, it is not only who you are that makes a difference in life, but what you actually do. And if you do what others do, you increase your chances of getting similar results.

This approach to living also applies to the arena of relationships. Study the qualities and behaviors of longtime couples, especially those who report that they are still in love and happy together. Elderly couples like my parents, who have been married for nearly sixty years, have learned that making love is not just about sex—that love must be made and remade. Since love fades like any other feeling, thriving long-term relationships are nourished by restimulating feelings of love. The heart is not just awakened; it must be reawakened again and again. Based on my observations, experience, and research, longtime couples share many of the following behaviors that restimulate feelings of love:

- They offer kind, complimentary words of appreciation.
- They withhold words of nagging and criticism (or deliver criticism in a soft, gentle, considerate manner).
- They kiss or touch one another with caring and affection, whether or not the touch is sexual.
- They remain loyal and supportive friends.
- They express their feelings and needs.
- They frequently say "thank you" and "I apologize."
- They forgive and ask forgiveness.
- They listen well and pay attention to the feelings and needs of their partner.
- They maintain a sense of humor about themselves.
- They value and consider their partner's needs not as less or greater, but as equal to their own.
- They demonstrate sexual caring, compatibility, and communication.
- They accept their partner's imperfections rather than trying to control or change their partner to suit their own preferences.
- They have their own interests and friends, give each other the space to pursue those interests, then share their interests with one another.

In light of this wisdom of longtime partners who have kept the lamp of love burning, here are some simple practices you can do:

- Make sure to kiss or embrace your partner (and children) every day.
- When appropriate, give your loved one(s) a one-minute back, neck, or foot massage. (Can you spare one minute to keep love alive?)
- Do something special on birthdays, anniversaries, and Valentine's Day, and also spontaneously surprise your loved one with a flower, a note, poem, or book—a tangible sign of your love.
- No matter how busy you are, especially if you have children, make a date to go out together, even if it's just for a walk, at least once a week.
- When your partner is upset with you or just feeling blue, ask questions, then let your partner speak and just listen.
- Look for things to appreciate and offer words of kindness, praise, and affection.
- When you must complain, use the word "I" more than the word "you"—such as "I have a hard time with this" instead of "You really frustrate me when you . . ."
- Be quick to offer thanks and equally prompt to apologize; make your comments specific rather than general—such as "Thank you for making my favorite meal" instead of "Thanks for all the work you do" or "I apologize for telling Burt what you had asked me not to tell him" instead of "Sorry I talk too much."

According to the U.S. Forestry Service, embers can burn all winter beneath the snow; the same is true of the embers of relationship. As long as a single spark remains, couples can reawaken the fire of a love that seems to have died. Sometimes love is smothered by criticisms, nagging, or belittling or doused by a thousand little hurts. Words of gratitude, appreciation, apology, and sincere forgiveness reignite the fires of passion and devotion.

Love as an Action

Talk is easy, but love is difficult. Awakening your heart requires more than sweet sentiment or fine intentions. It requires time, energy, and attention—treating your loved ones with the care you offer to honored guests. We cannot build relationships on words or feelings alone. True love is not feelings or flowery words; it is action. Love is as love does.

You now understand that you have no more control over feelings of love than you do over the weather. You cannot fall in or out of love just by willing it. But you can control behavior—you can behave with kindness, care, and compassion whether or not you happen to feel loving in a given moment. This is the beginning of unconditional love and unreasonable happiness.

As it happens, the words "love" and "happiness" express the same state of being, with the same physiological fingerprints; the same chemicals are secreted in the bloodstream. When you love, you feel happy; when you are happy, you feel loving. To awaken the heart is to be unreasonably happy. As you master the will to act loving—to show kindness and compassion in any moment despite feelings to the contrary—you develop the capacity to give unconditional love.

Conditional and Unconditional Love

Conditional love is attached to one particular person to the exclusion of others. This is the beginning stage of love. It may include positive feelings of deep, tender regard, of passion, affection, and solicitude, arising from kinship or from devotion, desire, attraction, fondness, or warm personal attachment, which can fade over time.

In marriage ceremonies we promise to honor, love, and cherish till death do us part, but such promises are unrealistic. Ask nearly any divorced couple. Because conditional love is *personal,* attached to specific qualities, appearance, and other attributes of a particular person, when these qualities, appearance, or attributes change or fade, so can the love.

Until we move from conditional to unconditional love, stores will be full of books and techniques to help struggling, suffering couples wondering whether or not to stay together because they don't feel fulfilled.

Unconditional love has no bounds, limits, strings, or conditions. It loves without reason, whether or not it is loved or even appreciated in return. It asks for nothing but gives what it can. It may be tough or tender, but it is always kind. It values the lives of others as equal to—not less or more than—one's own.

And unconditional love extends to all souls, even while living with one chosen partner. Loving everyone does *not* imply having sexual contact. As most of us have intuitively learned, sexuality best serves our spiritual evolution within a single, committed relationship. We can express nonexclusive love to friends, acquaintances, and other members of our human family without threatening the sanctity of our primary relationship, which remains the exclusive domain of sexual intimacy.

Parenthood serves as a primary theater and school of unconditional love. Words we have all heard uttered with great solemnity at wedding ceremonies apply most universally to our love for our children, whom we love fiercely, with all our hearts, for better, for worse; for richer, for poorer; in sickness and in health . . . till death us do part. Our children teach us how to love more than we could ever teach them.

If you can love even one other person with a fierce, sacrificial, unconditional generosity of spirit, then you can love many as you learn to cast your net of love wide enough to embrace all people as your children, as your brothers and your sisters. This is no idealistic wish; this is a preview and prediction of your destiny.

Transpersonal Love: The First Mystical Practice

True love is rare, but it exists, and not just in fairy tales. Each of us has known moments of true unconditional (unselfish) love, pure altruism. Such love draws you upward toward the higher planes of experience, the meeting place of flesh and spirit, where you contact the higher self described in the ancient traditions. Thus love is the first mystical practice.

Transpersonal love represents a paradox of two apparently incompatible ideas. Transpersonal means "transcending or beyond the personal," whereas we normally think of love as very personal. (How would it sound to say, "I love you, but it's nothing personal"?) Transpersonal love takes us beyond our egos, beyond the separate self. From that awareness you look with love upon all souls, wrapping them in a cloak of kindness and compassion. You love all women through your wife, all men through your husband, all children through your children, all people through your friends. In those moments that awareness awakens your heart, you find the will to act in a loving manner despite your moods, feelings, or preferences.

Love and Will

The bridge of will transforms love from something you seek to something you bestow, from dependence on changeable feeling to reliance on compassionate behaviors. But feelings, as you know, are fickle and undependable. Feelings of passion, commitment, and desire may turn to indifference, jealousy, and animosity. True love cannot wait for the right mood; it is fanned by the fires of your actions. When you can show love, act compassionately, behave with kindness whether or not you feel that way, you will know the plateau of human maturity. This does not mean you behave as a saccharine saint, but that even occasions of anger, criticism, sadness, and other natural feelings you may express are genuinely rooted in love. If your spouse, child, friend, or partner is yelling at you, blaming you, you are not likely to feel love and compassion for them in that moment; still, you never lose the power to act with kindness.

In the practice of everyday enlightenment, the process of awakening your heart, love and happiness are no longer passive feelings you hope or wish or wait for. Love becomes an action; happiness becomes a behavior. You love without reason and behave with unreasonable happiness.

This practice takes getting used to and bears repetition: To awaken your heart, you do not have to (nor can you) consistently generate loving feelings—you only have to *behave* with lovingkindness. The saints also felt anger, sorrow, and fear, since no one can control their feelings; but they spoke and acted with love, and that is what made them saints. In any moment you behave with loving-kindness even when you don't feel like it, you have ascended, for that moment, to sainthood.

This is the great secret of love: Loyalty is not something you feel; it is something you do. Kindness is something you do. Fidelity and friendship are things you do. This is why love is the greatest and most difficult spiritual discipline of all.

> It's a bit embarrassing
> to have been concerned with the human problem
> all one's life and find at the end
> that one has no more to offer by way of advice than
> "Try to be a little kinder."
>
> **—Aldous Huxley**

Love as a Spiritual Practice

There can be no spirituality without loving-kindness. The benefits of sitting alone in one's room meditating on a blue light or on ultimate truth are far less than forming an open relationship with life, moment to moment. Everyday enlightenment is, above all things, a loving embrace of the moment. It is possible to practice such love in everyday life while shopping, riding on a bus, making dinner, or working with colleagues or clients.

In the fifth gateway, *Tame Your Mind,* you learned that you have some degree of control over where you place your attention. Using this ability, you will find it possible to use your voice, touch, sight, hearing, and even thought as forms of everyday spiritual practice.

Your heart is not just a muscle in your chest; it is also the mystical center of love. You can love as, from, and with your whole body and being, but every culture I've visited associates love with the heart. That muscle, quietly beating, pumping life through your body, is the center of love. Even children know this. One evening several years ago, while at a gathering of friends, I found myself sitting next to a three-year-old boy as we listened to a master cellist from China. On impulse I asked the little boy where he felt the music. "Here," he said matter-of-factly, touching his chest, "I feel it here."

The heart is God's calling card. It beats the rhythms of the mystery of life, hope, inspiration, and love. Normally you have your attention not in your heart, but on your thoughts and actions. By placing your attention in your heart while speaking, seeing, hearing, touching, and thinking, you engage in a simple form of meditation to awaken your heart.

The theme from the beginning of this book has been the liberation of attention. This is the goal of the twelve gateways not just in and of itself, but so that your attention is free to rise into the heart and so you naturally speak, think, hear, touch, and act from the heart. Until such moments occur spontaneously, you can practice everyday enlightenment by placing your attention in the heart and experience love's awakening.

- Right now, instead of focusing your attention on this page or on your thoughts, place your attention in your heart. Feel your heart. (It may help to place a hand there at first.)
- Are you aware of a subtle shift in the quality of your awareness when you become aware of your heart? Notice this purified form of feeling above fear, sorrow, or anger.
- Notice that it is not a difficult or esoteric exercise, but rather a simple act of remembrance you can do instantly, at any time or in any circumstance.

It is known in numerous ancient spiritual and mystical traditions that we first connect with and experience the love and inspiration of our higher selves at the heart center—not in the realms below. Love, as I have said, is the beginning of mystical practice, the first stirrings of unity, of transpersonal life, where the language of the spiritual teachings, from the Bible to the Bhagavad Gita, begins to make sense. Thus this simple practice can change the quality of your life, to the degree you remember to do it.

Having practiced shifting attention to the heart a few times, you are ready for the following mystical practices that serve to awaken your heart.

Speaking from Your Heart

When you place two guitars (or other stringed instruments) next to one another, and you pluck, for example, the "D" string on one guitar, the "D" string on the nearby guitar will also begin to vibrate. This is known as sympathetic or harmonic resonance. This harmonic resonance also applies to the human voice, in the following way: When you speak from your mind (with your attention on your thoughts) you resonate the minds of others. When you speak from your heart (with your attention on the heart) you resonate the hearts of others. This conscious and deliberate act of remembrance—placing your attention on (or in) your heart as you speak, or visualize, or see, or touch, or listen—spiritualizes your senses. This act of feeling-attention is a key practice of everyday enlightenment.

There is nothing wrong with speaking from the mind. If someone asks you for information, for example, you may think about it (put your attention in your mind) and speak from your mind as you answer.

However, when you speak from your heart, you create a bridge of love and understanding between you and another person, connecting your higher self with theirs. This act of speaking from your heart is not merely sentimental or personal, but rather transpersonal. You don't need to use any special tone of voice; you can speak in a matter-of-fact way. The quality of your feeling-attention makes the difference. This practice is extremely simple, but new for many of us, so I summarize the key points here:

- Put your attention in your heart—feel your heart.
- Speak normally as you remain aware of your heart.
- In other words, you connect your voice to your heart as you speak, letting your voice carry feeling-attention.

When I first learned this method of speaking from my heart, I did it as a practice or a technique, in order to awaken my heart, as I recommend to you. Today I can't *help* but speak from my heart; it has become natural, as my attention abides in the heart more and more. When I speak to groups of people, I may relate material that I have written about; yet it has a special impact because of where I'm speaking from—a heart-to-heart transmission takes place that transcends the information conveyed.

You can incorporate this mystical practice into your everyday life and work, whether speaking with your children, friends, clients, neighbors, or clerks at the store. While you are apparently shopping, selling products or services, or engaged in meetings, your voice can become part of a secret, underground spiritual moment, touching others' hearts as it awakens your own, bringing more love into the world. With this practice you are never again only teaching or selling or coaching or managing or building or consulting; rather, your work and life become a source of love and light for others.

Inner Speech: Visualizing from Your Heart

Once you are aware of your heart, you are not limited by speech at all. You can also connect your heart to your thoughts and send inner speech, such as healing wishes or blessings, to others. When using inner speech, you are not limited by time or space. You can send messages of love and goodwill to someone nearby (in the same room or lying asleep next to you), or you can send an internal message of love to someone a thousand miles away, to someone in a coma, even to someone who has passed away.

The method is the same as with auditory verbal speech:

- Put your attention in your heart. Feel it.
- Visualize that person or those persons surrounded by light.
- Internally think/say words such as "I love you, I support you, God bless you." The specific words you use aren't critical—the key is remembering and feeling your heart as you send your wishes.

Do I know for certain that your words will reach someone who has passed away? No. But I am more certain, from experience and from reports of many others who have applied this simple practice of love, that whether people are near to you or on the other side of the world, they will get the message. They may not know it consciously, but I have gotten too many telephone calls out of the blue, and seen too many adversarial relationships suddenly healed, to doubt its efficacy. Ultimately you need to test it in your own experience.

Seeing from Your Heart

In my book *Sacred Journey of the Peaceful Warrior,* the Hawaiian kahuna named Mama Chia used the phrase "seeing with the eyes of the heart." I took it as a poetic metaphor until I learned how to do it.

- Put your attention in your heart. Feel it.
- Look at the world with eyes of wonder and love.

You can do this now, by becoming aware of your heart and gazing from the eyes of the heart at anything you see. You can look upon a tree, another person, or a piece of crumpled paper on the floor. You may view an automobile or a building, and consider the human effort, creativity, and labor required by people from many walks of life to create such wonders out of raw materials, drawn from the earth. Consider the spirit and dedication required. If you see something from the natural world—a stone, a tree, a cloud—consider how these were created and by whose hand.

There is another way to connect your eyes to your heart that enables you to connect spiritually with another human being. Consider first how little time we spend actually looking into the eyes of others. We may steal a glance, then quickly avert our gaze—or we look, but we do not feel. This is strange, because the eyes are indeed the windows of the soul. To learn to see in a new way, try the following practice and experience the results:

- Make eye contact with someone. It doesn't have to be for a long time, nor does it need to be some kind of self-conscious stare or involve any special facial expression. Just relax, open, and connect your heart to your eyes.
- As your eyes meet, let that person see your heart through

your eyes. You make no attempt to project love or anything else out of your eyes. This is a receptive exercise, where you feel your heart and open your eyes, letting another see the love and compassion you have for that person as another human being. Again, this is a transpersonal practice, *not* a personal flirtation. It matters not whether the person with whom you connect is the same or opposite gender. Seeing from the heart—letting others see your heart through your eyes—creates a bridge between two souls and reflects our common humanity.

Touching from Your Heart

It is no accident that when something stimulates your heart, you may say you were touched. Our tactile sense—our need to touch and be touched—is essential to our psychological and even our physical survival. Numerous studies have shown that baby monkeys deprived of touch languish or die; the same can happen with human infants.

You spiritualize your sense of touch by doing the following:

- Put your attention in your heart. Feel it.
- As you touch someone, maintain awareness of your heart.

Does it really make a difference whether you are aware of your heart when you shake hands with someone or touch in some other way? That question can be answered only in your own experience. I suggest that you will feel the difference in your own heart, in the quality of your attention and connection. And that the other person will feel it as well.

Listening from Your Heart

Many Buddhists believe that by listening deeply—by listening alone—we alleviate suffering. The practice of listening from your heart may be for many of us the most important practice of all. For many of us, listening is nothing more than a chance to think of what we are going to say next while the other person is speaking. Before some people become hard of hearing, they become hard of listening. We forget people's names because we hardly heard them in the first place, since our attention was elsewhere. The following practice can strengthen, mend, or even save relationships:

- Put your attention in your heart. Feel it.
- Consciously connect your heart with your ears by this act of attention.
- Placing feeling-attention on your ears (rather than on your thoughts), just listen.

Although others don't always acknowledge it, a part of them knows whether or not you are truly listening. A quality of heartful attention—treating what they say as the most important thing in the world in that moment—is one of the greatest gifts you can give to another. It values and validates them and encourages them to open up and express their truth.

When you listen from your heart, you listen without judgments, expectations, or opinions. You enter their world without demanding that they enter yours. And without knowing why, they are likely to find you one of the most charming conversationalists they have ever known.

The Healing Heart

These simple, pleasurable practices of connecting your heart to your voice, thought, sight, touch, and hearing are forms of spiritual practice that produces emotional healing in relationships. When your attention rests in your heart, it has risen above fear, sorrow, and anger. These heartfelt practices enable your attention to rise above emotional weather into the infinite space of love. Whether or not you experience their impact on others, you will soon know their impact on your awakening heart.

> Love cures people, the ones who receive love
> and the ones who give it, too.
>
> —Dr. Karl Menninger

Hearts, Flowers, and Global Shifts

As your heart awakens, and your sense of separation and isolation begins to fade, you will experience a variety of perceptual and behavioral shifts.

From Differences to Common Humanity

Those you previously viewed as strangers, you will come to see as members of your human family. Even as you appreciate and value our rich global heritage of religious, cultural, racial, and collective diversity—humanity's treasure house of wisdom—you will see beyond these differences to connect with people at the deeper levels of our common humanity.

Even as we speak different languages and practice different customs, religions, and rituals, we have infinitely more in common than we have differences. As your perception shifts, you will come to see every human as a brother or a sister, all in this adventure together, seeking meaning, purpose, happiness, love— sharing the same Mother Earth, seeing the same sun rise in the morning and set at night, feeling the same rhythms of nature and human life, loving our children, sitting under the same moon and stars at night, and wondering, and dreaming, and weaving our stories.

From Competition to Cooperation

As your heart awakens to our essential unity, you will begin to lose your taste not for excellence or achievement, but for the competitive mind. Instead you will find a growing commitment to cooperate with others toward common goals. The shift will come from within (rather than be imposed by an outside authority)— not from philosophical or political abstractions, but from a realistic understanding of how to survive and thrive together in the new millennium. The natural urge to join together as strong, unique individuals in cooperative communities will lead to new sports and games, institutions, and ways of being and doing that will reflect your evolving awareness, values, perceptions, and behavior.

From Personal to Transpersonal Love

So many songs and books about romantic love focus on satisfying the separate self. The promise of the eleventh gateway—transpersonal love—means recognizing the same consciousness alive in others as in yourself. We continue to love our mate, our children, our relatives and friends, but love our extended human family no less. Love becomes a way of life, no longer something we dole out only to a special few. Transpersonal love is the recognition that every soul is

- looking to find happiness
- seeking to avoid suffering
- fighting our own battles with fear, insecurity, self-doubt
- searching for greater meaning, purpose, and connection
- climbing our own mountains
- awakening to the truth that we are, each and all, fellow schoolmates on planet Earth.

Such a series of recognitions wakes the heart from its slumber. Love breaks through the walls of divisiveness and separation. Fragmentation gives way to unity. A transcendent worldview emerges, based on the connection of all creation, so that you finally see all people, all life, as the same Consciousness, the Light of God, manifesting as billions of beings, shining through each and all of us. You finally realize that you are that Light.

Even after this awakening, the everyday world and all its challenges reappear. But with the eleventh arrow of enlightenment in your quiver, you are ready to give back to the world. For the heart, awakened by love, turns naturally to service.

Love and do what you will.

—St. Augustine

THE

TWELFTH GATEWAY

Serve
Your World

❧

*Service is an attitude
founded on the recognition
that the world has supported you,
fed you, taught you, tested you,
whether or not you earned it.
Understanding this simple truth
can move you to do what you can
to repay a boundless debt of gratitude.
Service is both a means and an end,
for in giving to others,
you open yourself
to love, abundance, and inner peace.
You cannot serve others without uplifting yourself.*

Completing the Circle of Life

*The purpose of life is not to be happy—but
to matter, to be productive, to be useful,
to have it make some difference
that you lived at all.*

—Leo Rosten

Road Map: Enlightenment in Action

We come to the final gateway, the final step up the stairway to the soul, the completion of a journey preparing you for the ultimate practice of everyday enlightenment.

I first glimpsed the power of service as a collegiate gymnast. At first, most of my attention was dedicated to myself—my progress, my body, my problems—until I realized that I enjoyed helping others learn new elements even more than learning those elements myself. When I learned a skill, one person benefited; when I taught that skill, many could benefit. I didn't know it then, but once I stumbled upon the satisfaction of helping others, my life as a teacher had begun.

Years later, after a lengthy search for personal enlightenment, my exclusive self-focus again shifted to learning not only for my sake, but for the sake of others. Coincident with this shift, extraordinary teachers began to appear in my life, and doors opened within me and in the world.

Submitting ourselves to the needs of others makes heroes of us all. There are countless ways to make a difference—like stopping to assist someone in need, reaching down to pick up a piece of litter on the street, sharing your talents and energy with others

309

in practical ways—this is what it means to be a part of the human family. Making our every interaction with people at the grocery store, the print shop, the bank, the hairdresser, a chance to leave someone feeling a little better is serving our world, enlightenment in action.

Again I repeat: You are not here to contact your higher self; you are here to *become* it. And there is no surer or greater path to embodying the courage and love of your higher self than self-sacrificing service. Serving those around you in the spirit of love becomes everyday enlightenment.

As you discover the joy of service, your life may or may not experience dramatic shifts or monetary abundance. But you won't care about that any more than Mother Teresa cared if she was having a bad hair day when she tended the sick or blind or lame. You'll be too busy making a positive difference in this world, connecting to the circle of life.

We begin *Serve Your World* by resolving the apparent contradiction between working on oneself and serving others, followed by a reflection on the gift of life; finding your calling; putting your money where your heart is; and how small, everyday acts can make a big difference in the world. Throughout this gateway you will find stories about the kindness of strangers, as a reminder to create and share stories of your own.

The Heart of Service

Let's start with the words of Lynne Twist, a founder of the Hunger Project, on "The Heart of Service":

> People think service is a kind of charity—strong people giving to weak people, healthy people giving to sick people, rich people giving to poor people, together people giving to people who aren't so together.
>
> To me, true service is an experience of wholeness, fulfillment, fullness, self-reliance, and self-sufficiency for all parties—an experience of the magnificence and infinite capacity of human be-

ings. When I'm really in service, I disappear. My identity is no longer present. I am one with he or she or that which I am serving. It is actually an experience of God, of unity and wholeness. There is nobody giving and nobody receiving. None of that is happening. There is only an experience of unity. We begin to see that we are the expression of one soul.

An act of service is an act of love and of trust. It's also an act of responsibility and of courage . . . a stand for the integrity of human life.

Service Is an Attitude: Questions to Ponder

Until your attention, energy, and heart are free, service appears as either a guilty omission or a social obligation. Or you may not appreciate the service you already provide in the world, in everyday ways at home or work. Consider these questions to reflect upon your relationship to service:

- When you hear or read the phrase "serve your world," what are the first five words that come to mind? (Say them quickly, now.)
- Do you do any volunteer work? Why? Why not?
- Beyond services you normally provide at work or at home, name three forms of service, large or small, you've provided in the past twenty-four hours.
- If you were independently wealthy, how would you spend your time?
- How would you spend your money?
- Do you help others when it is convenient?
- Do you help others when it is inconvenient?
- How did it feel when you've done someone a service?
- When you do someone a favor, do you expect thanks? Is it possible you should be the one thanking them?
- Name your three best accomplishments. Pick any one of them. Can you think of at least ten people whose skills or services helped you to accomplish it? (There are many more than ten.)

● Whether or not you are paid, your work in the world is a form of service. What form of service would you most like to provide in the world? What have you done to set this in motion?

These questions serve as an entrée into a new experience of living and open the twelfth gateway within your psyche. Let's now explore what may be the ultimate purpose of human life.

Self-Service and the Leverage for Change

Social activists argue that in the real world we need to focus our efforts and energy on helping others, political action, striving to make peace among nations. Mystics claim that we will not find peace in the world until we find it within ourselves.

Years ago, a single incident reconciled for me this apparent conflict between social activism and inner work. It happened during a period of intense spiritual growth work on myself—meditation, prayer, contemplation, visualization, bodywork, and self-analysis. One afternoon, as I was walking with an old man I called Socrates, we came upon several large posters on the side of a building. One showed the gaunt faces of starving children; next to it was a plea to help oppressed people around the world; the third pictured the plight of endangered species.

"You know, Socrates," I said, pointing to the posters, "I feel guilty, or selfish, doing all this work on myself when there are so many people in need—"

Soc stopped abruptly, turned to me, and said, "Take a swing at me."

"What do you mean, take a swing at you? Did you hear what I said?"

"Come on," he urged, moving like a boxer, goading me. "I'll give you five dollars if you can slap me on the cheek."

I figured this was some kind of test, so I took a swing—and found myself on the ground in a painful wrist lock. As Soc helped me to my feet, he made his point. "You notice how effective the right leverage can be?"

"Yes," I said, shaking out my wrist. "I noticed."

"Before you can help others, you need to understand them. Before you can understand them, you need to understand yourself. Then you will know how to exert the right leverage at the right place and at the right time. The more clarity and courage your actions reflect, the more impact your efforts will have."

Ben Franklin once wrote, "God helps them that help themselves." This is a self-help book in the best sense in that it can help you cultivate the heart and will to help others. As you transcend your own limitations and tendencies, you will naturally show loving-kindness to others. As your own light shines more brightly, you illuminate the world.

Rabbi Hillel wrote, "If I am not for myself, who will be for me? If I am for myself alone, what am I?" If you help only yourself, constantly looking out for number one, you lose your connection to the human family and tear the fabric of which you are one thread; but if you serve only others while remaining a stranger to yourself, your service remains a hollow act of separation, a dismal chore devoid of healing power.

A Story of Service: It Is Good

James from Texas wrote:

Four years ago, on a cold and wet Sunday, where the plains of East Africa meet the forested slopes of Mount Kenya, my motorcycle broke down. Getting it to a garage cost me my last shilling. Stranded fifty miles from home, I knew no one with whom I could stay until morning, [so] I chose to spend the night in the doorway of a small church.

Near dusk, a threadbare, elderly Kikuyu man walked by and we struck up a conversation. Njoroge was the pastor of a tiny church. When he learned of my predicament, he invited me to spend the night at his house. He and his wife were squatters in a dilapidated, abandoned European farmhouse. We warmed ourselves around a cooking fire beside the porch. They apologized for having no tea to serve me. I noticed that they had nothing in which to boil water, anyway. Njoroge's wife, who spoke neither English nor Swahili, cooked me an immense mound of potatoes mixed with corn and beans.

Although my Swahili is limited, Njoroge and I talked late into the night about religion, white settlers, freedom, and the tragedy of people so desperate for firewood that they cut down the forest. Njoroge and his wife insisted that I take their bed—newspapers and cardboard covered with a blanket.

The next morning, my host served me a cup of tea he had purchased at a mud-and-thatch hut a half-mile away. Afterward, I hitchhiked home, grateful to this old man and his wife, and chastened by the knowledge that they had given me a larger portion of their belongings than I had ever given anyone, stranger or best friend.

When I returned the following weekend to retrieve my motorcycle, I took the old couple an aluminum tea kettle, a strainer, tea, and some sugar. Njoroge wasn't home, but his wife greeted me warmly. Some people say that the Kikuyu are an ungrateful people because the words "thank you" don't exist in their language. The expression they use instead means "it is good." Njoroge's wife shyly accepted my gift and smiled, and we both said that it was good.

How Will You Spend Your Life?

Millions of people in this world have earned or inherited enough wealth so that they never again need to work for money. Some then give of their time and talent in creative service to the world. Others, because they have not yet seen their shadows or awakened their hearts, may remain self-absorbed, idling their time on amusements, esoteric pleasures, traveling, collecting sensory experiences, playing with power and status and influence. Such people are lost and need our compassion more than our misguided envy or quick judgments. Their naked pain, clothed over with the trappings of wealth or power, will eventually lead them to a form of useful service.

> There must be more to life
> than having everything!
>
> **—Maurice Sendak**

Millions of people are born into a culture of poverty. Preoccupied with the struggle for survival, dealing with pressure of relationships, assailed by worries, they are not yet free to consider the power of service to the larger world. For them, God is bread and service is the struggle to survive another day, another season. Abundance to share with others is not yet even a dream. Yet they, too, are led to sacrifice and serve in order to feed their families and cling together for the common good.

Thus the winding paths of both wealth and poverty lead to service, as do all the paths of life.

Love and Do What You Will

Once you establish physical and spiritual sufficiency, and find enough free attention, self-worth, and will to cultivate a balanced, energized body; once you rise above the storms of the mind and emotions to trust your intuition, meet your shadow and face your fears, embrace both your sexuality and your humanity, and awaken your heart—you will have nothing left to do, and nothing that gives you greater meaning or joy, than simple service.

> What you are is God's gift to you;
> What you make of it is your gift to God.
>
> **—Anthony Dalla Villa**

Given that no one ever perfectly masters all the gateways, and that work in each gateway contributes to mastery of all others, ask yourself: How can I begin now to share my energy, my talent, my heart, with others? What would I choose to do if I were already whole and complete? How would I spend my time, my energy, my life? What will be my priorities?

Even as we hike up, sometimes struggle up, the mountain, we can help others to do the same. Once we awaken to the reality that we are responsible for our own life, we come to realize that we are, in a larger sense, responsible for the care of our entire human family.

A Story of Service: A Simple Act of Kindness

Susan from Washington wrote:

My friend Murphy was broke. He was teaching one night class at college, and it didn't pay much. One of his students was a long-haired, barefoot-in-winter guy who looked to be in his thirties—a thoughtful, hardworking student whose life seemed generally disorganized. In this respect, he was like Murphy, who had a big warm coat and not much else besides a great education.

The barefoot student kept Murphy after class one evening with questions. When they walked outside it was snowing, and the guy asked if he could get a ride. Murphy said, Sure. As they drove toward the student's home, Murphy began talking about a beautiful piece of land he wanted to buy—a steal, but still beyond his means. The guy asked how much it cost, and Murphy told him, a little apologetically. It seemed greedy to want it, considering how little this other guy had. After all, Murphy did have his big coat, a twenty-year-old VW bug, a paycheck, and a room to live in. It wasn't a very nice room, but hell, he had shoes.

Anyway, this guy without shoes was a great listener. Murphy appreciated it, and was getting ready to see what kind of shelter or food he could offer when suddenly the guy said, "Well, I can help with the land." Murphy smiled at the jest, but the guy explained that he had a lot of money and hadn't thought of a good way to use it, except to take courses sometimes and help out people who knew what they wanted.

The guy ended up buying the land in Murphy's name on a no-interest loan. Murphy kept driving the VW bug and wearing the big old coat. He paid off the loan, built a cabin, got married, began raising kids, and got a job he adores. It began with a simple act of kindness.

The Gift of Life

Imagine for a moment that, through a strange twist of fate, you wake up one morning and find yourself imprisoned in a nameless country and for political reasons scheduled for execution at midnight. You gaze out through prison bars and see the first rays of your last sunrise. A rooster crowing in the distance sounds poignantly sweet. You feel greedy for every sight, every sound, taste, and aroma. You eat your last meal as the shadows grow long outside. And as the sun sets, you say your final farewell to the light of day, for you will never again see the sunrise. Each passing minute draws you closer to your final good-bye, your last prayer, and, finally, your last breath.

A final day awaits us all.

We may know in advance when our end is near, through declining health, a terminal illness, old age. Or we may have only a few seconds' notice, or none at all.

When the executioner raises his scythe, how many of us may want to say, "Wait! Just another moment, please! Let me take one more sweet breath! Give me one more sight, sound, touch of my beloved! Wait, please! Just one more moment!"

Now is the time to see, to listen, to touch—bring our best to life while we have the life for it. How much we have, no one can say. Life itself is a near-death experience.

Consider how we appear from nowhere, as microscopic specks on a minuscule, blue-green dot moving through the infinity of space and time. Our lives are ephemeral and brief, each of us one cell among billions on the planet, and yet we strive to love, to serve, to find meaning and fulfillment while we live. Life itself is a hero's journey.

Contemplating how we came to be here is like trying to find the ends of space. We find no answers, only wonder and awe and gratitude for being invited. Counting our blessings leads to a desire to give something back. Thus begins the path of service, the fruit of our journey, the gateway to joy.

The purpose of life is a life of purpose.

—Robert Byrne

A Story of Service: Giving and Receiving

Pete from North Carolina wrote:

I decided to pick him up because I knew it wasn't easy to get a ride if you had a dog. His name was John, and he was wearing old, dirty jeans, a beret, and no shirt. His torso was tan and lean. I was reminded of Christ's long body hanging from the cross.

He put his sheep dog named Sailor in the back. In the rearview mirror, Sailor's big stern face, with one ear hanging down and the other standing up, was deadly serious, as if he were watching over John, who had a very different demeanor.

I tried to make small talk, but nothing he said in response made any sense. When I asked him about his childhood, where he had grown up, he squinted. "I remember the archery," he said, then paused before continuing solemnly, "The Red Cross can't help me."

I gathered that he was penniless and homeless and that he had probably been released from a mental institution. He said he'd go as far as I was going.

That night I stopped at a McDonald's. I asked if I could get him a couple of burgers. He said no, but he dug into his pocket, pulled out a quarter, and asked if I'd get him an ice-cream cone. I went inside, deciding to buy some extra burgers and then pretend to be too full to eat them.

When I came out, feeling ticklish with covert kindness, I found John and Sailor gorging on burgers from the garbage.

From the Dumpster, he said, "Do you want any?"

Late that night he said that soon time machines would be commonplace. He told me he was going to Canada to see a cousin who would give him some plywood so he could make a boat from it, and all orphans would be welcome.

I let him out under a bridge on the interstate. Clumsily, I tried to give him money, but he said no. Instead he would sell me his beret. Deal.

Five years later, I saw John again. I was driving down the interstate with a van full of kids, so I couldn't stop. Sailor was with him, one ear still up, one down. John had on a new hat, a brightly colored beret embroidered with gold. I think I helped him out a little that day; I think he helped me, too.

Follow Your Heart to Find Your Calling

When, through accident, intent, or design, you feel the call to serve others, your dilemma becomes, How can I best serve? Just as most of us search for or stumble upon a form of livelihood, so we come upon ways to make a difference in the world.

Some people have written me to suggest that I make a career presenting peaceful warrior trainings to prison inmates. Others have proposed that I make youth my mission. Still others have suggested that I could do the most good working with corporate executives or with men's groups. I have in fact spoken with inmates and corporate executives and with youth and men's groups. But my calling involves working with people from *all* walks of life who are drawn to my writings, talks, or audio programs. There are other people who have been called to working with prison inmates, or the ill or dying, or with youth or executives in the corporate world. We each need to follow our own mission and heart's desire rather than be driven by the dictates of guilt or obligation. It is unlikely, for example, that Mother Teresa got up each day and said, "Oh, darn, I've got to go work with these lepers again." On the contrary, she said she saw the face of Jesus in everyone she served.

Find a form of service that calls to you, that suits your abilities, aptitudes, qualities, and interests, that makes time fly, that draws forth your best effort and energy, that tells you you've arrived home and found yourself.

Service and Self-Worth

In the final gateway you have come full circle, in the sense that the action of service provides the ultimate means to establish a solid sense of self-worth, which, you have learned, can favorably impact every facet of your life—so much so that it is questionable whether the receiver or giver of service should offer the most thanks. The following letter I received several years ago stands as a testament to the power of service in helping to enhance our sense of worth and the quality of our lives.

A Story of Service: Surprising Change

Todd from Kansas City wrote:

About two years ago, I called your office, Dan, and asked to speak with you. You happened to be in the office, and we spoke briefly. I remember telling you that I was twenty-eight years old, and feeling kind of lost. My girlfriend wasn't sure whether she wanted to stay with me, and I was sick of my work but didn't know what I wanted to do with my life. I'm not sure what else I said, but I remember that you said something that really irritated me. You said that I might want to consider volunteering some-where—at a hospice, or a hospital, or an organization I believed in—some kind of community service. I felt like you were brush-ing me off, since you didn't respond to the problems I had raised. I was really surprised how angry I was that you would make such an irrelevant suggestion that didn't help me at all.

The reason I'm writing now is that about six months after that phone conversation, I found myself volunteering at a youth center—you know, helping kids in sports. A lot of them didn't have fathers around or other male figures in their lives.

I just wanted you to know that volunteering at that youth center changed my life. Everything seems to be working better now. I don't know what happened, but I just wanted to thank you.

Ways to Serve

When you ask the question "How can I help?" you may look for a local charity or organization that accepts volunteers. They are available in every city and town. In fact, many groups and organizations can exist only if supported by a core of volunteers, and your help is needed and appreciated. Some opportunities include

- working with environmental organizations
- visiting homes for the elderly
- working with youth at recreation centers, or as a Big Brother or Big Sister
- staffing a suicide prevention hot line
- painting, repairing, or decorating a homeless or women's shelter
- helping build a home with Habitat for Humanity
- working as a teacher's aid at a local school
- helping in hospitals
- working at a hospice
- creating your own ways to serve and to help (since the preceding list only touches the tip of the iceberg).

The Internet or local library can provide a list of many possible organizations seeking volunteer help. It sometimes happens that volunteer work turns into a career, or at least helps clarify your purpose and direction, while also making a difference to others.

An act as simple as giving a gift increases serotonin levels in the blood, releasing endorphins (natural opiates) that produce a natural high. Perhaps that explains the comment of my friend, Swami Beyondananda, who said he was angry with his higher self because "it's always getting high without me."

A Story of Service: Common Ground and Compassion

Ann from Washington wrote:

My husband, Mark, was in and out of the hospital for three

years with leukemia. During one two-week stay, he shared a small room with a man named Paul, who had lymphoma. The first day, he watched Paul dab cotton balls in lotion and carefully stroke his skin. Then Paul rubbed moisturizer on his face and slicked back his hair with a sweet-smelling oil. When he began buffing his nails, Mark yanked the curtain shut between the two beds.

"It's not enough that I'm sick, but I've got to share a room with some fag," he whispered. He pointed to the curtain. "We're keeping this closed."

I visited every day, and the curtain was always closed. I could hear Paul's bottles and jars clink together during his cleaning routine, and Mark banged his shaving gear around in response.

But on the tenth day, I walked in to find the curtain open. It was hot in the room, and both men dozed without even sheets to cover them. Mark's long legs had lost all their muscle tone, and tiny bruises were sprinkled over his skin like grains of purple pepper. Paul's face was jaundiced, and a bit of blood dripped from his mouth. Wet towels, dirty pajamas, and newspapers were heaped on the floor near Mark's bed, but Paul's clothing and toiletries were neatly arranged on the wide shelf. This was the original Odd Couple, I thought—the only thing these men have in common is cancer.

When Mark left for chemotherapy, I visited with Paul. "Last night," he said, "I was throwing up, and crying because I wanted to go home. Mark got out of bed and wheeled his IV over here and sat with me until I calmed down."

Later I told Mark what Paul had said, but Mark brushed it off. "Just returning the favor. A few nights ago I was puking and bawling, and Paul opened the curtain and came over and just sat here."

At home a month later, Mark got a postcard from Paul. It said he would be hard pressed, if hospitalized again, to find another roommate as kind as Mark.

Mark has since died. I assume Paul did, too. But their encounter reminds me that a simple act of kindness can somehow make the worst of times endurable.

Putting Your Money Where Your Heart Is

Is it better to pick up a hammer and nails and volunteer to help build a house or to donate money so a professional carpenter can do it? The answer: They're both valuable. Building a house involves your direct energy and time, but so does earning the money to write a check. And helping to hire a professional carpenter may get the house built better and faster than if you volunteered.

Money can be a powerful form of service. Sending money to a homeless shelter may not be as satisfying (from the viewpoint of the sender) as putting on overalls and joining others in painting the shelter, but from the viewpoint of those receiving the funds, it makes a big difference. Ask any charity what donors mean to them. Countless charities are crying out for financial aid. As much as they appreciate volunteers, few can exist on volunteer labor; they need the lifeblood of funds to do their work.

Those of you whose seeds of creativity, initiative, intelligence, ingenuity, and labor have reaped an abundant harvest can make a real difference in the world through charitable enterprise. One of the greatest joys and blessings of making a lot of money is in sharing it—not because you have to or should, but because you realize your interconnectedness and appreciate the chance to show love and compassion in action.

The Dilemma of Philanthropy

How do you know where your money will do the most good? Is it best to give most or all of your charitable donation to a single organization or spread it among many? Shall you support the poor or the environment or human rights organizations or medical research? Shall you focus on local, national, or international charities? Is it best to give to the same organizations year after year or stagger your donations? Which is more useful, helping someone go to college who couldn't otherwise afford it or helping the poorest of the poor find shelter and food?

I wouldn't even attempt to answer these agonizing questions—but I know how good it feels to reach out a helping hand when that hand can offer financial support to those in need.

If you had a million dollars to give away, how could you produce the most good? Probably not by giving one dollar to each of a million people. Giving ten dollars to each of one hundred thousand people still wouldn't have much impact. If you gave one hundred dollars to each of ten thousand people, you would probably bring a smile to many faces, but the money would soon be spent. If you gave one thousand dollars to one thousand people you would produce greater impact for those who made wise use of their gift. If you gave ten thousand dollars to each of one hundred people, you would reach fewer people but might make a real difference—perhaps helping to bring families out of debt or sending children through college. If you divided your million by giving one hundred thousand dollars to each of ten people, it might well change their lives.

Ted's Excellent Idea

The hand of billionaire Ted Turner shook when he signed the papers giving more than $200 million to charity—to universities and the environment. "I knew I was taking myself out of the running for the richest man in America," he said. But Mr. Turner had found that giving away money can be even more satisfying than making it. He has challenged his fellow billionaires, or ol' skinflints, as he calls them—to open their purse strings wider. Mr. Turner then suggested we start an annual list of the most generous patrons, offering an Ebenezer Scrooge Prize that embarrasses stingy billionaires and a Heart of Gold Award to honor philanthropists. "What difference does it make," he said, "if you're worth twelve billion or eleven billion? With a billion dollars you can build a university!"

You don't have to be a millionaire to make a difference. Giving ten dollars here and twenty dollars there can work wonders. Even people on the line of poverty express their human dignity and worth by giving what they can to causes they believe in. If ten thousand poor people each give ten dollars to a charity they believe in, they would have given a hundred thousand dollars. Not too bad for poor people with generous hearts.

If you have much give of your wealth,
if you have little give of your heart.

—Arab Proverb

A Life-Changing Gift

Even those of modest income have been shining examples of putting their money where their hearts are. Oseola McCarty, an aging washerwoman who had lived alone since 1967, felt at eighty-eight years of age that her life was nearing its completion. Since she had no living relatives, she decided to give $150,000—her entire life's savings, putting away one dollar at a time—to the University of Southern Mississippi.

Oseola did this simply because it seemed the right thing to do. Her generosity touched so many people that she found herself flying across America, accepting humanitarian awards and meeting many famous people, including Whoopi Goldberg, who knelt at her feet; and Roberta Flack, who sang for her. Harvard University gave her an honorary degree; President Clinton asked to have his picture taken with her; she even carried the Olympic torch a little ways. And Oseola McCarty's portrait now graces the wall in the administration building at the University of Southern Mississippi—the first portrait of a black person to do so. She appeared on *Good Morning America*. Her story was on the front page of *The New York Times*. Barbara Walters named her one of the Ten Most Interesting People of 1995. She was also featured in numerous magazines, such as *Ebony, People, Guideposts,* and *Glamour*. She even appeared on British television.

Other donors have followed Oseola's gift with more than $250,000 to her original endowment, all due to the generous heart of a hardworking woman who wanted to make a difference before going to the next world.

Story of Service: Words of Encouragement

Jim from Washington wrote:

I was in my early teens in a mall on Long Island where I grew up. I was sitting on a bench reading an Edgar Rice Burroughs paperback I'd just purchased, when an old man of African heritage, wearing a well-worn suit, sat down next to me and asked me what I was reading. I showed him. He complimented me for being a reader and strongly encouraged me to continue to read as voraciously as my heart desired. Then he said he had to go, but that if I was ever in a town called Wyandance I could visit him at the school where he was the principal.

That this man stopped to talk to me and offer words of encouragement touched me then, and it touches me now, as I remember it. I still love to read, and write as well. I make my living operating a bookstore.

Small Acts That Make a Big Difference

Volunteering at an organization is one way to serve your world. You can also do any number of little things in daily life that have great spiritual significance: a kind word to a stranger, a note of appreciation to a bank clerk, waiter, or postal carrier, even letting someone into your lane on the highway—these are among the most important forms of everyday service you can contribute.

Small acts of service not only make a big difference to others; they also transform our own lives. Because what we need even more than personal happiness is a sense of meaning, purposes, and connection—a sense provided by small, everyday acts of service.

Small services anyone can do to uplift others include

- paying more than is charged for a service
- writing a note thanking a waiter or waitress, postal carrier, trash collector, bank teller, gardener, or someone else for a specific service he or she provided
- putting a quarter into an expired meter

- buying a sandwich and giving it to a hungry person
- picking up litter
- cleaning up a rest-room sink after using it
- making a donation, whether identified or anonymous
- when buying tickets, getting extras and giving them to someone
- passing by a parking space and letting the person behind you have it (when they won't even realize you did them a service)
- practicing the spiritual senses you learned in the eleventh gateway—speaking, seeing, touching, and listening from your heart
- spending a hundred dollars a year buying gift certificates to a movie theater, coffeehouse, bookstore, or candy store that you pass out randomly or to people who do you a service
- offering a silent (or audible) blessing, warm greeting, or even a smile to people you meet.

A Story of Service: A Sermon in Action

Sandra from New York sent me the following story:

One afternoon years ago, reporters and officials gathered at a Chicago train station, awaiting the arrival of a Nobel Prize winner. He stepped off the train—a giant of a man, with bushy hair and a large mustache. As the cameras flashed, the officials extended their hands and began telling him how honored they were to meet him. The doctor thanked them and then, looking over their heads, asked if he might be excused for a moment.

Walking through the crowd with quick steps, he soon reached the side of an elderly woman who was having trouble trying to carry two large suitcases. He picked up the bags in his large hands and, with a kind smile, escorted the woman to a bus. As the doctor helped her board, he wished her a safe journey. Then, since the crowd had tagged along behind him, he turned and apologized to them for keeping them waiting.

The man was Dr. Albert Schweitzer, the famous missionary-physician who had spent his life helping the poorest of the poor in Africa. Said a member of the reception committee to one of the reporters: "That's the first time I ever saw a sermon walking."

A Lifesaving Smile

Some years ago, after finishing a talk in a Southern California bookstore, a woman came up to me and said in a voice so quiet I could hardly hear her, "Excuse me, Dan—could I have just a moment?"

I said yes and waited. It took her another moment to speak: "What you said—about little things making a big difference? Well, I just wanted you to know, I suppose this sounds melodramatic, but I wanted you to know how a man's smile once saved a life—my life."

She had my attention as she continued. "I've always been shy. About four years ago I was also suicidal—I had made two half-hearted attempts, but I had decided I was going to do it once and for all. I didn't believe anyone cared whether I lived or died, so I didn't care, either. I was on the way home where I was going to do it, when I saw a man—a nice-looking man, walking in the opposite direction. I don't usually look at people, but in the state I was in, it didn't matter, so I looked at him and he looked back and smiled at me." She smiled as she said this. "He had a wonderful smile, and then he was gone.

"It sounds crazy, I know," she said, "but his smiling at me—it was something I wanted to hold on to for a while, so I—I didn't kill myself that day, or the next. Then I decided to stick around and get some help. Things are better now. I have a boyfriend I love a lot, and a job I like. I just wanted you to know that little things sure can make a difference. Oh, and my name is Cheryl," she said, smiling.

Cheryl's story has a clear moral: Although a few of us have an exaggerated sense of self-importance, most of us don't have enough self-importance. We forget that people are watching us, learning from us, being affected and influenced by our example.

Few of us really understand how a kind word, a note to a waiter or waitress, the act of picking up some litter in the street, or flashing a smile can offer needed encouragement, lift someone's spirit, or make their day. And who knows? It might even save a life.

Practicing Everyday Enlightenment

The student has hindsight;
. the teacher has foresight;
the master has insight.
In the school of daily life,
you are here to become
a student, a teacher, and a master—
one who learns from the past,
foresees the consequences of your actions,
and finally, looks within
to discover the Universe.

Daily Life as Spiritual Practice

I died as a mineral and became a plant.
I died as a plant and rose to animal.
I died as animal and I was human.
Why should I fear? When was I less by dying?
And when I die to what is human,
to soar with angels blessed;
and even from angelhood I must pass on,
to become what no mind ever conceived.

—Rumi

Reaching the Summit

In exploring the twelve gateways—completing this journey up your inner mountain, the soul's stairway—you have reached the summit and accomplished more than you may yet realize. Your psyche has changed; your vision has expanded to new horizons; you have seen the bigger picture, purpose, and promise of everyday life.

Yet the twelve gateways are not a destination; they are a process, an ongoing journey. Before we look ahead, let's stop, as we might on a mountain peak, and take a panoramic look at where we have been.

Discover Your Worth: You are no more or less worthy than any other person or part of reality. Your sense of worth grows by doing what is worthy. But you do not have to *feel* worthy; you need only treat yourself as you would a loved one or honored guest, ending self-destructive behaviors or cycles of self-sabotage, opening to life's opportunities.

Reclaim Your Will: When motivation lags, your willpower takes over. You will use your will when you stop waiting to feel motivated. Life has always come down to this: The ripest fruit grows on the highest limbs of the tree of life. To pick the fruit you make the climb, step by step, day by day.

Energize Your Body: Your body is all you have for a lifetime. Attend to the holy trinity of health: light diet, regular exercise, and rest. Practice full breathing and you will maximize your genetic potential, find greater health, vitality, and energy for life's many facets and adventures.

Manage Your Money: First rise above negative, hidden attitudes about money. Value and use money wisely, as you would any other form of energy. Stretch your talents and abilities to produce stable, sufficient, even abundant income, then spend, give, and save.

Tame Your Mind: Remember that the world is not what you think. Look beyond your filters to grasp the world as it is, in its moment-to-moment simplicity. Let thoughts be, focus your attention on the matter at hand in this moment, and you will find inner peace and illumination.

Trust Your Intuition: You know and can access far more than you have read or studied or been told. Trust this deeply rooted, ancient human capacity. Become whole by using, respecting, and trusting both sides of your brain, but not at the same time. Listen to your mind, but trust your heart.

Accept Your Emotions: Life without emotions would be as calm as death, like a world without weather. Accept feelings as they are; pleasant or painful, they are natural and don't need fixing. Let them rise and pass without allowing changeable emotions to run your life.

Face Your Fears: Fear is a chameleon that can be a wise guide in one moment and a terrible tyrant the next. Respect fear, but never let it be your master. If physical danger is involved, listen well; if psychological danger challenges you, then do what you most fear—live as a peaceful warrior.

Illuminate Your Shadow: You have to deal with the darkness before you see your light. The image you present to the world is but the visible tip of the iceberg. Embrace all your opposites;

illuminuate the darkness of your psyche so that you live consciously in the light, finding wholeness, authenticity, compassion.

Embrace Your Sexuality: Your approach to sexuality mirrors your relationship to life. Sexual enlightenment transcends both self-denial and self-indulgence to find a full and balanced expression of sexual-creative energy, forming an intimate bond between you, your partner, and Spirit.

Awaken Your Heart: As you have seen, the emotion of love comes and goes like waves. Enduring love of the awakened heart is not a feeling but an action. Combining love and will, you walk the same path as the saints by showing loving-kindness to all other beings whether or not you feel like it.

Serve Your World: When you have seen what there is to see, when life has revealed you to yourself as you are, your search becomes how to best serve. Life itself—your work, family, and every interaction—is a chance to serve, to connect, to find meaning in the moment and purpose in the play.

Now that you have reached the summit of the twelve gateways, you are ready to understand and apply the practice of everyday enlightenment. Let's consider what that means. You know that life is made up of a series of moments and that no one is nice, or intelligent, or dull, or neurotic, or enlightened all the time. It is simply not realistic. So the practice of enlightenment should not be taken as some kind of idealized, all-the-time-pie-in-the-sky perfection. Rather, the title and promise of this book—*Everyday Enlightenment*—is about creating more enlightened moments every day, moments that illuminate and complete each of the twelve gateways. One moment you come from a place of infinite worth; in another moment, when most needed, you call forth a will of iron—and moments of free-flowing energy, intuition, authenticity, courage, love, and service. Every single day. Improving over time. Remember that life is a work in progress and that you are a HIT—a human-in-training. Trying to "have it all together" all the time is like trying to eat once and for all.

Now that you understand the practical context of everyday enlightenment, we turn to the most transcendent everyday practice you may learn in this lifetime.

The Ultimate Awakening

In the spiritual traditions, "enlightenment" is often referred to as the endgame, the highest human destiny, surpassing every achievement or pleasure and transcending life and death. Enlightenment is most often described as a state of self-realization, unity, awakening, nirvana, satori, or grace. The main problem with such important-sounding words is that none of them sound relevant to addressing the practical challenges of everyday life. To many of us, this whole idea of enlightenment seems irrelevant, elsewhere, out of reach, or only at the summit of a secret mystical path traveled by a rare few. But to what end?

Even in the spiritual traditions, a hundred different teachers give a hundred different descriptions, ranging from "the ultimate realization" to "nothing special."

In the *Way of the Peaceful Warrior,* the following story illustrates the paradoxical nature of enlightenment:

> A young man searching for enlightenment comes upon an old man walking down a mountain path, carrying a heavy sack on his back. The young seeker senses that this wise-looking elder has been to the summit and has found illumination.
>
> "Please, sir," he asks, "can you tell me what enlightenment is?"
>
> The old man smiles, takes the heavy burden off his back, and stands up straight.
>
> "I understand!" cries the young man. "But, what is after enlightenment?"
>
> The old man simply swings the heavy sack up his shoulders and continues on his way.

Enlightenment makes no difference at all. Enlightenment makes all the difference in the world. Both of these statements are true. The Chinese sage Lao-tzu said this of enlightenment: "He who knows does not speak; he who speaks does not know." But Lao-tzu himself presumably knew *and* spoke, pointing again to the paradoxical nature of enlightenment.

Cover your ears and listen. You will hear only silence at first.

Continue to listen and you eventually notice a high-pitched tone or buzzing sound. You can find more sounds, some say up to twelve, which were there all the time but had escaped your notice. Enlightenment is like that.

With enlightenment, everything changes and nothing changes. And that makes all the difference in the world. You already have it. You already are it. And you must find it.

There is no higher truth than awareness of what is.

There is no higher practice than embracing what is.

There is no higher realization than this: You *are* that awareness, which shines through all beings.

If these words make no sense, trust your process and be patient.

If these words are obvious, live your life and be aware.

One day you happen to notice that Awareness-Consciousness-God-Spirit is living as you. You may laugh aloud because what made no sense before will have become the single most obvious, ordinary, and wondrous reality.

If existence is something like a cosmic joke, enlightenment may be getting the punch line.

In the meantime, you do not have to seek or wait for a dramatic moment to become enlightened—to realize what is already the case—to become aware of awareness. You can practice enlightenment (only) here and now in everyday life.

The Practice of Enlightenment

Your journey through the twelve gateways has prepared you for a practice that bridges heaven and earth, blends body and mind, and heals the rift between flesh and spirit. I call it the practice of enlightenment. It is nothing special. In fact, you have been practicing enlightenment every day for most of your life. I wrote this book to help make your practice conscious, and effective, and fruitful.

Before you learn this practice, consider these questions:

- With whom would you prefer to live—an enlightened person who acted crazy or a crazy person who acted enlightened?
- What if, while continuing to experience fear, sorrow, envy, resentment, doubt, insecurity, you still *behaved* in an enlightened way?
- What if you moved with grace even though you felt like a klutz?
- What if you treated yourself with kindness even when you felt undeserving?
- Would it matter what you happened to be feeling or thinking at the moment as long as your actions reflected loving-kindness and illumination?
- Is behaving like an enlightened being when you don't feel like one an act of falsehood or an act of self-transcendence?

Behaving As If

For most people, enlightenment requires that you work from the inside out, *first* clearing your body and psyche, which *then* enables you to behave in an enlightened way. I propose that you can work from the outside in. *Behavior* can precede realization. You can fake it till you make it; just do it until more enlightened behavior becomes a habit.

A gymnast doesn't have to understand all the laws of physics to learn a full-twisting somersault. A singer doesn't have to understand theories of vocal acoustics to inspire an audience. You can practice enlightenment by living it every day, *behaving* as if you were enlightened, whether or not you understand it or feel like it. Clearly there are hurdles to overcome:

- If you're feeling afraid, or angry, or sad—or if your mind is filled with negative thoughts—you may not have enough free attention even to *remember* the practice.
- Most of us would agree that enlightenment involves, among other things, being completely who you are—real

and authentic—responding naturally and appropriately to whatever arises. So if you are feeling upset by acting enlightened, would you only be pretending?

Yes, you would be pretending, in the best possible way—like a shy youngster at a school dance, who pretends he is confident as he asks a girl to dance; like the nervous new employee who speaks up at a business meeting and dazzles everyone with her knowledge; like the terrified soldier running through a firestorm, who despite his fear acts bravely and pulls a comrade to safety.

Meanwhile, instead of waiting to *feel* enlightened, peaceful, blissful, or wise, by *behaving* in an enlightened manner, you become a positive influence on those around you. Your life begins to change as you set up a positive chain of cause-effect reactions. Acting kind when you don't feel kind *is* kindness; acting brave when you don't feel brave *is* bravery; acting decisive when you feel confused *is* clarity.

Thus the practice of enlightenment is not about positive thinking, grandiose beliefs, or denying your interior reality (which can be chaotic at times). The practice has nothing to do with how you feel or the thoughts passing through your mind. It is about what action you bring into the world. You have learned that love is an action; that happiness is an action; that courage is an action; that peace is an action; that service is an action. So is enlightenment.

Declaring yourself enlightened will no more make you so than declaring yourself to be a pineapple. Saying or believing you are enlightened does not make it so. Practicing enlightenment, living it, makes it so.

Enlightenment is as enlightenment does.

If you practice enlightenment in this way, your actions will shape your thoughts and feelings rather than the other way around. Accepting thoughts and feelings as they are, without denial, you persist in your practice, behaving as if enlightened to the best of your ability.

But how can you be kind if you don't feel kind or be brave if you don't feel brave? Try acting. Act the role of an enlightened being.

Acting as a Transcendental Art

Acting is a shamanistic, shape-shifting art that enables you to transcend your personality by stepping into the body and life of another—to animate any quality you can imagine, to reinvent yourself, to become who you wish to be, explore and express your shadow side, to change your views, attitudes, and behaviors. It is also a key to the practice of enlightenment.

But what if you are not a very good actor?

As it happens, you are a consummate actor, having practiced most of your life. You play one role at parties or social occasions, another with your family, and still another at work. Each one of us plays countless roles in a lifetime. As Shakespeare reminds us, "All the world's a stage, And all the men and women merely players. . . ." The roles you have typically played, however, have often been automatic and unconscious. The practice of enlightenment involves making your roles intentional, powerful, even fun.

Beyond the roles you play, you are, of course, yourself—but what does "yourself" mean? Are you a static, unchanging personality or constellation of shifting roles, varying with your surroundings?

> "Who are You?" crooned the Caterpillar.
> Alice replied rather shyly,
> "I—I hardly know, Sir, just at present.
> I know who I *was* when I got up this morning,
> but I think I must have changed several times since then."
>
> **—Lewis Carroll**

Former alcoholics create new identities as nondrinkers; the same is true for former addicts, smokers, and spouse abusers. Changing behavior changes identity. Each time you behave in an unaccustomed way—like changing your posture or your job or adapting to a new exercise regimen—it feels awkward until it becomes natural—difficult until it becomes easy.

If your role becomes your reality, you can change your reality by changing your role. You can play any role you choose, including that of a fully conscious, courageous, clear, wise, enlightened human being. Your past does not have to become your future.

Who but yourself is stopping you from doing what you want to do, what you need to do, being who you want to be? The question is not whether you *can* do this practice, but whether you *will*. For all practical purposes, *enlightened beings are those simply willing to behave in an enlightened way.*

The Role of a Lifetime

If a film company cast you in the role of a police officer, you would naturally want to research the part and learn as much as you could about a police officer's life. But suppose you were cast in the role of an enlightened being? Whose behaviors do you study? Enlightened beings, it turns out, aren't so easy to find. In fact, since life is a series of moments, there *are* no enlightened beings— only people who have more enlightened moments. So let's define an enlightened person as someone who has many enlightened moments, just as an intelligent person is someone who has many intelligent moments.

Since you cannot imitate someone else's thoughts or feelings, you would need to observe and model that person's *behaviors*— how he or she moves, responds, and speaks—in order to achieve a more realistic portrayal. Therefore for the sake of your role, let us agree for the moment that an enlightened person is someone who behaves in an enlightened way.

Enlightened Behavior

Now comes the biggest question: How do we determine enlightened behavior? Trying to do so is like trying to grasp water in your fist. The moment we idealize enlightenment as never getting upset or smiling blissfully, we go astray, because enlightened behavior isn't always blissful—it is flexible, chameleonlike, adapting naturally to the shifting sands of circumstance.

Enlightened behavior is not about perfecting one's personality or becoming more likable or popular. To convey its transcendent rather than its conventional nature, I share the following story:

> I first met Bud in the mid 1970s, when we attended a forty-day intensive training in spiritual growth. Before long it became obvious that Bud had a speech disability—he stuttered badly. In that the training featured an unusually broad array of disciplines for body, mind, emotions—deep relaxation methods, personal insight work, a variety of meditations, bodywork, exercise, breathing methods—my other trainees and I assumed or at least hoped that as a side benefit, Bud might rid himself of his speech impediment. But at the end of the forty days, he still stuttered.
>
> I saw Bud two years later, in an advanced training. Near the end of that training, I had a chance to speak with Bud, who had done much personal growth work in the intervening years, but still stuttered as much as ever.
>
> "Bud," I said at one point. "After all the processing you've done, I notice that you still stutter."
>
> "Y-y-yes," he said, matter-of-factly. "B-b-but n-n-now I d-d-don't g-g-give a hoot!"

In that moment, Bud was an enlightened being who stuttered, and simply didn't give a hoot.

Do enlightened beings behave in *any* predictable, consistent ways?

Yes. And no.

Enlightened behavior is almost certainly natural, no longer in conflict with itself or with life. It rises to meet circumstances in the best possible way. Such behavior reflects maturity in the twelve gateways in acting with energy, authenticity, discipline, courage, and kindness. But whether that kindness takes the form of tough love or gentle sentiment is impossible to say.

Since enlightened action is spontaneous and intuitive, it is also unpredictable—sometimes eccentric, sometimes ordinary, sometimes contradictory. To avoid idealizing enlightenment as "never getting upset" or "always being calm and blissful," enlightened teachers have been described as having no consistent image at all.

So whose behavior are you to observe? You may wonder, are such beings married or single, sexually active or not? If you research historical models of reputedly enlightened beings such as Jesus, Buddha, Krishna, Muhammad, Zoroaster, Saint Teresa of Avila, Joan of Arc, or illumined teachers such as Chuang-tzu, Lao-tzu, or more modern examples such as Anandamayi Ma and the Dalai Lama, you will find no consistent role model or behaviors.

A seeker once asked the Buddha what made him different from other men. He said only three words: "I am awake." He didn't say, "I am kinder, gentler, have a more beatific smile, have powers, can do miracles, am calm and blissful all the time, have a charming personality," or even, "I am always happy or loving." He only said, "I am awake." But since life is made of moments, we cannot know whether an enlightened being is awake in every moment or less awake some moments than others.

Our task appears more difficult, it turns out, than role-modeling police officers.

One of the best ways to understand enlightened behavior is to compare it to the behavior of water flowing down a mountain. In one shallow stream the water runs smooth and rapidly, spilling over into small waterfalls; in another stream the water meanders down a shallow grade; in a trickling brook the water gurgles over a bed of stones; then the streams join and the water becomes a surging river.

It is doubtful that the water shows more enlightened behavior in one stream than another. But in every case, the water demonstrated enlightened behavior in being itself completely yet responding naturally to gravity and its environment, changing shape, adapting perfectly to its environment. The water's direction remains constant, abiding with the natural law of gravity, flowing downhill to a lake or to the sea, merging with other water. But its behavior and functions change—helping things grow, eroding topsoil, sustaining the life of thirsty creatures, polishing stones—running slow and then fast, rough and then smooth, flowing around obstacles in its path.

Enlightened behavior is a natural and realistic response to each moment, including full and natural participation in life with all its ups and downs, just like water flowing down a mountain. The best answer to the question "What is enlightened behavior?" is this: *It depends upon the situation, the circumstance, the moment.*

As you prepare for your role, there is more help on the horizon.

You Already Know What to Practice

As it turns out, even though an enlightened being may choose to behave in almost any manner, each of us has an intuitive, archetypal understanding of the qualities and behaviors associated with one who is awake. If you have any doubts of your intuitive knowledge, take the following quiz.

Would an enlightened person generally

- act constructively or destructively?
- speak in a rushed or unhurried way?
- behave in a judgmental or compassionate manner?
- appear tense or relaxed?
- breathe slowly and deeply or take rapid and shallow breaths?
- smile or frown more?
- seem more serious or good-humored?
- exemplify self-denial, self-indulgence, or a balance?
- act aloof and superior or treat everyone as equals?

Even if this quiz had fifty questions, you could answer them all, because a part of you knows—*the part of you that is awake.* Still, everyday life may bring circumstances for which an enlightened response is not at all clear. In moments like these, you can draw upon one or more of these four models:

- Respond as if you have mastered the twelve gateways— someone who has worth, will, energy, sufficiency, clarity, intuition, passion, courage, authenticity, pleasure, kindness, and service—someone with free attention and expanded awareness. Someone who is awake.
- Ask yourself, "What might my higher self—the part of me that is courageous, altruistic, and wise—do in this moment?" And then do it.

- If you have a strong connection to a religious leader or other person, living or dead, who represents to you the divine human prototype, you can also ask, "What would that figure [such as Jesus or Buddha] do?"
- Or you might just say, "Thy will be done," and trust, and act.

Whether you draw upon any of the foregoing models or upon your own intuitive inner knower, the cameras are about to roll. Preparation is over. Now, the play's the thing.

Back on the Set

You have probably never before consciously modeled enlightened behavior, because you've never been given that assignment.

Until now.

Now you are about to play the role of a lifetime. In your first scene you enter a room, walk across the floor, greet a small group of people, then speak with another character who is upset and hostile.

The problem is that you, yourself, are feeling extremely upset. The past few weeks you've been having heated arguments over your spouse's late hours at the office with a very friendly assistant. A few moments ago, on the telephone, after another fight, your partner told you that your relationship was over. You just hung up the phone.

The shot is ready. Your partner's words still ring in your mind: "This relationship was over a long time ago." You feel the tension in your body—the hurt, the anger. But the show must go on; the moment of truth has arrived.

The director yells, "Roll cameras. Action!"

And on cue, you step into your role. You take a deep breath, relax your body, and walk into the scene with grace and clear attention. You greet the group of people with a pleasant nod. You listen well and show kindness to the hostile character. You are present, fully in the moment, giving yourself to the situation at hand, moving, speaking, responding directly to this person in your most enlightened manner, despite your upset of a few minutes before.

Notwithstanding your emotional turmoil—the doubt, the anger—you play your role flawlessly. It isn't until after the scene ends and you walk away from the set that that voice on the telephone begins to replay itself in your mind.

Everyday Enlightenment

What if, when the scene ended, *no one ever yelled, "Cut"?* What if you choose to continue the same impeccable role as you walk off the set, get in your car, drive through rush-hour traffic, and find your partner packing a suitcase? What if you choose to continue your enlightened role at work the next day and the next? It is, of course, more difficult to play an enlightened role in difficult or stressful circumstances. You will blow many scenes, step out of character, and forget your lines. You can only give it your best shot. In doing so, you will improve over time, become more like flowing water.

Always remember that *you don't have to think or feel enlightened. You only need to behave that way,* as much as you can, whenever you remember to do so. This practice, which you can engage in each and every gateway, animates and celebrates the best of the human spirit.

The practice of enlightenment is the simplest and most transcendent spiritual practice I can share. Infinitely challenging and varied, supremely interesting, you are never bored because you have, in any moment, something to do. Calling forth all you have learned on your journey, you can transform everyday life into a path of personal evolution imbued with new meaning and purpose.

> For the things we have to learn
> before we can do them,
> we learn by doing them.
> **—Aristotle**

As you practice, you will find that your (more enlightened) behavior begins to heal your mind and emotions. You may also discover that life is not quite as serious as you were led to believe—that you are not (and have never been) a human working to be enlightened, but, rather, you are, ultimately, pure awareness now playing the role of a working human.

Start Now

This book has been about the courage to play a starring role in your own life. Do it now, while you have the time, the body, the heart, the life for it. The road is open, the pathway clear. You understand the practice. Now live it. Notice your options in every situation. How will you behave? See what intuitive answers come, and act accordingly. Ask your heart, where the higher self speaks. Then practice.

Practicing Everything

If there is a key to a life well lived, if there is a single culminating insight I have gained from all my years of study and teaching it is this: Just as musicians practice music, as poets practice poetry, as athletes practice sports, the practice of enlightenment involves *practicing everything*—walking, speaking, breathing, sitting, standing, eating, writing, making love, doing the dishes, everything.

Practice, unlike those times we go on automatic, involves attention and refinement. When we practice anything, we pay special attention, with the intention to refine a quality, skill, or aptitude.

One key to paying attention, as you have learned, is remembering to breathe, to relax, and to do whatever you are doing with grace and quality. Practicing all that you do brings a variety of blessings into your life I will let you discover for yourself.

Practicing everything is *not* about turning life into a series of routine drills, chores, or drudgery. On the contrary, a reawakened interest in the quality and refinement of your actions and words brings new levels of involvement and makes an art of living. You become a master athlete in training, your sport is everyday life, and the prize is a fuller experience of all the moments of which life is made.

When you practice everyday enlightenment, play and practice become one. Your practice is a creative adventure in the quality of each moment. And you play with the intense concentration of a young child first learning the skills of life. As a young trampolinist, I never remember practicing—I only played—right up to winning the world championship. So play in the spirit of practice, and practice with the joy and spontaneity of play.

Be Gentle with Yourself

If this practice does not interest you in any moment, then attend to what does interest you. Don't turn practical guidance into a masochistic, perfectionist, obsessive-compulsive, self-defeating self-improvement game. ("Oh, no! I lost my temper! Gandhi would never do that! Messed up again!") Instead, take it easy. Life is to enjoy. Enlightenment also means forgiving your own and others' unenlightenment and continuing to do what you can. Remember that enlightenment neither achieves nor demands perfection. It simply embraces life as it is and participates fully, with faith and trust in life itself. So have fun with it! Approach this practice in the same way you might learn a somersault or a new dance step. I am practicing, stumbling, practicing.

Now you have a bridge between heaven and earth, between flesh and spirit, that transmutes each day, each moment, into a sacred practice. Practice is the catalyst of transformation. Play is the celebration of our humanity. This is your training and your destiny. Welcome to real life.

Having passed through the gauntlet of the twelve gateways, knowing what you now know, what will you do?

Polar Shifts for the New Millennium

Time is a surging river, bringing change to each and all. Cultures come and go; the face of the world changes. Humanity moves forward, accelerating, evolving, not toward larger heads or bigger brains, but toward higher consciousness and open hearts.

This book places an emphasis on you, the individual—on your personal evolution and destiny. But no one is an island; each of us influences those around us. By awakening, you become a spark that sets others aflame. The individual touches the community; the community touches the region; the region touches the nation; the nation touches the world.

Individual change precedes global change. Every one of us counts; each of us contributes to the beauty of the whole. We change the world by changing ourselves. And if we do nothing more than offer a smile to a stranger or utter a kind word to someone in need, we make a difference. And as humanity learns the lessons of the twelve gateways, we will see a shift of awareness that transforms our politics, entertainment, media, medicine, military, and the way we do business with one another.

We are evolving from exploiters to plunderers to protectors and caretakers of the earth. Acts of slavery, war, bigotry, and callousness once considered acceptable in some circles will soon be mourned by an awakened humanity as periods of madness. We are growing out of childhood toward maturity. Yet we are racing against time to find ways to correct and transcend our mistakes before the clock strikes midnight. Enlightened civilizations appear only when enough individuals behave in enlightened ways. The dawn of our destiny awaits us.

The Native American peoples have scattered to the winds; the great horse culture has vanished, but the Great Spirit is alive and well within each of us and growing stronger in the world. The same species that created TV dinners and hydrogen bombs is undergoing a metamorphosis no less profound than that of a chrysalis turning to a butterfly. The same species whose powers may destroy life on this planet may yet develop the wisdom and will to nourish it.

Journey's End

Many years have passed since my experience in that forest grove. It seems like lifetimes. Enlightenment is no longer a faraway or otherworldly experience; it has become an everyday practice that you or I can do in any moment. When you forget—when the light grows dim and you seem to lose your way—hold to this vision:

You are in the cellar of a building, stumbling in the darkness, bruising your body as you bump into unseen obstacles. Suddenly a door opens at the top of the stairs, and you catch the briefest glimpse of twelve stairs, illuminated for only a moment, before the door closes again. This is a moment of understanding.

It becomes dark once again, but *now you know that the stairway exists, and you know its direction.* There will be more bumps and bruises, but everything has changed, for you have hope and knowledge and memory of the light at the top of the stairs.

Now we arrive at the completion of our journey together through the pages of this book. The end of one journey is the beginning of another.

The practice of these gateways, which is the practice of enlightenment, the practice of life, is a cycle without end, like the changing seasons. You will pass through each gateway not once but many times, each time learning more, until practice becomes play, and play becomes life, and life becomes illumined. As you travel the winding roads ahead, remember your sense of humor, your sense of perspective, your simple humanity.

Ultimately, nothing can block you on your quest, because nothing is stronger than the human spirit that links us all. You are a seed of what is to come, stretching upward, reaching to the Light.